3rd EDITION

FINAL CUT STUDIO

ON THE SPOT

TIME-SAVING TECHNIQUES FOR USING FINAL CUT PRO AND THE STUDIO APPLICATIONS

Richard Harrington

Abba Shapiro

Robbie Carman

ELSEVIER

AMSTERDAM • BOSTON • HEIDELBERG • LONDON • NEW YORK • OXFORD
PARIS • SAN DIEGO • SAN FRANCISCO • SINGAPORE • SYDNEY • TOKYO

Focal Press is an imprint of Elsevier

Focal Press

Acquisitions Editor: Paul Temme
Associate Acquisitions Editor: Dennis McGonagle
Publishing Services Manager: George Morrison
Project Manager: Kathryn Liston
Assistant Editor: Chris Simpson
Marketing Manager: Rebecca Pease

Focal Press is an imprint of Elsevier
30 Corporate Drive, Suite 400, Burlington, MA 01803, USA
Linacre House, Jordan Hill, Oxford OX2 8DP, UK

 Recognizing the importance of preserving what has been written, Elsevier prints its books on
acid-free paper whenever possible.

Library of Congress Cataloging-in-Publication Data
(Application submitted)

British Library Cataloguing-in-Publication Data
A catalogue record for this book is available from the British Library.

ISBN: 978-0-240-81007-2

For information on all Focal Press publications
visit our website at www.books.elsevier.com

07 08 09 10 11 12   10 9 8 7 6 5 4 3 2 1

Printed in Canada

Working together to grow
libraries in developing countries

www.elsevier.com | www.bookaid.org | www.sabre.org

ELSEVIER   BOOK AID International   Sabre Foundation

Dedication

This book is dedicated to my wife, Meghan,
our children, Michael and Colleen, and our family.
−Richard Harrington

This book is dedicated to my children, Daniel and Ian, and my family.
−Abba Shapiro

To my parents, John and Marcia, for supporting me in my dream to do what I
do. To my beautiful wife, Catherine, for her undying support, and
to Jason Osder for his help throughout.
−Robbie Carman

Contents

Introduction

Why did we write this book? We love this application. We use it ourselves almost every day to edit and to create programs for our clients. We teach Final Cut Pro classes, give lectures, and consult one-on-one. And you know what makes us feel really good? When people learn a new trick or tip, smile, and say, "Wow!"

We still learn new tricks every day, and we still smile and say, "Wow!" We wanted to pass that excitement along. As much as we love this program, we can't teach everywhere, we can't answer the phone every night at 3 a.m. (our families would kill us), and we can only get across so many tips in the time allotted to us at conferences.

So we wrote a book. The idea was to give the reader the cream off the top of the milk—just the good stuff. Final Cut Pro is a great program with tons of features and shortcuts; the problem is separating the cream from the skim milk.

If you read every tech document on the web, perused every page of the manual, attended all of the Apple certification courses, and hung out with all the other FCP uber-geeks, not to mention the Final Cut Pro people at Apple, you'd have a bounty of knowledge (trust us, we have and we do). But you have a life, a job, and no time to dig to find those gems.

If you're impatient, on a deadline, or just can't stand to look at another "Getting Started with Final Cut Pro" book, this book is for you.

We've used Final Cut Pro from the beginning; in fact, we've got more than 40 years combined experience with nonlinear editing and 50 years of hands-on Apple usage. And we've distilled that knowledge into this book, giving you the best tidbits and secrets we have.

All we ask is that you tell your friends about this book, and that when you win your first Oscar/Emmy (or make your first million dollars), you remember us—or, better yet, just smile and thank us at the next NAB, DV, or Apple trade show.

Who Is This Book For?

If you've edited nonlinear video for a while and feel comfortable editing, you can get a lot out of this book. If you're a seasoned editor, we may help break you of some extremely slow habits and show you some really cool techniques. This book will help you move to a higher level.

If you've never opened the manual, read another Final Cut Pro book, or taken a training class, don't start here. You must learn to walk before you can run. If you're a "newbie," this book may leave you a bit overwhelmed. Buy it anyway, but read it after you've had some walking lessons.

With that said, don't try to read the book linearly. Shop for ideas, jump around a lot, and work your way through the chapters you need most. We've left extra space by the tips so you can jot down your own notes. If you're a mobile editor, this book should fit nicely in your bag. Hit a tough spot? Just pull the book out when the client leaves the room to check for a new idea or a troubleshooting tip. Have a few minutes to kill? Read a tip. We bet you'll return to the application with some new ideas and new energy.

If you're looking for the little sidebars or tips in the margins, there aren't any. This whole book is filled with more than 500 tips. Get reading already–you've got a deadline to make.

–Richard Harrington, Abba Shapiro, and Robbie Carman

ON THE SPOT

Plugging In
Mastering Final Cut Pro's Interface

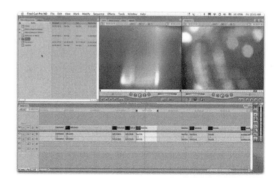

So you want to be fast? A virtuoso of the Final Cut Pro keyboard? A concert pianist doesn't see the piano as a tool, but as a conduit for the music. In the same way, Final Cut Pro is a conduit for your show and your creativity. Mastering the interface will keep you from stumbling in the dark, hitting the wrong keys, and making a lot of noise. You have to know what all your tools do, where to find them, and how to access their power instantly.

Over time, you'll gain confidence with all the controls. You want to be able to make the interface "disappear," which will allow you to reach "inside" the computer and create. Great editors know that the more brainpower they can put toward their edit session (not edit system), the better their show turns out.

Practice your scales. Don't skimp on learning Final Cut Pro's interface—after all, you paid good money for a Baby Grand, so learn to play it well.

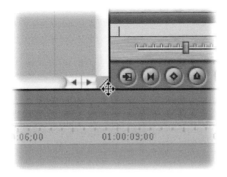

Get Dynamic with Interfaces

One of the coolest features of Final Cut Pro is the dynamic resizing of the interface. You can now quickly adjust the size of windows using dynamic resizing. Clicking between two windows or at the intersection of multiple windows allows you to drag and resize all windows. You no longer have to resize one window at a time.

Need more space in the Timeline? Just grab the top edge, and pull upward. Want to see more in the Viewer? Grab the edge, and pull to the right. It's simple to quickly change the size of a window and view exactly what you need.

Better Bins

Want to open a bin without eating up more window space? You can hold down the Option key and double-click a bin's icon to open it as a tab in its parent window. This helps keep your interface lean and clean.

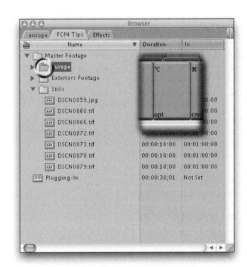

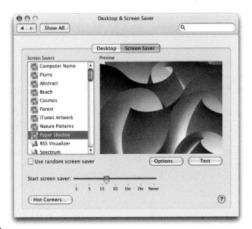

Save Your Monitors

This one comes from first-hand experience. Screensavers serve a greater good than entertainment (though we still see those Flying Toasters from time to time in our dreams). You'll want to set your screensavers to trigger automatically (30 minutes of inactivity is probably enough time to stare at the screen). Otherwise, you can get monitor burn that leaves a ghosted image on the screen.

Make It Big—Part 1

Depending on your work style, you may like to make your tracks taller or shorter. Tall tracks are great when you are looking at your audio waveforms. Shorter tracks are helpful when you're trying to composite multiple layers. Previous versions of Final Cut shipped with four preset track heights, but now you can change them individually.

Click on the thin gray line between tracks and grab. You can now drag and size the height of each track individually.

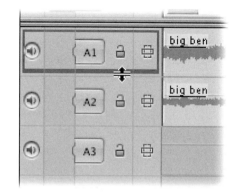

Make It Big—Part 2

Hold down the Option key and you can size all of your video *or* audio tracks at once.

Hold down the Shift key, and you can size *all* tracks at once.

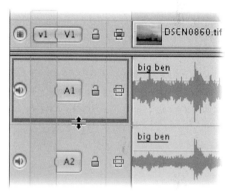

The First Thing You Should Do: Save ... No, Save As

We admit, sometimes we get a little excited when we sit down to edit. It's time for the magic to happen; all of the preproduction and production is about to come together into our latest masterpiece. New project, check. Tapes loaded and labeled, check. Start to capture—WAIT!

The problem is that Final Cut Pro assigns clips to a folder on your drive based on the project name. Without a project name your clips will get stored in the ever deadly, "Untitled" folder. ALWAYS choose Save As from the File menu as soon as you create a new project. This way your clips will have a project association and get stored in the right place.

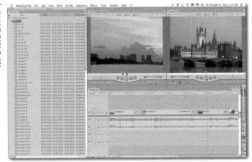

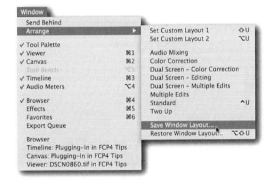

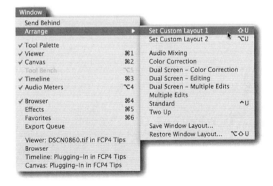

That's the Spot

You've perfectly configured your windows. Every palette is exactly where you want it. The Timeline has just enough room and you've got the audio meter exactly where it should be. Now save that window arrangement.

Long-term storage

❶ Choose Window > Arrange > Save Layout. This setting is stored by default in your Window Layouts folder.

❷ Final Cut Pro also has custom layouts at the bottom of the list with a new keyboard shortcut automatically assigned.

❸ Now call up your Button List (Tools > Button List) or Option + J and type the word **window**. Grab the Window Layout button and drag it to a convenient button well.

> Note that the Custom layout is an alphabetized list. Number your layouts when saving them: Editing 1. Effects, 2. Compositing, and so on.

Short-term storage

Still testing the layout to make sure you like it? You can save it temporarily in one of two custom positions. Hold down the Option key, and choose Window > Arrange > Set Custom Layout. Now when you return, you will find the Custom Layouts have been set.

Move the Dock

The Dock was not designed for use with Final Cut Pro. Seems like it's always popping up and getting in the way. In its default position (bottom of the screen) it can eat away valuable monitor space that you could use for your Timeline. But like most things in OS X, there's a preference that can be changed.

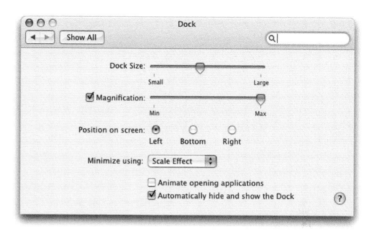

① Go to the Apple menu and choose System Preferences and click the Dock button.

② Tell the system that you want to automatically hide and show the Dock. This will put the Dock away when it's not in use.

③ Change the Dock's position. Placing the Dock on the left or right side of the screen will allow you to have more screen real estate for your Timeline.

When the OS Guys Don't Talk to the Pro App Guys

A great feature in OS X called Exposé allows you to quickly see all of your open windows or hide everything to get to the desktop. We find this feature very useful in applications like Photoshop or Word when we have a bunch of documents open, but it's a bear in FCP when all of your windows start flying around the screen. To make things worse, Exposé uses F9, F10, and F11, which Final Cut Pro uses for Insert, Overwrite, and Replace Edit.

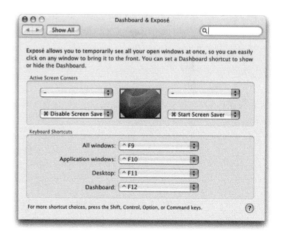

① Launch the System Preferences from under the Apple menu. Click on the Exposé icon in the first row.

② Hold down the Control key and click on the drop-down menus under Keyboard.

③ Change All windows to Control F9 (^ F9), Application windows to Control F10 (^ F10), Desktop to Control F11 (^ F11), and Dashboard to Control F12 (^F12).

④ Edit away like you used to—the feature is there when you need it.

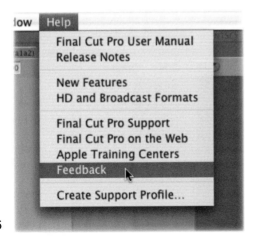

Bring It With You

One issue that freelance editors come across all the time is making the machine they're using on any given day feel like theirs. We're not talking about a dirty keyboard, we're talking about Final Cut Pro settings!

Many people realize that in FCP you can create custom keyboard layouts, window layouts, column layouts, Timeline track layouts, and button bars, but many people don't realize how easy it is to take these custom settings from place to place. The first step is knowing where these files are stored.

- By default, FCP stores custom settings in User > Library > Preferences > Final Cut Pro User Data. In this folder you'll find subfolders for window layouts, etc.

- To take these layouts with you, simply attach a drive (a USB thumb drive works well) and copy the subfolders onto your drive.

- When you arrive at your next editing gig, simply load your custom settings by choosing the appropriate window to load them, i.e. Window > Arrange > Load Window Layout. Navigate to your thumb drive and choose the file that matches what you want.

One thing to note is that even though FCP likes to save these files by default in the folder listed above, you don't have to save your settings there. When you create a custom setting, you can choose any location to save the new file, including in this example, the USB thumb drive. If you do that, it eliminates the copy to the drive step and eliminating steps is good!

Gee, I Really Wish ...

Something about Final Cut Pro bother you? Really wish something were different? Well, Apple does listen ... you just need to know the secret knock.

❶ Choose Help > Feedback.

❷ Fill in your comments and submit (don't expect a phone call, but the comments DO get read).

Lock Down—Part 1

Want to preserve a video track? Then lock it. Hold down F4 and then type a track number using the top row of number keys. You can lock tracks V1–V9. For audio locking, use F5 and a number key. This is a great way to avoid "accidental" edits.

Lock Down—Part 2

Need to work on one video track without affecting any others? Hold down the Option key and click on your desired track's lock icon. All other video tracks will be locked. To unlock all tracks, simply hold down Option and click the lock icon again. This trick also works on audio tracks.

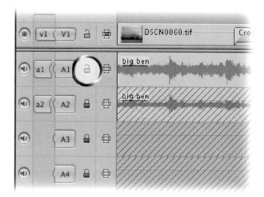

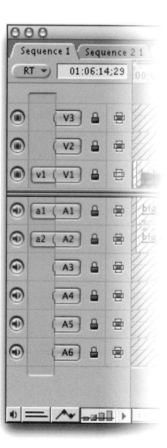

Global Lock Down

Need to lock all your video or audio tracks? Simply press Shift + F4 to lock video tracks or Shift + F5 to lock all audio tracks. Repeat the key combo to unlock all tracks.

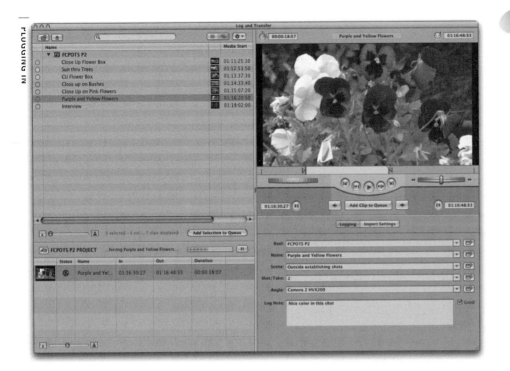

A New Way to Ingest

In the past few years, tapeless acquisition and post-production have really taken off. One really popular tapeless format is Panasonic's P2. Capable of shooting DV all the way up to 1080p, it's one cool format! Apple recognized this format and built the Log and Transfer window (although Log and Transfer does support other tapeless formats).

It's called Log and Transfer because you're simply just transferring digital files from disk to disk. This is unlike tape-based media that you have to capture into a file on disk, i.e. Log and Capture. To launch Log and Transfer choose File > Log and Transfer or Shift+Command+8.

Overall, the Log and Transfer window operates like the Log and Capture window. The big difference, of course is how it ingests the media. Unlike Log and Capture where you have a few options for how to get the footage on to disk, with Log and Transfer you simply log your clip and then click Add Clip/Selection to the Queue to begin the transfer to your scratch disk.

A Bit of Scale

Maybe you get stuck bringing a lot of work home on the weekends (Never happened to us! Yeah, right!). At work, perhaps you use a big 30" Cinema Display, but at home you're working off your laptop.

You're already hip to saving custom window layouts, but when you get on your laptop and load your favorite layout, it's gigantic and set up for your work monitor.

The one thing you might be missing is changing the format of your custom window layouts. Here's how to do it:

❶ Arrange your windows as you see fit.

❷ Choose Window >Arrange > Save Window Layout.

❸ Choose a location for the layout (maybe a USB thumb drive discussed in a previous tip).

❹ Before you click OK, notice the format pull-down at the bottom of the dialog box.

When it says Fixed Aspect Layout, FCP will remember the exact size of the layout when you save it. If you open a Fixed Aspect Layout on your laptop it will be HUGE!

If you change this pull-down to Auto-Aspect Layout, FCP will attempt to keep the window arrangement the same as it is now when opened on screens with different resolutions by changing the size of windows. This is the option to choose if you find yourself opening up window layouts on different monitors all the time.

Custom Views in the Audio Mixer

If you're using the Audio Mixer, you know that it can be a pretty powerful tool. Like many things in Final Cut Pro, the Audio Mixer is customizable. Let's see how.

Launch the Audio Mixer by choosing Tools > Audio Mixer or Option + 6.

The Audio Mixer shows you the controls for all the tracks you have in your project, but if you take a closer look, on the top of the bar of the Audio Mixer there are four view buttons. Using these buttons you can create up to four custom views. Why do this?

Well, maybe in view 1 you want to see all of your tracks, in view 2 just your dialog tracks, in view 3 just natural sound tracks, and in view 4 music and effects.

That sounds great, but how do you actually choose which tracks get assigned to each view?

The trick is the black circles next to each track in the track visibility area. Note: If your track visibility area is not being shown, click the disclosure triangle next to the top of the first track strip.

❶ First select the view you'd like to edit.

❷ Next, using the black circles next to each track in the track visibility area select which tracks you want in this view. A black filled in circle will include that track in the view, while an empty circle indicates that track will not be part of the view.

A Window to the World

One window layout that many find confusing is the Multiple Edits layout. While we agree that at first it can be a little hard to figure out which window is which, this layout is really powerful for comparing edits to your current playhead position, as well as to see what you have loaded in the Viewer.

To load this view, choose Window > Arrange > Multiple Edits. Oh, boy! What did we get into here? There are all sorts of windows displaying things. Take a deep breath—let's break it down.

- The window layouts from left to right (excluding Timeline and Browser) are the Viewer, a Frame Viewer that shows the previous edit relative to the current location of our playhead in the Timeline, the Canvas which shows our current playhead location, and a Frame Viewer that shows the next edit relative to the current location of our playhead in the Timeline.

- As you navigate the Timeline you'll notice that the Canvas window updates as it normally would, and the Frame Viewers on either side of the Canvas window update automatically, showing the previous and next edits respectively.

- If you find yourself doing a lot of color correction, this is one of the best views you can use. It is also particularly useful for trying to match the flow of action between a group of shots.

Keys to the Locks

If you find yourself needing to lock and unlock tracks often, remember you can customize your keyboard layout. We suggest mapping the toggle track locks to a Function Key combo. For example, try mapping Toggle Track Lock V1–V8 to Option + F1–F8. You can then map Toggle Track A1–A8 to Option + Command + F1–F8. This will significantly speed up your Timeline editing ability.

Here or There?

It's important to realize the difference between working with Browser clips and Timeline clips. This is critical when creating titles. When you generate a title, you should immediately cut it into the Timeline and then reload it into the Viewer (by double-clicking it in the Timeline). That way you can see how your modifications look against the final image. You can do the same with filters. Conversely, if you drop a filter on an item in the Browser, it's available in all future uses of the clip.

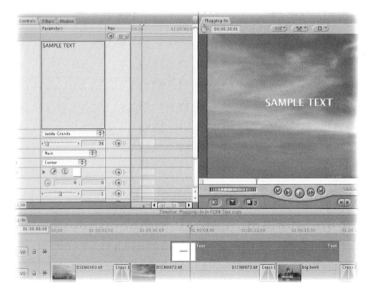

Exposé: Part Deux

If you have a mouse with more than three buttons, such as Logitech, Keyspan, etc., you can map these new Exposé keyboard shortcuts right to your mouse. Simply open the control panel that you installed when you got your mouse and assign it to, say, your thumb button.

Wow, now if you need to grab a clip, image, or project file off your desktop, you can Exposé your desktop from your mouse, grab that file and drop it directly into your browser ... all without touching your keyboard!

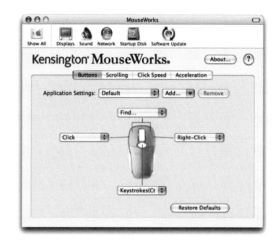

Clean Your Room

Creative people are often messy; it's much more fun to create than it is to clean. While building an effect or tweaking an audio filter, it's not uncommon to tear the Audio, Filters, or Motion tab off to have greater access to controls. But what about when it's time to go on to the next challenge? Not to worry—just double-click to load the next clip into the Viewer. All of your tabs restore themselves into their default position. Now if our desks could only stay so clean.

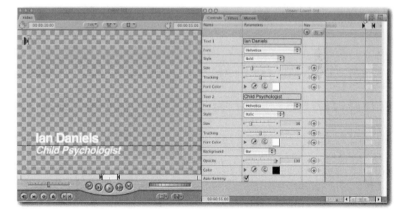

OS X: Child-Proof Windows No More

Miss the ability to roll a window up? The window shade feature of OS 9 was a nice way to keep a window open but out of the way (allowing you to quickly jump into your Finder without having to hide Final Cut Pro or minimize a window). Until Apple decides to put this feature back, there's a great alternative. WindowShade X from Unsanity.com is a reasonably priced option that allows you to collapse windows. As a bonus, it also can make windows transparent or minimize them in place. Our favorite feature is the ability to disable the Minimize to Dock option. This will prevent you from accidentally banishing a bin or window when you click its title bar.

Time on Your Side

Are you the decisive type? Know exactly what you want? Then this shortcut is for you. It's possible to specify the exact duration for a shot, quickly.

❶ Mark an In point by pressing I in the Viewer.

❷ Press Tab; the duration field is now highlighted.

❸ Type in the desired duration, but omit any colons or semicolons (for example, type **315** for a duration of 3:15).

❹ Press Enter. The new Out point is marked.

> Note: You can reverse this tip by marking the Out point first if its more to your liking.

What's Your Destination?

Need to define on which track your video edit will occur? Then you need to set its destination. Hold down F6 and then type a track number using the top row of number keys. You can set tracks V1–V9. For setting an audio's destination, use F7 to patch A1 and F8 to patch A2. If you want to switch tracks again, you will need to press the F key again. Laptop users will need to use the fn + the F key to get the same results.

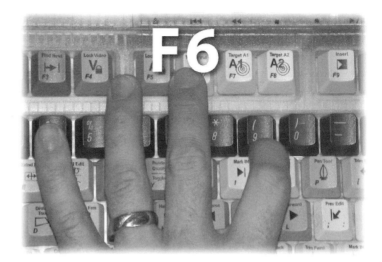

Am I Loaded?

You're working on a clip in the Viewer, but you can't remember if you loaded it from your Browser or the Timeline—not a problem. Final Cut Pro distinguishes between clips opened from the Browser and clips opened from the Timeline. Clips opened from the Browser have a plain scrubber bar; those loaded from the Timeline have two rows of dots in the scrubber bar, similar to the sprocket holes in a strip of film.

Gear Down

When using filters, you'll often want to make "fine" adjustments. You can always switch to numeric entry, but most users find the graphic interfaces more intuitive. Simply hold down the Command key to "gear down." The sliders or control points will move much more slowly. This tip works in several places, including audio.

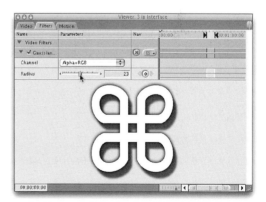

ON THE SPOT

Setting Yourself Up for Success
User Settings for Best Performance

Preferences, preferences, preferences. These are the settings that turn an off-the-lot car into a supercharged racing machine. User settings not only make Final Cut Studio work better and faster, they make it work better and faster for you. They tune the engine to your style of driving.

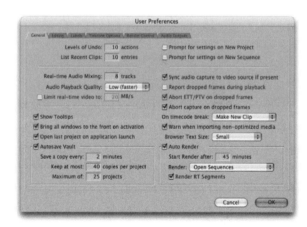

One of the beauties of Final Cut Pro is that it's "plug and play." You can literally edit DV right out of the box. What's even better is how flexible and scalable it is. You can work with DV, SD, HD, film, 24p, internal drives, external drives, PAL, NTSC ... the list goes on. But all that flexibility means you need to configure your system. Beyond hardware configuration, there are even more options to set. How do you want Final Cut Pro to modify graphic files? How often should it save a backup copy? Do you want your Motion projects to back themselves up? What's the default number of audio tracks in a new sequence? You can customize hundreds of settings. This chapter will help you fine-tune your NLE system's performance and ensure fewer headaches down the road.

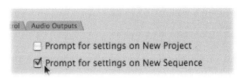

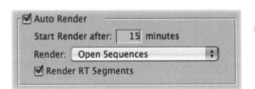

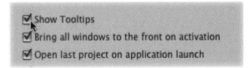

Get It Right from the Start: Using Presets

If you're working with multiple formats and resolutions, this is a critical preference: It's easy to create a new sequence and have it set up improperly for the media you are working on. So under User Preferences, check the Prompt for settings on New Sequence checkbox, and Final Cut Pro will ask you to set your sequence settings each time you create a new sequence. You'll want to pick the preset that matches the primary media format of your Timeline. If you know you'll only work with one type of sequence, you can uncheck Prompt for settings on New Project.

Even Forgetful People Can Be Efficient: Auto Render

This feature is made for long client phone calls, unexpected staff meetings, or alien abductions. Even if you forget to render, Final Cut Pro can automatically render your work for you. Simply check the Auto Render box on the General tab of the User Preferences panel. Tell Final Cut Pro how long to wait and which sequences to render. You can also choose whether to render real-time segments—we usually do.

Tooltips Give Psychic Powers

Want to quickly learn the name and shortcuts for your tools? That's why Tooltips are there. Just hover over an unknown button, and you'll often discover its name and keyboard shortcut. If this isn't working, check the Show Tooltips box on the General tab of the User Preferences panel.

Batting Lefty: Customizing the Keyboard

J-K-L editing is the most useful shortcut for fast editing. But a lot of lefties find it fatiguing to drive right-handed—harness Final Cut Pro's mappable keyboard. Go to Tools > Keyboard Layout > Customize (Option + H), and unlock your keyboard. Now drag the J, K, and L keys to A, S, and D, respectively. While you're there, set W and E to be In and Out, respectively, and then edit away.

Foreshadowing: Using Pre-roll

We usually find that Final Cut Pro shows too much Preview Pre-roll. When trimming on the fly or reviewing an edit point, Pre-roll allows you to review what happens before an edit. Simply choose the Editing tab of the User Preferences window and modify the default preference of 5:00. We usually find that two or three seconds is adequate. And, hey, every second counts when trying to meet a deadline.

A "Dupious" Achievement: Dupe Detection

Dupe detection has its origins in film editing. If you repeat a shot, you need to duplicate that clip because the physical film can't be in two places at once. Dupe detection is designed to warn film editors of this problem.

Video editors can benefit, as well. Think of this as a "dummy" switch. When enabled, dupe detection alerts you if you've used a particular shot already in your Timeline by placing a red bar at the bottom of the clip. This can be useful when cutting B-roll into a long-format show.

If you have duplicate frames in a transition, look for white dots to the left and/or right of the transition.

Give Me a Break: Timecode, That Is!

"Oops ... bump ... bang ... pardon me ... excuse me ... ah, sorry."

If DV tapes could talk, this is how many people's tapes would sound, filled with huge chunks of timecode and control track breaks. The Make New Clip on Timecode Break feature works well, but it can only do so much.

Sometimes you need to go to plan B or C. If you only need to grab a clip or two, try Capture Now. If your tape is really hosed, get a 4-pin to 4-pin FireWire cable, borrow a second camera, and CLONE your bad tape onto a new one. Create a new master with continuous timecode and no control track breaks. The trick here is to start recording the new master first so that the camera generates new timecode instead of cloning the bad timecode.

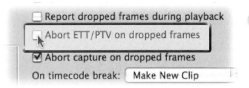

How to Miss FedEx: Abort on Dropped Frames

You're rushing to get a rough cut out to the client for review purposes. Maybe you've rendered everything or you've taken advantage of Final Cut Pro's ability to output frames without rendering. Then, 25 minutes into your 30-minute program, the Print to Video command aborts because of a dropped frame.

Yes, dropped frames are bad. But missed deadlines are worse. Disable the Abort ETT/PTV on dropped frames checkbox on the General tab of the User Preferences panel when you're making a rushed output on a deadline. This will keep the layout from being aborted. Restore the dropped frame option when making archival masters of your program.

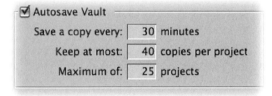

CYA: The Autosave Vault

Ever have a project go bad? A file get corrupted? Maybe the system crashed (OS X never crashes—it just has an undocumented close feature). Worse, you come back from lunch, and the client is standing over your editing system. "I just pushed a few buttons, really!"

It's okay if the Autosave Vault feature is turned on. This great feature will back up your project automatically. You tell it how often to save, how many versions to save, and how many total projects can be archived. This is a great way to cover yourself against unexpected events.

If things ever go wrong, simply choose File > Restore Project.... This way you can quickly access time-stamped versions of your project. After restoring a project, immediately select the Save Project As command and revert to the original name. Otherwise, the Autosave Vault feature will start building a new project folder for the project with a name such as FCP Tips_08_12_08_0241.

Use this the next time a producer pulls a 180-degree turn on you and wants to go back three hours in time.

You Do, He Do, She Do, Undo

If you've got RAM, you might as well use it. Final Cut Pro supports up to 99 levels of undo. Your safety net just got bigger. But remember, more undos will cut into your performance, so find a good balance that works for you and your machine.

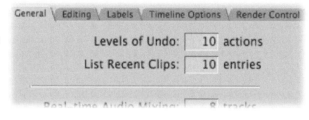

Hear More in Real-Time

While you can mix sample rates in your Timeline, it is taxing on your system. Switching your audio playback quality to the Low setting will allow you more channels of real-time audio. Don't worry; on a Print to Video or Edit to Tape command, Final Cut Pro will automatically switch to maximum quality.

"In a Vacuum"—Trimming with Audio

So you want to be a trimming god or goddess ... it's essential you set your trimming preferences correctly. Otherwise, you might as well wear earmuffs and pull a hat over your eyes. You now have a choice between a "global" or a "local" listen while in the Trim Edit window.

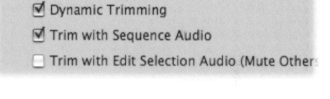

❶ Choose Final Cut Pro > User Preferences or press Option + Q.

❷ From the Editing tab choose from the following options:

- **Dynamic Trimming:** This allows you to use your J-K-L keys for trimming in the Trim Edit window. You can now ripple and roll the edit point back and forth.

- **Trim with Sequence Audio:** This is so you can listen to all sequence audio tracks while trimming.

- **Trim with Edit Selection Audio (Mute Others):** This mutes all audio tracks except those currently selected in the Timeline.

❸ Click OK.

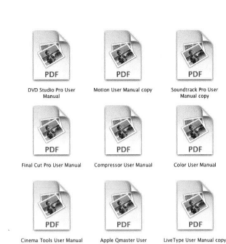

DVD Studio Pro User Manual   Motion User Manual copy   Soundtrack Pro User Manual copy

Final Cut Pro User Manual   Compressor User Manual   Color User Manual

Cinema Tools User Manual   Apple Qmaster User Manual   LiveType User Manual copy

Make More Room for Final Cut Studio

So, you might think we're obsessive, but we try very hard to keep our laptops clean and uncluttered. Enter Final Cut Studio, with its 59 GB of installed content (no, that's not a typo); it's a good idea to trim. Here are two ways you can make space.

METHOD 1 – Do a Spotlight search for PAL (or NTSC), depending upon which country you live in. Chances are you don't need to make content for both. Select the files in the Spotlight window and Press Command + Delete.

METHOD 2 – Trim those user manuals. The Final Cut Studio manuals clock in a 788 MB (that's a lot for a few PDFs).

❶ Right-click on each user manual; you can choose Show Package Contents. Inside there are copies of the manual in several languages. Unless you enjoy switching your native tongue, toss 'em.

❷ Choose Contents > Resources > [Languages]. Select the ones you don't want and throw them away.

The results: 788 MB becomes 168 MB. Not too shabby for 3 minutes of cleanup work.

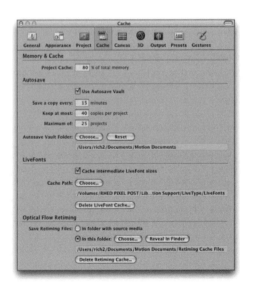

Keep It Safe in Motion

Looking to keep your work backed up when building graphics in Motion? Don't worry, it's simple.

❶ Choose Motion > Preferences and click on the Cache tab.

❷ Check the box next to Use Autosave Vault.

❸ Specify how often to save and the number of copies to store.

❹ Click the Choose button to specify a location.

Limit Real-Time Video

Final Cut Pro offers the ability for dynamic playback of content without the need to render. The number of real-time streams is a combination of several factors including the speed of your machine, disk speed, and network connection. If you are trying to playback a sequence using the Unlimited RT options, and the sequence performs unsatisfactorily, you can manually limit the real-time data rate.

❶ Call up the User Preferences window by pressing Option + Q.

❷ Check the box next to Limit real-time video to: # MB/s.

- The number to enter is determined by the number of streams that consistently play well for you and the data rate of the material.

- You can determine the data rate of a clip by looking in the Data Rate column in the Browser.

For example, you could try to play a sequence with five simultaneous video tracks containing DVCPRO HD 720P media, if Final Cut Pro warns you that frames were dropped during playback, then you then try to play a sequence with four simultaneous video tracks. If no frames are dropped, you know that your disks are at their limit.

Since DVCPRO HD 720P at 24 fps has a data rate of 5.8 MB/sec., you can set the Limit real-time video to option and enter 24 MB/sec. (4 × 5.8 MB/sec. with a little headroom) in the number field.

Avoiding the Capture Blues

Nothing is more frustrating than having a clip abort capture, especially if that clip is a long performance piece that you're loading and it bails after only 16 minutes. Be sure to select Make New Clip from the On timecode break setting.

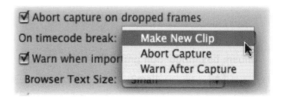

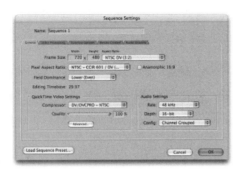

Seeing Red: When Sequence Settings Go Wrong

If you've customized your sequence settings and you're getting red bars across nearly all your footage, you're probably not configured correctly. It's likely that the last project you worked on used a different configuration (such as Widescreen or Offline RT). Check your sequence's settings (Command + 0 (zero)).

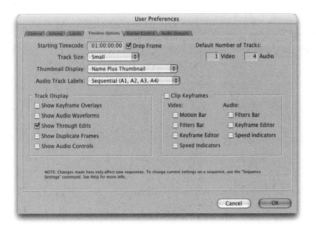

Sequence Settings

There are a few places to change sequence settings. The important detail to remember is which settings you want to change.

Selecting Final Cut Pro > User Preferences and going to the Timeline Options tab allows you to modify all future sequences.

Selecting Sequence > Settings (Command + 0) or selecting the Timeline submenu allows you to modify the current sequence only. You must have the Canvas or Timeline selected for this command to work.

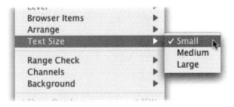

Give Your Eyes a Break: Adjusting Browser Text Size

Whether you're working on a high-res monitor (we are) or just getting a little older (us too), sometimes it gets a little hard to see things in the Final Cut Pro interface. Fortunately you can adjust how large text appears in the Browser and Timeline.

➊ Select the Browser or Timeline window.

➋ Choose View > Text Size and specify Small, Medium, or Large. (Alternately, you can contextual-click in the Browser and choose a text size.

Got a Broadcast Monitor? Then Use It!

All of the major applications in Final Cut Studio support the use of an external video monitor. However, each application is a little different in how you set it up and not all applications will support every configuration of hardware cards or decks. Be sure the hardware is powered on and properly connected before launching an application.

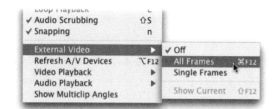

Final Cut Pro

1 Choose Final Cut Pro > Easy Setup. Pick the profile that matches your hardware.

2 Choose View > External Video > All Frames (Command + F12).

3 If you have more than one device, you can specify it by choosing View > Video Playback > and choosing the device.

Color

1 Choose the Setup Room by pressing Command + 1.

2 Locate the Video Output menu toward the right edge.

Note: Color currently does not support FireWire monitoring of any kind including DVCPRO HD and AJA IO devices.

Motion

1 Choose Motion > Preferences and click the Output tab.

2 Select an Output path based on your active hardware.

Soundtrack Pro

1 Choose Soundtrack Pro > Preferences and click the Video Out tab.

2 Select a device from the popup menu.

DVD Studio Pro

1 Choose DVD Studio Pro > Preferences. and click the Simulator tab.

2 Choose a Video and Audio path for the Simulator and click OK.

3 To invoke, click the Simulator button and use the virtual controls on the Simulator window.

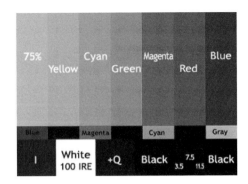

Calibrating Your Monitor Using Color Bars

While it's not quite a "user setting," you'll want to get your monitor calibrated from the get-go. Otherwise, you'll make bad decisions regarding color and exposure. Color bars are used to calibrate the monitor, but the bars have to come from a source that is known to be accurate.

You can use a Color Bar generator, which is a specialized piece of test equipment that few people actually own. Fortunately there are other sources of accurate color bars. You could use taped color bars but you would have to be sure that they were recorded correctly and that the playback deck is also calibrated. Recorded color bars are not recommended as a source of bars because there is no easy way to be sure the source of the bars and the deck are accurately calibrated.

Fortunately we do have a ready reference. Final Cut Pro and most NLEs can produce color bars using the Color Bar generator, which can be selected from the Generators menu in the Viewer window. The color bars generated in Final Cut Pro are an accurate reference to use to calibrate the monitor.

You can feed the output from the NLE to a digital-to-analog converter or from the outputs of your capture card. Be sure that any digital-to-analog converter adds the necessary setup to the signal if you're using NTSC.

NTSC and PAL Bars

The main difference between the NTSC bars shown and PAL bars is that NTSC bars have "blacker than black" bars in the black at the bottom right. PAL does not have "setup" so there is no need for these blacker than black bars. Note that the "white/gray" in the main bars segment can be 75% or 100%—both are correct as long as you know which you are using. Once you have a source of color bars you know are accurate, then calibration of the monitor is pretty straightforward once you now how. All you need to do is follow these simple steps:

❶ Turn on the monitor and allow it to run for about half an hour to stabilize the temperature.

❷ Connect the output from Final Cut Pro to the monitor via any converter device or from your capture card.

❸ Play back bars in your NLE or from tape, suitable for your television system from the Viewer's Generator menu.

❹ Start with the color to zero saturation while you adjust the black level. At the bottom right of the color bars image there are three black bars known as the PLUGE bars —Picture Lineup Generating Equipment.

❺ Adjust the brightness control until the middle bar at 7.5 IRE bar is not quite visible, i.e., adjust it so it's just visible, then back it off a bit.

❻ The 11.5 IRE bar should be barely visible. Adjust brightness until you can just see a difference between the 7.5 and 11.5 IRE bars.

❼ Adjust the contrast to maximum. The 100% white bar will bloom or appear to glow. Adjust the contrast down until that white bar just responds with no blooming and no darkening.

Adjust color hue. With the saturation set back to normal levels, switch the monitor to Blue only (if you have the Blue-only option). If you don't have a Blue-only option, use a deep blue lighting gel in front of the monitor so you can see only blue. PAL users do not have to adjust Hue because it is automatic in PAL, and not user adjustable, so they can skip this and the next step.

❽ Adjust the Hue control on the monitor until the Yellow, Green, and Red bars show equal brightness of Blue.

After this adjustment, you might want to compare skin tone, and make any final adjustments, based on skin tone, from a source that you know to be accurate. Reference monitors should not need any tweaking. Calibrate every monitor to the same source and never adjust the setting on the monitor between calibration sessions. Calibration should be checked every six months, as electronic component values can drift slightly as they age.

> Tip: Once a monitor is calibrated, tape closed the controls (other than those necessary to change source) on the monitor. You should never, under any circumstances, adjust the monitors so "the picture looks right." If it does not look right on a correctly calibrated monitor, then the picture is not right and should be corrected in the NLE.

Phil Hodgetts – http://www.digitalproductionbuzz.com/BuZZdex/

27

How to Close a Project Fast

How many times have you needed to close a project, only to find out that the Close Project keyboard shortcut doesn't work. Wait, there is no Close Project keyboard shortcut key. Well, why not map "Command + P" to close project, and while you're there, make a Close Project button too!

1 Press Option + H to customize the keyboard.

2 Click the Lock button to unlock the keyboard.

3 Select the Command tab to switch to those keys.

4 In the Search field, type close to quickly find Close Project command.

5 Switch to the Command tab.

6 Drag the command onto the P key in the keyboard layout.

7 You can also drag the button into an empty button well (such as the area in the upper right corner of the Browser).

Get to the Good Stuff: Using Search Folders

If you have several drives or a large storage network hooked up to your edit system, finding files or reconnecting clips can be very time-consuming. You can streamline the search process by harnessing the power of Search Folders. By customizing the Search Folder list with specific directories (such as drives or project folders) you can limit your media searching to a specific destination. When reconnecting offline media you can use the Search Folder list to speed up the re-linking process.

To add or replace a search folder:

1 Open up your System Settings window by pressing Shift + Q and choose the Search Folders tab. It is empty until you add a search folder.

2 Click the last Set button in the list to add a new search folder. You can click the Set button next to an existing search folder to change it.

3 Use the File dialog box to select a folder. Select a folder, then click Choose.

4 Click OK to store the list of search folders.

More Than Meets the Eye: Inside the Package

Warning: Throw out the wrong things, and you can really mess up your applications.

In OS X nearly every native application is really a folder containing all the resources it needs to operate. But every time you click that "folder," the application launches. The trick is to go to the Applications folder and Control + click the Final Cut Pro icon. You'll see a pull-down menu. Click the Show Package Contents command. Inside you'll see a Contents folder—welcome to Pandora's Box.

Warning: Throw out the wrong things and you can really mess up your applications.

When You Don't Want Your PALs Around
(or NTSCs If You're from the Other Side of the Pond)

Warning: Deleting your Final Cut Pro preferences deletes all sorts of stuff. You'll lose your Recent files, Favorites, Custom effects, Motions, and Transitions.

So you only work in NTSC (you may substitute PAL throughout) and want to rid your Audio/Video Settings folder of those options? Here's the trick: You need to remove these presets in the package located inside the Contents folder by drilling down this path: Resources > English.lproj > Final Cut Pro Settings > Hardware Settings. You'll see several presets—delete the ones you don't want.

Now comes the second part: You need to delete and rebuild the User settings in your User Preferences folder. This is located in the Final Cut Pro User Data folder in your User settings. Just search for Final Cut Pro 6.0 Prefs, and delete. The next time you start Final Cut Pro, all your PALs will be gone.

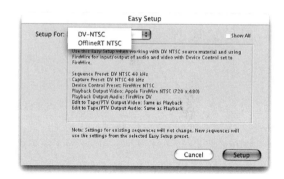

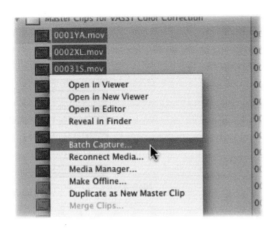

Look Before you Dig: Capture Settings ...

Surprise! You have a choice to make when digitizing (okay, you have LOTS of choices to make). But here's one more that's important. When batch capturing, you need to specify whether you want to Use Logged Clip Settings or not. This is an important decision. You are telling Final Cut Pro to capture with the settings used while logging, or to override and use the current capture settings.

- Use Logged Settings if you are sure the clips were logged properly.

- Uncheck this box if you'd like to capture at an alternate resolution, like OfflineRT.

- You should uncheck this box if you captured your clips as video only and need to capture audio as well.

Streamline Your Presets

Now let's say you want to rid yourself of all those other pesky settings you never use, such as OfflineRT NTSC (Photo JPEG) – 23.98. Drill down to <system drive> > Library > Application Support > Final Cut Pro System Support > Custom Settings. Now duplicate the Custom Settings folder, and rename it **Custom Settings Backup**. Open the original Custom Settings folder, and throw away any settings you don't want to clutter your settings. Once again, you need to delete and rebuild your User Preferences for these changes to take effect.

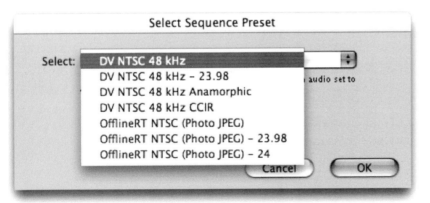

How to Kill a Hard Drive

The best way to kill a drive is to fill it up so much that it essentially locks up. Final Cut Pro seems to have a death wish when it comes to hard drives. Call up your system settings, and check the Minimum Allowable Free Space on Scratch Disks field.

Be sure to set the Minimum Allowable Free Space to at least 5 percent of a drive's capacity, whichever number is bigger. This way you'll have room for other files, such as graphics or music, associated with a project.

Danger, Danger (Aww, Shut Up)

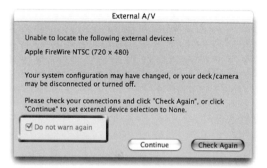

In the past, Final Cut Pro warned you when a device wasn't present—the thought being you might not actually notice that someone came in and walked off with your camera or deck. Fortunately, the engineers decided that we could have a choice.

If you're tired of clicking OK every time you launch Final Cut Pro on your laptop, check the Do not warn again box the first time you're presented with the warning dialog box. If you ever change your mind, call up your Audio/Video Settings and go to the A/V Devices tab to re-enable the warning.

MacBook Pro Users: Reclaim your F-Keys!

Want to use your F-Keys in Final Cut Pro so you can quickly access your edit commands? Well, then be prepared for keyboard calisthenics. You'll have to hold down the fn key and REALLY stretch to reach F9, F10, or F11 (you may even have to use both hands).

Fortunately OS X can fix this problem. Launch your System Preferences and click the Keyboard & Mouse button. From the Keyboard tab, just check the box next to Use F1–F12 for custom actions. Your F-keys will be F-keys again, but you will need to hold down the fn key if you want to change the volume or screen brightness.

31

Auto Conform Sequence

While you often get the best results by matching your sequence settings to the most prominent form of media in your Timeline, open format Timelines now give you a lot more flexibility. Now when media is added to a sequence, Final Cut Pro can automatically conform your sequence settings to match those of the clip.

❶ Open the User Preferences by pressing Option + Q and select the Editing tab.

❷ Make a choice in the Auto conform sequence popup menu.

- **Ask:** Final Cut presents a dialog asking if you want to conform your sequence settings to the first clip that is added. Clicking Yes will conform the sequence settings to the current clip. Clicking No will not change the sequence settings, but still add the new clip. This is the most flexible option.

- **Always:** The sequence settings will automatically be conformed to the settings of the first clip added without a dialog box.

- **Never:** Sequence settings are never changed by the first added clip. However, you can still modify sequence settings by pressing Command + 0.

What Happens with Auto Conform

When the automatic sequence conforming option is enabled, some rules apply when you first add a clip to an empty sequence:

- Only a sequence's video settings are conformed to the clip settings. Audio settings are not affected by Auto Conform.

- If a clip does not match any of the installed sequence presets, Final Cut Pro warns you. This means that the new sequence settings may not be compatible with your input and output hardware.

- If the selected clip uses an unsupported codec that is not supported or not installed, the sequence settings are not changed.

- Clips copied from the Browser and pasted into a sequence also trigger sequence conforming. If you edit multiple clips into an empty sequence, Auto Conform can also be triggered. However, it will only occur if all of the clips match formats.

Where'd My Stuff Go?

Many users choose to install or move their Application Libraries and Stock Content to another hard drive to save space. If you launch and the content isn't visible, you'll need to make a few fixes.

Motion

❶ Choose Motion > Preferences and select the General tab.

❷ Click the Library Path Choose button.

❸ Navigate to and select the destination for the Motion Library.

If you've moved LiveFonts:

❶ Select the Cache tab.

❷ Cache Path Choose button.

❸ Navigate to and select the destination for LiveFonts.

LiveType

❶ Choose LiveType > Preferences.

❷ Click the Plus symbol to add a directory.

❸ Navigate to and select the destination for the LiveType media.

Soundtrack Pro

❶ Click the Search tab.

❷ Click the Setup button.

❸ Click the Plus symbol to add a directory.

❹ Navigate to and select the destination for the Soundtrack Pro media.

❺ Click Index Now.

❻ When finished, click OK.

ON THE SPOT

CHAPTER 3

Notching It Up
Taking Effects to the Next Level

Is this the chapter you turned to first? Probably … it's the one we would've turned to first. As an editor, you want to dazzle your clients with effects and make your shows sparkle. You want to be the slickest editor on the block, with the biggest bag of tricks. No problem, you supply the bag, we'll supply the tricks. However, be prepared to push yourself. Good effects take more than drag and drop. They take time to learn and build. The more you use them, the faster you'll be able to create them and the further you'll go.

In this chapter, we've pulled together some of the top effects that our clients love, such as a film-look treatment and a blown-out treatment. More important, though, we'll teach you how the effect interface works. You'll learn techniques that increase your speed when building effects. You'll also learn strategies for faster renders and improved control. Go grab an espresso, Red Bull, or Jolt cola, fasten your seatbelt, and get ready to notch it up!

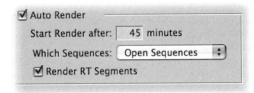

Auto Render

We love this feature, but use it wisely. In the User Preferences area, there's a checkbox to have Final Cut Pro automatically render your sequences after a certain amount of idle time (anywhere from 1 to 120 minutes.) You can have it render all open sequences, the current sequence, or all open sequences except for the current sequence.

So what does this mean to you? Well, if you wander away for a cup of coffee and get yanked into a meeting (or locked in a closet), your show could be rendered upon your return. This is very cool. However, you may not always want this to happen. Suppose you're just playing around with an effect or composite. If Final Cut Pro keeps rendering every time you're idle, your hard drive could fill up with out-of-date render files pretty quickly. So perhaps you'll want to set your preferences to Auto Render all the open sequences except for the current one just to be safe.

This is a cool and powerful tool, but like the magic wand in the Sorcerer's Apprentice, you could be up to your neck in water (or render files) if you aren't careful.

Illustration Done Easy

We've always wished that we were incredible illustrators. Alas the whole hand-eye coordination thing never really worked out. However, we have a nice, happy medium.

❶ Choose a clip you'd like to effect.

❷ Choose Effects > Video Filters > Stylize > Line Art. Whoa! Isn't that cool? Your footage has instantly been transformed into a moving illustration!

❸ Load the clip into the Viewer and click on the Filters tab. Here you can adjust paper color and opacity, and ink color.

❹ You can also control threshold and smoothness to adjust what is included as a line and the blend between the lines and the paper.

❺ Use the Mix control to blend in your original image.

Freeze Frame: Setting Duration of Stills

The Still/Freeze Duration preference has been around since version 1, but a lot of folks don't use it to its full advantage. Whenever you create a freeze of an image or drag in a still, such as a PICT, TIFF, PSD, or JPEG file, the resulting clip is your default still/freeze duration. This, by the way, is factory set at ten seconds (with total handles of 1:50 seconds, making the clip really two minutes long).

Suppose you're creating a slide show to music. Instead of leaving the default at ten seconds, set it to five. This way you won't have to readjust every clip you import.

Now suppose you're doing an animation. You could change the duration to one frame! Drag it into your Timeline, and you've just edited an animated sequence. (You can also use QuickTime to merge a sequence of PICT files into a QuickTime movie.)

The secret is Final Cut Pro will assign whatever the current default duration is to your images at the moment they're brought into the Browser. So feel free to change this throughout your project to meet your immediate needs.

Effects Tip—Moving Tab

A lot of folks still don't realize they can rip tabs off their Viewer window. This is helpful if you've loaded a clip from the Browser or have a generator loaded. So when you're editing effects, pull the Video tab off and place it next to the Filters tab. Now as you make changes, you don't need to toggle back and forth between tabs to see how your video is affected.

Photo credit James Ball

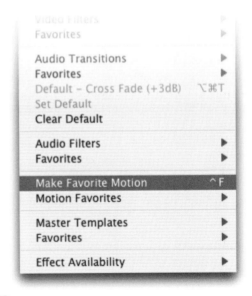

A/B Effect

Need to compare what a clip looks like with and without filters? Clients always seem to ask this question, so you might as well know the answer. You might think it's easy—just turn all the checkboxes off next to each filter name, right? But there's a better way.

In the Tool Bench is a Frame Viewer (Option + 7). This tool has several uses (especially for color correction). But when building effects, it's very useful. Follow these steps:

❶ Place the cursor over the clip you want to use. You may want to switch to the Color Correction workspace. When you do, you'll notice that the Frame Viewer is docked with the scopes in the upper-right corner.

❷ At the bottom of the Frame Viewer, choose what you'd like to see; in this case, that's the current frame and the current frame without filters.

❸ Select a V-Split or H-Split to view both states of the clip.

You can grab the blue or green squares and customize your split.

Remember That Motion

Often you'll find the need to redo a move. This might be something simple like sliding a piece of text on screen using keyframes for the center point, or something more complex. Either way, why waste time redoing your adjustments? Just like saving favorite filters and transitions you can also save motion parameters as favorites.

❶ Change parameters in the Motion tab, including setting keyframes if needed.

❷ Choose Effects > Make Favorite Motion or Control + F.

❸ Choose the Favorites bin in the Effects tab of the Browser. Find the motion you just saved (it defaults to taking the name of the clip to which you applied it) and change the name to something more descriptive.

❹ To apply the motion favorite either drag it from the Effects tab onto a new clip or load a clip into the Viewer and choose Effects > Motion Favorites > [Name of Your Favorite].

Note: A motion favorite doesn't save individual parameters; rather it saves all the parameters on the Motion tab. You might be saving more than you want.

Stealing Effects

Thanks to Final Cut Pro's media management, you can steal rendered effects from one sequence and place them in another. Perhaps you have a clip that has had several image effects applied to it; you can copy this to your Clipboard and paste it into another sequence. As long as you don't composite anything on top of it, your render files should stick. Any transitions will just need the overlapping handles rendered.

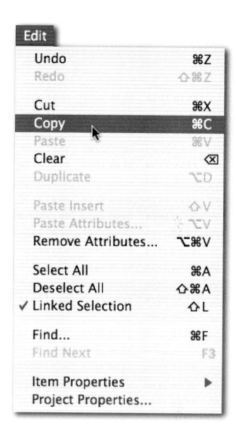

Effects Mode

Avid editors often complain that Final Cut Pro lacks an Effects mode. "Why must I double-click a clip every time to see its controls?" Well, we agree; all that extra clicking can get tiresome. Good news: So does Apple!

Follow these steps to create an Effects mode:

❶ In the middle of your Canvas is the Playhead Sync menu. Simply pick Open.

❷ In the Viewer, choose the Filters tab.

> Now every time you pause on a clip, the effect controls will pop open. Don't worry—Final Cut Pro will not try to open tabs when you're playing your sequence, only when paused.

When RT Extreme Is Not Enough

Ever want to preview an effect without rendering? Sure, you say, that's why there's RT Extreme. The number of effects, the data rate of the video files, and the speed of your machine all affect real-time preview. Things can get so demanding that your computer may not be able to keep up. Then what?

The solution is to force Final Cut Pro to Play Every Frame. To do this, simply press Option + P to invoke a non-real-time preview. You can now view every frame (at less than 1× speed) without dropping any frames.

The Quick "24" Look

So you've mastered motion favorites, right? Well, put them to use!

A popular look these days is multiple cropped windows on screen at the same time. This look has been popularized by television shows like Fox's *24*. Here is an easy way to quickly build the same look in a repeatable way.

❶ Stack 3–5 clips each on their own video track.

❷ Load each clip into the Viewer and scale and crop each one using the controls in the Motion tab. After you've adjusted each clip, choose Effects > Make Favorite Motion or Control + F.

❸ Choose the Favorites bin in the Effects tab of the Browser. Find each motion you saved and change the names to describe the crop and onscreen position; try something like "right crop use for upper right" and so forth.

❹ Now when you need to repeat the look, simply apply your motion favorites to your different tracks.

Now you can save the world, or at least your video ... again, just like Jack Bauer!

Smooth This

Got the shakes? Not quite sure where the cameraman got his inspiration for that "roving" shot? Well, the SmoothCam filter is for you! The new SmoothCam filter in FCP is leaps and bounds better than the stabilization filter found in previous versions.

❶ Load your shaky clip into the Viewer. Choose Effects > Video Filters > Video > SmoothCam.

❷ As soon as you do that a window pops up called Background Processes and the clip in the Viewer (and the Canvas if your playhead is on that clip) has an overlay indicating the status of the background process. These things are happening because the filter is analyzing the clip for changes in motion. As you might guess this process happens in the background so you can continue to work in FCP.

❸ After analyzing has finished, click on the Filters tab in the Viewer to control how SmoothCam is going to work.

❹ Use the Smooth controls to compensate for the amount of camera movement. Translation controls side to side and up and down movement. Rotation controls rotation around the center of the image. Scale controls forward and backward camera movement.

❺ Depending on how much smoothness you apply, you may have to adjust the Auto Scale parameter to control how much the filter zooms in on the image to compensate for motion change.

> Note: While the SmoothCam filter is a giant leap forward for stabilization, it can't work miracles. Don't expect footage from a drunk camera person caught in an earthquake while driving down a bumpy road to be fixed by this filter.

Final (Chroma Key) Salvation

Some of the best keys aren't chroma keys at all, but color difference keys. Two of the nicest are Keylight and Primatte. Both of these are part of Apple's Shake application. So you don't have Shake lying around? No worries. Motion has Primatte built right in. Not only can you pull a great key in Motion, but you can also watch it in real-time.

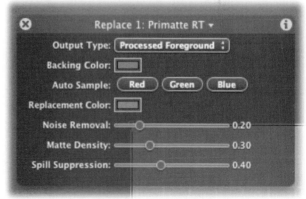

My Effects Are Broken

Every time we speak, someone asks us why sometimes their effects don't work. Upon further prompting we discover that they keep getting a black screen on unrendered effects. The answer: the Caps Lock key.

If you're using intensive effects, you sometimes want to disable them for faster navigation within the Timeline. This can also be helpful if you don't want to wait for screen redraw while tweaking an effect. Just press the Caps Lock key. All non-RT effects are disabled.

My Caps Lock Key Is Broken

For those in the know, the previous tip on the Caps Lock key is somewhat universal. In Adobe Photoshop it disables brush previews; in Adobe After Effects it disables screen redraw. So why, when you press it in Final Cut Pro, does it no longer work?

Only clips that require rendering for playback are disabled. If you've turned on the Unlimited RT feature, those clips that aren't true real-time will still play back in a limited fashion. You may want to switch to Safe RT mode using the RT popup menu.

Rack It

Rack Focus effects are often used by camera ops to add a feeling of movement in the image without actually moving the camera. Typically, these effects happen at the head of a clip to act as a transition. From time to time we've found the need to simulate a rack focus. Fortunately, this is really easy using a Gaussian Blur filter.

❶ Load the clip you'd like to effect into the Viewer and choose Effects > Video Filters > Blur > Gaussian Blur.

❷ Position the playhead at the head of the clip and set a keyframe for the Radius parameter with a pretty high value; something like 50 works well.

❸ Move about one second forward into the clip (further for a slower rack) and change the Radius parameter to 0 (a new keyframe is automatically inserted).

Play back the clip. Now that's Racking! Oh sorry, Rocking!

Effects Your Way

If you're anything like us, you keep adding and buying new effects and transitions and very quickly the Effects menu can get really full. The problem is, you probably don't use most of them on a daily basis. Well, there's help!

1 Choose the Effects tab in the Browser.

2 Open up the Video Filters bin (or any of the other bins in the Effects tab, including Master Templates and Generators) and then open a category.

3 Notice one of the columns in the Browser is called Preferred.

4 Check the boxes of the filters, transitions, templates and generators you use the most often.

5 Choose Effects > Effect Availability.

6 Here you can choose to show Recommended Effects, Preferred Effects, or All Effects (and Transitions).

7 If you choose Preferred Effects, only the items you checked in the Browser will be shown in the Effects menu (as well as the Browser).

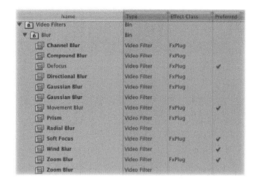

Steal from Yourself

It's okay to save time by lifting keyframes or parameters from one clip and pasting them to another. We use this all the time while editing audio or creating title effects. The simple truth, is this is one of the biggest time savers out there.

1 Select a clip that has the properties you want to access with the Select Tool.

2 Contextual-click the clip, and choose Copy.

3 Select the target clip, and contextual-click it.

4 Choose Paste Attributes, and select the desired parameters from the popup box.

Pack It (Using Filter Packs)

Perhaps you are familiar with creating a Favorite effect that you can then apply to other clips? Well, you might not know about a very cool and helpful feature called Filter Packs. Unlike plain vanilla favorite filters, Filter Packs allow you to save combinations of filters in the order that you applied them along with any keyframes that you've applied.

To create and apply a Filter Pack, simply do the following:

❶ Add filters to your clip as you see fit.

❷ Make sure you don't have any filters selected in the Filters tab of the Viewer (when a filter is selected FCP will make a favorite filter not a Filter Pack).

❸ Choose Effects > Make Favorite Effect or Option + F.

❹ Choose the Effects tab in the Browser and then open the Favorites bin. Inside the favorites bin notice that a sub bin that is named effects (Filters). This is a Filter Pack.

❺ Rename the Filter Pack to something a little more descriptive; for example, Widescreen with Color Corrector.

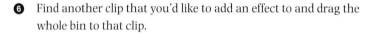
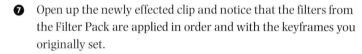

❻ Find another clip that you'd like to add an effect to and drag the whole bin to that clip.

❼ Open up the newly effected clip and notice that the filters from the Filter Pack are applied in order and with the keyframes you originally set.

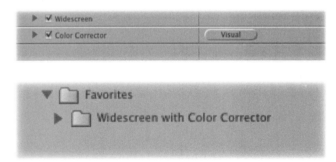

RT to the Max

RT Extreme is one of the biggest additions to Final Cut Pro. You not only get more layers of real-time effects, but you get real-time out to your NTSC monitor. How can you get even more layers of real-time effects? Final Cut Pro looks for the following:

❶ The faster the better. A brand-spanking-new eight-core Mac Pro is going to give you way more real-time functionality than your "ancient" G4 500. The more random access memory (RAM), the better. And every school kid knows the faster your bus is, the better off you are—but that's system bus, not school bus.

❷ Make sure the Unlimited RT feature is turned on and your playback quality is set to Low. You'll want to tell your system to ignore dropped frames (unless you enjoy clicking the OK button).

❸ Turn off your external monitor if you're not using it (by selecting View > External Video > Off). External monitoring can sap a layer or two from your real-time. (If you edit in Offline RT mode, you get even more layers.)

Remember, when you're pushing the limit of RT ... real-time, you may drop a frame or two. That's okay—you're building and designing the show, so you should always render before you output to a master tape.

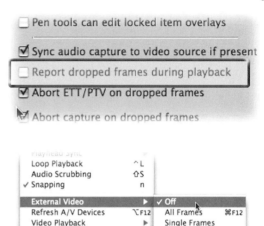

Fx from Motion

Although first introduced in FCP 5.1.2 you might not have realized that you now have a ton of new video filters that were previously only available in Motion, now in FCP.

The main advantage of these FxPlug filters, besides the fact they look really cool and do really cool things, is that they are hardware-accelerated, meaning that most of them will play in real-time.

Not sure which filters are FxPlug? Here is an easy way to check:

❶ Choose the Effects tab in the Browser.

❷ Open the Video Filters bin.

❸ Notice one of the columns in the Effects tab is Effect Class. If a filter is FxPlug it is noted here (filters that are not noted FxPlug use FxScript).

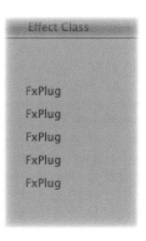

45

Motion, You Better Behave

Do you have keyframe-phobia? Don't worry, it's happened to the best of us. Fortunately, Motion provides a simple way to animate without setting a single keyframe. Sound too good to be true? It's not!

❶ Right-click on a clip and choose File > Send to Motion.

❷ Select the clip in Motion and choose the behaviors pull-down in the toolbar.

❸ WOW! Look at all those sexy behaviors! Choose a behavior that works for what you're doing. For this example choose Basic Motion > Throw.

❹ The Throw behavior does exactly what it sounds like. It literally throws the image across the screen.

❺ Make sure your HUD (heads up display) is open by pressing F7.

❻ Using the radar-like screen, drag out from the center in the direction you choose. The direction is which way the clip will be thrown and the distance from the center is how far it will travel.

❼ Play back the Timeline by hitting the space bar and watch the image fly across the screen. Yes! It's that easy.

❽ When you're done, simply save. The file will update back in FCP.

Some behaviors will only work with specific types of objects. For example, behaviors in the text categories only work with text. Also, because Motion 3 now also includes the ability to design in 3D space, many of the behaviors (Throw included) will operate three-dimensionally.

Put a Little Curve in that Line

One problem with animating things on a television screen is that it's sometimes hard to make those animations look natural. This is due to the fact that the default behavior of Final Cut Pro is to create linear keyframes. In other words, if you scale something from 0% to 100% it will happen in a linear fashion with no variance in how it scales.

To fix this issue just put a little curve in the line. Here's how:

❶ Choose the keyframes you want to alter (in the Filters tab, the Motion tab, or in the Keyframe Editor in the Timeline).

❷ Right click on a keyframe and choose Smooth.

❸ Handles will appear on the sides of the keyframe. If you have an adjacent keyframe on either side, you will have handles on both sides; if you have an adjacent keyframe on only one side, you will only have a handle on that side.

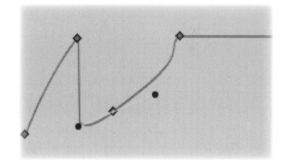

❹ Now you can manipulate the shape of the line between keyframes by dragging the handles out from the keyframe as well as up and down.

❺ To manipulate one handle only, hold Shift + Command and drag one handle or the other handle.

❻ However, not every keyframe can be manipulated in the window. For example, center point cannot be smoothed in the Motion tab, but it can be smoothed in the Video tab of the Viewer. Right-click on a keyframe in the Video tab of the Viewer (the green dot) and choose Ease In/Ease Out.

❼ You now have handles that you can control just like described above, but in addition, you can control the speed through the keyframe by manipulating the inside handles. Essentially, the closer the inside handles are together, the faster through the keyframe, the further apart, the slower.

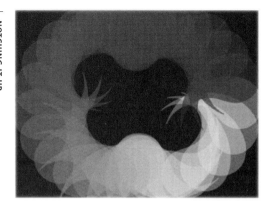

Replication in Motion

Need a little bit of texture for an abstract background? Not getting the look you want from applying different filters? Give Replicators a chance. Replicators in Motion are a way of taking a simple geometric shape (a square, for example) and replicating that shape in a pattern that can be animated.

Like particles, you can build your own, but Motion ships with quite a few that you can combine or even use standing alone.

❶ In Motion, choose the Library tab in the Projects pane (Command +2).

❷ Then click Replicators and choose a category you like.

❸ At the bottom of the Library tab you should now see all the Replicators for that category. Click on one and at the top of the Library tab you will get a preview of that Replicator.

❹ Drag the Replicator you like into the Canvas.

❺ To customize the Replicator, select it in the Canvas and click on the Inspector tab in the Project pane (Command +3).

❻ From here you can adjust parameters as you normally would in the Properties tab or for more specific controls, click the Replicator tab.

Choke It

No, we're not advocating violence unless you're trying to beat some ugly edges on a key! A common problem when keying video is fringe at the edges of the subject where it meets the matte. Not to worry! There is a quick and easy way to get the fringe out.

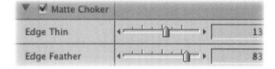

❶ With your keyed clip already in the Viewer, choose Effects > Video Filters > Matte > Matte Choker.

❷ Use the Edge Thin control to adjust the edges of the matte. Higher values will eat into the alpha channel, eliminating the fringe on the edges of the subject.

❸ Edge Feather smoothes the effect.

❹ Be careful, don't push the values too far or you will be eating into the subject.

The Effects Project

So you've become an effects guru and are making Favorite filters, Filter Packs and Motion favorites. Then all of a sudden your FCP system starts doing some funky things. As a troubleshooting measure you delete your preferences.

Everything seems to have returned to normal and you start working again. You find a clip that would work well with your favorite Filter Pack (the hot pink widescreen border!) and go to your Favorites to apply the Filter Pack.

Oh no! Where did your Favorites go? Well, FCP saves Favorites as part of its preferences, so when you deleted your preferences, you also deleted those Favorites. It was only a dream, it's okay! To prevent this from happening, here is an easy fix:

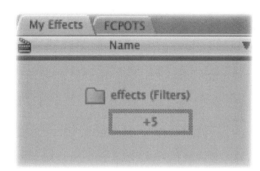

❶   Create a new project.

❷   Drag the Effects tab off the Browser so you can see it a little better.

❸   Drag all of your Favorites into the main level of the Browser for the new project.

❹   Save the project and give it a name like MY FILTERS.

Now, because all of your Favorites are located in a project and not the Favorites bin they're safe. You can carry this project around with you and then, when you're on a new machine, simply copy the filters back to the Favorites bin to use them.

Plug This Script

Not satisfied with the standard effects and transitions in FCP? Did you know that you can make your own filters and transitions in Final Cut Pro? Using the FxScript language for FCP, you can write your own FCP native plugins. Choose Tools > FXBuilder. Confused about where to start?

Check out http://developer.apple.com/appleapplications for more information.

Already the uber programmer? Then take advantage of Apple's new FxPlug architecture that makes it possible to create hardware accelerated effects. FxPlug takes advantage of other technologies such as OpenGL and CoreImage.

For more information on FxPlug, check out http://developer.apple.com/appleapplications/FxPlugsdk.html.

Precision Preview

Wouldn't it be nice to preview your complex effects without actually rendering to disk? It's a pain getting your hard drive all cluttered with extra render files that eat up drive space. Well, you have a solution; you can render to RAM.

The QuickView is a great way to view your sequence outside of the Canvas window. It caches frames into RAM as you play it:

1 The QuickView creates no render files, which is good for media management.

2 If you preview an effect and like it, you'll still have to render before you can do final output. QuickView is for previewing only.

3 You can choose Full, Half, or Quarter as your viewing resolution. Lower quality will speed up previews but may impact certain effects that contain mattes or fine edges.

4 Be sure you have specified which video to cache:

- Auto chooses the Viewer or the Canvas, whichever is active.
- Viewer or Canvas caches from the selected window.

5 None disables preview (we know ... silly choice).

6 When finished, be sure to close the QuickView window and free up your RAM.

7 If you misplace the QuickView window, select Window > Tool Bench. Otherwise, you'll open a second (or third) QuickView window.

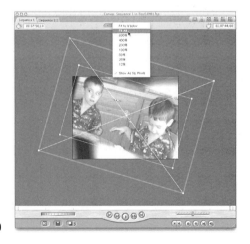

Pull Back to See More

Compositing or setting up an animation path? You'll want to choose Fit All from the Canvas's View menu. This allows you to see the bounding boxes of all elements, even those dragged partially off the screen.

How Much Is That Preview in the Window?

When using QuickView, you must specify how much area to preview. Only preview what you need because the rest is just wasted time. There are four ways to set a preview duration:

- **Using both In and Out points:** Set a specific range in your Timeline for QuickView to use.

- **Using an In point:** QuickView will preview the number of seconds specified with range slider, beginning at the In point.

- **Using an Out point:** QuickView will preview the number of seconds specified with range slider, ending at the Out point.

- **Not setting any marks:** QuickView will cache the duration set with the range slider. The preview will be split in half using the playhead, half occurring before and half after.

The Light at the End of Tunnel

Two new filters that we've used to easily create abstract backgrounds are the Slit and Tunnel Scan filters. These filters trace their way back to special effects traditionally done with motion control cameras (think *2001* the movie). Both of these filters can be found in the Stylize group. Both filters can turn ordinary footage into really neat backgrounds, but by default, they might not give you the results you want. Here are some tips to get better results:

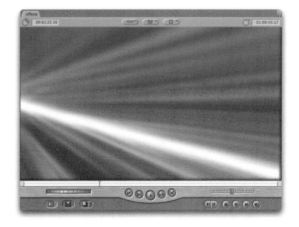

❶ Position the center point off screen or the sides of the viewable area. This "hides" the strong light of the slit or tunnel.

❷ Slow the speed way down. With the default speed, the effect can be distracting.

❸ Apply a Gaussian Blur to soften hard edges in these effects.

Easy as that! You now have a nice simple abstract background.

Vector Me

Recently we've been inspired by some commercials for a financial firm that use a real stylized look. Recreating this look combines the previously mentioned Line Art filter with another filter called Vectorize Color that gives the effect a cool abstract look.

❶ Load a clip into the Viewer and apply a Line Art filter; adjust the threshold and smoothness values (low values work better for this effect). Make sure that you lower the mix value to something like 50% to blend in some of the original image.

❷ Choose Effects > Video Filters > Stylize > Vectorize Color.

❸ Using the Vectorize Color controls in the Filters tab use the Resolution, Smoothness and Curvaceousness controls to set the look of the video. For more abstract looks set your Resolution slider to a higher value. For more realistic looks try a lower value. Adjust to taste with the other two sliders.

❹ Choose four different colors to vectorize—adjust how you see fit, keeping in mind that these colors are mapped over the entire range of color in the image.

❺ Adjust the mix down to around 50% to blend in the original image.

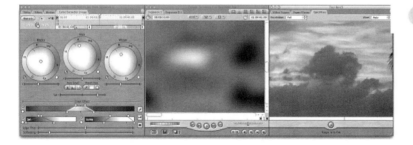

Stay on Target

Zoomed all the way into an effect while editing a motion path? Up close working on a matte effect such as a chroma key? You can see the effect play, in its entirety, without having to zoom out.

❶ Mark an In and an Out point on the area you'd like to preview.

❷ Call up the QuickView window by pressing Option + 8.

❸ Set the resolution of the effect and click Play. The first time through, the effect is building (and not playing in real-time). Subsequently, the effect will loop and play back in real-time.

Digital Concealer

Little too much detail in your skin tones? If the subject's pores are just jumping off the screen, you can use this effect to soften skin. This can be useful when polishing a shot or as a precursor to additional effects work.

❶ Select the clip to be processed.

❷ Apply the Channel Blur filter by selecting Effects > Video Filters > Channel > Channel Blur. This effect allows you to blur a specific channel of information.

❸ Be sure to view this effect in High Quality mode to make the best judgment. The best way to do this is to view the clip while paused.

❹ By default, a two-pixel blur is applied to all channels. Adjust the blur on individual channels to reduce noise. For skin tones, you'll usually blur the blue or green channels. Be sure to reduce any blur on the red channel.

Photo credit James Ball

Make Your World 3D

So, have you heard that Motion can now operate in 3D space? Well, placing objects in 3D is a piece of cake. Here's how you do it:

❶ Simply select an object that you'd like to manipulate in 3D space.

❷ Choose the Adjust 3D Transform Tool (Q).

❸ Now select the object that you'd like to manipulate in 3D space.

❹ Notice how the object now has three open circles. Clicking on the circle to the left controls X rotation, the circle to the right controls Y rotation, and the circle on top controls Z rotation.

❺ If dragging is not your thing, simply click on the Inspector tab in the Utility pane and then, Properties. From here you can control XYZ Rotation, XYZ Scale and XYZ Anchor Point.

   Note: Many other aspects of Motion can operate in 3D space, like particles, replicators, and behaviors.

Like a Kid in a Candy Store ...

Because there are now so many versions of "real-time" in Final Cut Pro, several colors became necessary to mark them in the Timeline. The old colors made sense: Green = Go, Red = Stop. But now, even we have to stop and think.

Here's a short guide to what all those colors mean:

Dark Gray	No rendering needed.
Steel Gray	Already been rendered.
Light Green	The effect is at Preview quality. It will play, but should be rendered for final output.
Dark Green	Real-time effect that can be output to video at full quality without rendering. Green will play back in the computer in real-time. However, when going out over FireWire or qualified card, the effect will play at a lower quality.
Yellow	The effect you see is an approximation. Final Cut Pro may revert to default angles for transitions or may remove soft edges. The effect plays, but not all parameters are displayed while the effect is in motion.
Dark Yellow	The effect has been rendered at a lower frame rate or quality setting than the current sequence settings. Render files are now preserved after switching resolutions.
Orange	The effect has exceeded your machine's real-time ability. However these effects are partially enabled because of Unlimited RT being chosen. You are likely to drop frames on orange clips, but this is a useful way to preview without rendering.
Blue	You've installed unsupported real-time enabler files. These blue bars indicate areas of your Timeline that may drop frames if not rendered. Blue bars are rare and may be an indication that a hardware device is no longer installed or is malfunctioning because the drivers are trying to process real-time effects but can't access the required power.
Red	You broke it! The RT ability of your machine has been exceeded. The red bar may come sooner than you'd like on older machines, but newer processors have shown significant ability to playback with Unlimited RT turned on.

Film Look: Soft Bloom

On several occasions, there's been a crazy notion that Digital Video signals can be somehow manipulated (mangled?) into the look of a film. Although we don't subscribe to this belief, it's quite possible to achieve a nicer look for your video images.

The trait that people often are trying to achieve with their "film-look" filters or recipes is an increase in saturation (intensity of color). You can easily accomplish this look in Final Cut Pro using built-in filters and features. Follow these steps:

1 Using the Selection Tool, select the clip you'd like to process using the film look.

2 Drag straight up while holding down the Option key. This clones the shot.

3 With the clone highlighted, apply a Gaussian Blur effect. Crank the filter up between a radius of 15 and 90 pixels. Don't worry if it looks awful.

4 Right-click the clip in your Timeline, and try different composite modes (Overlay, Soft Light, or Multiply). You may want to try all of the modes to see which one you like. Depending on your source, you may want to try different modes.

5 Adjust the opacity of the top clip to taste.

6 If you need to color correct the combined shot, nest it first.

Big Effects:
More Room to Keyframe

On a one-monitor system or laptop? Trying to keyframe filters in the Viewer is tough. There's not nearly enough space to view effect parameters and keyframes. You can scroll back and forth all day long and drag windows constantly.

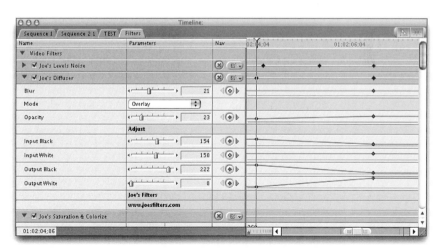

Film Look: Blown-Out

So you want to create a blown-out look and still keep your clip broadcast legal?

Here's a quick way to do it:

❶ Open the Color Correction window arrangement so that you can see your scopes.

❷ Take your clip and duplicate it on the track above (by pressing Shift + Option and dragging).

❸ Now, on the upper clip, add a Gaussian Blur filter with a radius of about 20.

❹ Pull the opacity of this layer down to about 35 percent. (These numbers will vary depending on your image.)

❺ Now drop on a three-way color corrector. Use it as a proc amp to reduce the luminance of the whites circle and raise the luminance of the midtones.

❻ Now the fun begins. Control + click the upper clip, and change the composite layer to Add. You'll see that your whites are starting to get blown out but that you've exceeded broadcast safe on your overall luminance levels. Fear not, the next step contains the trick.

❼ Use the Color Corrector 3-way and Broadcast Safe filters to bring everything into a legal zone. But it won't work by dropping it onto just one or both clips; you must nest the two clips together before you drop the Broadcast Safe filter. Select both clips, and press Option + C to collapse the two tracks into a nest. Ah ha ... a blown-out image that still caps at 100 IRE.

Chroma Key is Not Just for Weather

Creating a chroma key in Final Cut Pro is pretty easy. The trick is to use a filter under the Key drop-down called Color Smoothing – 4:1:1 (for DV-25) or Color Smoothing – 4:2:2 (for DVCPRO-50 and 8-bit and 10-bit uncompressed clips). Remember, use this filter before using the Chroma Keyer filter.

Now, drop the Chroma Keyer filter onto your shot, and click the eyedropper to sample the color you want to key out. You can press Shift + click with the eyedropper to select an even wider range of colors. We often zoom the image 200–400 percent so that we can sample all the pixels. You should also tweak the Edge Thin and Softness sliders, which gives you a cleaner key. (Remember, with these sliders, a little goes a long way.)

Blue and Green Screen
Chroma Keyer
Color Key
Color Smoothing – 4:1:1
Color Smoothing – 4:2:2
Difference Matte
Luma Key
Spill Suppressor – Blue
Spill Suppressor – Green

Grain the Easy Way

Seems like everyone is talking about making their video look more like film these days. One characteristic of film is grain. There are lots of fancy (read expensive) filters out there for simulating film grain, but here is an easy and free method for creating grain.

1. Determine the clip you want to effect.

2. Select either the Generators pull-down in the Viewer or choose the Video Generators bin in the Effects tab of the Browser and choose Render > Noise.

3. Edit the clip on the track above the video clip you want to effect, making sure it's the same length as the video clip below.

4. Toggle your clip overlays on (Option + W).

5. Adjust the opacity of the Noise generator in the sequence down to a low value (10–15).

6. Right-click on the Noise generator and Choose Composite Mode > Screen.

7. If needed, go back and adjust the opacity level of the noise generator to taste.

> Note: You might have two Noise generators in the Render category. One of them is a native to FCP (FxScript) and the other is from Motion (FxPlug). It's easy to distinguish them, the FCP one is black and white and the Motion one is color.   This tip used the FCP Noise generator.

ON THE SPOT

A Cut Above

Building Better Transitions

"Oh, a star wipe transition ... pretty!" If you hear this from your client, run away as fast as you can. We've found one good use for this transition in the past 20 years, and that was marginal. However, good transition skills can really impress your clients.

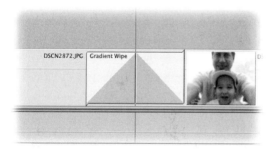

This chapter goes miles beyond "If you can't solve it, dissolve it." We'll teach you customizable effects such as a Gradient Wipe as well as custom-built transitions available nowhere else. We'll explain when to cut and when not to cut. We'll even teach you the "secret of the wells" (hmmm ... sounds like an adventure movie). Following the techniques in this chapter will put you on the fast track to a better-looking show.

Just one word of warning: If you're the type of person who drags their shots to the Timeline, you'll have problems with transitions. When you load a shot into the Viewer, you can set In and Out points that include handles (extra frames beyond your marks). These handles become the overlap where the transition occurs. Remember: No handle, no transition.

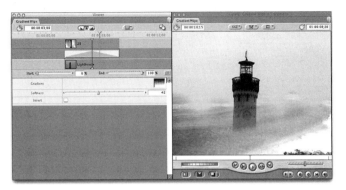

Photo credit Time Image: http://www.timeimage.com/

Gradient Wipe

The Gradient Wipe is the most useful transition inside Final Cut Pro (after a Dissolve of course). Don't be turned off by how the effect looks on its own; without an image dropped in the well, it's useless. The effect creates a transition between two clips by using a luminance map. The transition will occur between the darkest and lightest areas in the map. Why is this so cool? You can create as many transitions as you like using graphic files. Make your own or download away.

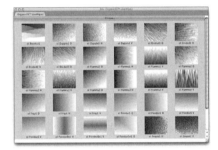

What's My Wipe?

If you want some idea of what your imported Gradient Wipes will look like, change your view. By looking at a Gradients icon, you can "see" the shape and direction of the wipe. Simply contextual-click, and choose the View as Large Icons command. By default, the wipe will travel from the darkest areas to the lightest. Remember, you can change the direction of the wipe by clicking the Invert button within the transition controls.

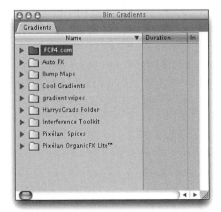

Need Gradients?

Need some inspiration on making gradients for use in transitions? Not sure where to begin? Don't have time to make your own? Visit the following websites for free gradient patterns you can use:

- http://www.photoshopforvideo.com

- http://www.autofx.com

- http://www.thepluginsite.com

- http://www.pixelan.com

Filters as Transitions

You can use any filter as a transition. You just need to combine it with a segment edit and layer the two clips. Throughout this chapter we'll refer to this as a Layered Transition Stack (LTS).

❶ Place the outgoing clip above the second clip in your Timeline.

❷ Adjust the edit points so the two tracks have at least 20 frames of overlap.

❸ With your Blade Tool or (better yet) the Add Edit command, create segments that are precisely overlapped.

❹ Apply a filter to one or both tracks, and experiment with the effect parameters (we'll show you more examples in the next few pages).

❺ Use opacity keyframes on the top track, or a cross-fade on both tracks, to create a smooth transition between clips.

Power Blur #1

This creates a nice transition between two clips. It's particularly effective to signify a major transition in time or space and can help if the handles of your clips are very short.

❶ Overlap the two tracks with a Layered Transition Stack (LTS).

❷ Apply a Gaussian Blur filter to the top track.

❸ Keyframe the track to start with a radius of 0.

❹ Apply a second keyframe at the end of the track with a radius of 50 or higher.

❺ Apply a fade to the track by keyframing the opacity.

Optionally, apply the blur in reverse to the lower track as well, and make the opacity ramp up quickly. You'll get a dissolve from one blur to another before the incoming shot is revealed, thus creating a more complex transition.

Power Blur #2

When a simple blur transition begins to look stock to you, take it one step further.

❶ Overlap the two tracks with an LTS.

 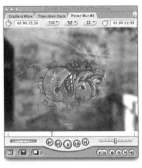 

❷ Apply a Gaussian Blur filter to the top track.

❸ Keyframe the track to start with a radius of 0.

❹ Apply a second keyframe at the end of the track with a radius of 25 or higher.

❺ Add a Gradient Wipe at the end of the outgoing clip. Experiment with different patterns in the well in the Filters tab. Also adjust the softness settings until you get a nice "melting" effect.

Roll It

So you've applied a great transition but now you realize something is just not working about the edit. You realize that you need to roll the transition about half a second to the right. But how can you do that with a transition without covering the edit points?

We can still roll edit points under a transition. Here are four ways to do it:

- Position your cursor over the edit point. The cursor becomes the Roll Tool automatically without having to choose it.

- Select the edit point (single-click) and type +/- and a timecode to roll the edit forward or back, or use the bracket keys to roll the edit forward or backward one frame at a time (shift + bracket for multiple frames).

- Select the edit point and choose F7 or double-click the edit point to launch the Trim Edit window.

- Double-click the transition (not the edit point) to load it to the Viewer. Position your cursor on the transition (above the start and end controls); your cursor becomes the Roll Tool automatically.

The Fly By

Here's a transition you see all the time on TV that's easy to create. We call it the Fly By.

❶ Choose your Effects tab in the Browser > Video Transitions > Slide > Push Slide. Double-click Push Slide to load into the Viewer.

❷ Make the duration of the transition something short (four frames works well).

❸ Change the angle to 90 for a Fly By to the right or −90 for a Fly By to the left.

❹ Locate an edit point you want to add a transition to.

❺ Drag the transition from the Viewer (use the little hand in the upper right-hand corner) to the edit point on the Timeline. Make sure that you don't center the transition on the edit; you want to start on the edit. If you're not sure what you did, right-click on the transition and choose Transition Alignment > Start on Edit.

❻ Position your playhead at the end of the transition you just added (it helps to have snapping on) and press Control + V to add an edit (make sure you either lock your audio tracks or toggle Auto Select off or you'll be adding the edit to your audio as well).

❼ Drag the transition from the Viewer to that edit point again, making sure it starts on the edit.

❽ Repeat the process one more time.

Play back your Timeline and you should see the image Fly By the screen a few times. One trick to make this process easier in the future is to save the Push Slide as a Favorite.

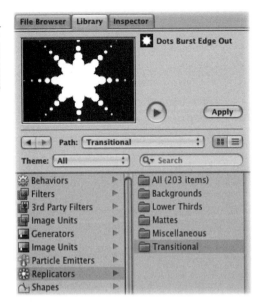

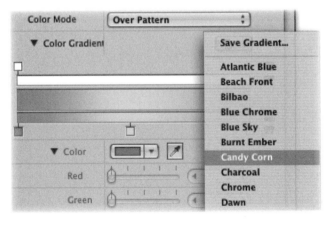

Replicate for Fun Transitions (With Motion)

The Replicator in Motion is a very cool tool for creating patterns out of shapes. It also happens to be a cool way to create a custom transition. Worried you don't know Motion? Don't worry, we're simply going to use Motion's prebuilt Replicators to create a semi-custom transition.

❶ Launch Motion and create a project to match your FCP project size.

❷ In the Utility pane click the Library tab (Command + 2).

❸ Choose Replicators > Transitional.

❹ Click on one of the prebuilt Replicators listed. As you choose different ones, they will be previewed in the top part of the Library tab.

❺ Choose one you like (we chose Dots Burst Edge Out) and drag it to the Canvas.

❻ Play back the Canvas with the space bar. Pretty cool right? Problem is, it's just a little boring. Let's fix that.

❼ Click on the Replicator in the Canvas.

❽ Choose the Inspector tab in the Utility pane (Command + 3) and then the Replicator tab.

❾ About three quarters of the way down, find the Color Mode pull-down. Here you can keep the original (white); Colorize it, which lets you pick a color; Over Pattern, which lets you create or choose a pattern of color by picking a number of repetitions; or Pick From Color Range, where you can choose or create a range of colors for the Replicator.

❿ Let's choose Over Pattern. Notice below the Color Mode pull-down a new parameter appears called Color Gradient. We could make our own gradient but for simplicity's sake, let's choose a prebuilt one from the Gradient pull-down to the right of the display of the gradient.

⓫ Choose one you like (we chose Candy Corn).

⓬ Next, setup the Timeline for export. To do this simply drag the playhead in the mini Timeline (which is right above the transport controls) to immediately after the transition ends. Now type Command + Option + O to make an out point.

⓭ Choose File > Export and choose a name for the file and a location to save it. The default settings are fine for our purposes, except we want to check the Use play range box. Click the Export button.

⓮ Back in FCP import the file. Edit the transition onto the layer above your video clips. Align the transition clip to the clips below as you see fit.

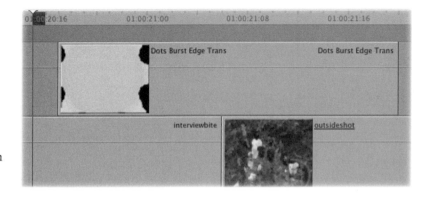

Fade Through

Performing a luminance key is a useful way to drop the darkest or lightest elements from a shot. Also, adding keyframes to a luminance key can create a nice transition effect.

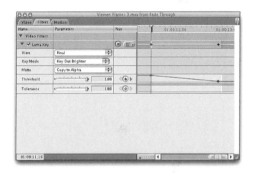

❶ Overlap the two tracks with an LTS.

❷ Apply a Luma Key filter to the top track (by selecting Effects > Video Filters > Key > Luma Key).

❸ To create a light to dark transition, set the effect to Key Out Brighter.

❹ Set the tolerance to 100 to soften the effect.

❺ Apply a threshold keyframe set to +100 at the start of the transition stack.

❻ Apply a second threshold keyframe set to –100 at the end of the transition stack.

Optionally, you can swap the direction of the transition by setting the Luma Key filter to Key Out Darker. Start the effect with a keyframe set to –100 and end with +100.

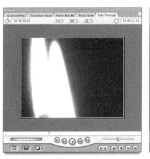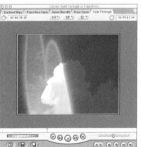

Retro is Not Always Cool

Most transitions have hard edges; that looks bad enough. Avoid the temptation to add a colored border, or you'll really be traveling back to the days of clunky tapes that were heavier than a MacBook. Instead, try feathering the edges and adjusting the width of the border. In our experience, the client will find the effect far more pleasing.

Want some retro wipes, then try out these:

- Wrap Wipe
- Zig Zag Wipe
- Venetian Blind Wipe

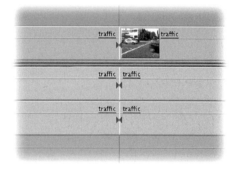

Through Edits

If you've ever bladed a segment in half, you'll see two red triangles facing each other. That's a through edit. (Through edits are turned on in your preferences by default.) This lets you know that even though you see an edit point, there's continuous timecode, so the video will play through uninterrupted.

Un-Blade

Chopped a track to perform a segment effect, such as a multitrack transition? Changed your mind? No big deal ... as long as you see the through edit triangles, simply click the edit point to select it. (Make sure you're using the Selection Tool (A)). Then simply press Delete. The edit is now removed, thus joining the two pieces back together.

A Better Cross Zoom

The Cross Zoom transition is a standard transition that pushes the outgoing shot toward the Viewer and then snaps back with the incoming shot. The default settings for this transition are okay, but the following tips will make the transition work for you and your clients:

- Keep the effect short; a duration of 15–20 frames works well.

- Change the center of the effect. With the crosshairs, set the center of the effect in a large area of similar color (such as a region of sky or shadows). This will minimize pixilation during the zoom.

- Adjust the Blur setting to Maximum on the effect.

Don't Forget About QuickTime Transitions

Most users avoid the QuickTime transitions folder. We're not sure why—perhaps it's because the transitions are oddly named. Try the following transitions out when you seem to be running low on ideas:

- **Explode:** This warps the outgoing clip into a tunnel-like wipe. We find this particularly useful when going between graphics and an incoming clip. Offset the center of the wipe to match the focal point of the incoming clip.

- **Iris:** The QuickTime Iris transition is worlds better than the Final Cut Pro Iris transition. Choose from 26 different shapes. Particularly nice is the ability to repeat the Iris pattern with separate controls horizontally and vertically. Be certain to check this one out.

- **Radial:** With similar options to the Iris transition and 39 patterns to choose from, this effect needs to be on your radar screen.

- **Wipe:** This one transition has more options and possibilities of all the transitions contained in Final Cut Pro's wipe category.

Additive Dissolve: An Effect with No Reason

Perhaps someone far wiser than us can come up with a reason to use the Additive Dissolve. This effect adds the brightest areas up to cause a flare in the middle of the transition. The problem is, you always seem to switch into a nonbroadcast-safe color space. Just forget this one exists.

While we're at it, what's a Non-Additive Dissolve do? It's really hard to see any difference from Cross Dissolve transition and pretty impossible within one second of playback.

Transitions ... Line Up Here

Here's a neat trick: You have a series of clips in your Timeline, and you want to add the same transition effect between all of them. Well, if you select all the clips and drop your transition on them, you'll soon discover that Final Cut Pro only puts the transition on the first clip. Not good. Most people we've talked to say this feature is impossible in Final Cut Pro. We disagree.

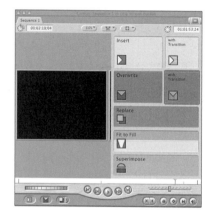

Create the transitions you want for all these clips, and make it a Favorite (in case you want to use it in another show). Then contextual-click on its icon in the bin, and make it your default transition.

Now place the playhead at the beginning of your group of clips. Highlight the group of clips in the Timeline that you want, and drag the group up into the Canvas. Drop the group on the Overwrite with Transition box. Bam—the clips fall back into the Timeline with your default transition between each clip.

More Transitions?

If you need more wipes for your system, be sure to check out these websites:

- **FX Factory** – http://noiseindustries.com/

- **Too Much Too Soon** – http://mattias.nu/plugins/

- **CGM DVE Complete** – http://www.cgm-online.com/

- **Big Box of Tricks** – http://www.nattress.com/

- **The Complete Collection** – http://www.chv-plugins.com/

Turn Off the Telly

Want your video to end like you've pulled the plug? It's not too difficult to simulate a television being switched off.

❶ At the end of your clip, create a segment by adding an edit point.

❷ Load the segment into the Viewer by double-clicking.

❸ On the Motion tab, set initial keyframes at the start of the clip for the following categories: Scale, Aspect Ratio, and Opacity.

❹ At the desired end of the transition, add three more keyframes for the aforementioned categories.

❺ Set the Scale keyframe to 20.

❻ Set the Aspect Ratio keyframe to –10000.

❼ Set the Opacity keyframe to 0.

❽ Drag the first Opacity keyframe closer to the second to delay the fade until the effect is approximately halfway completed.

❾ Check the Motion Blur box.

To further enhance the effect, consider adding multiple keyframes for Opacity and Aspect Ratio. Better yet, adding the sound of the television clicking off really helps the effect. In Soundtrack you'll find Click Off FX.aiff or Lighter Click FX.aiff, which should work nicely.

69

The Flash

You're bound to get requests from clients to reproduce this transition. Here are a few ways to do it—take your pick and use the one you like the best.

- **Dip to Color Dissolve:** Apply a Dip to Color Dissolve but change the color to white by loading it into the Viewer. Also change the duration to something quick like 5–10 frames.

- **Use a Color Generator:** Either from the Generators pull-down in the Viewer or the Video Generators bin in the Effects tab of the Viewer, choose Matte > Color. In the Filter tab of the Viewer, change the color to White. Click back on the Video tab and change the duration of the generator to something like 7 frames. Edit the generator onto the track above your clips, align it to the clips below as you see fit. Lastly, add a short 2 or 3 frame dissolve to either side of the generator so it fades up and down.

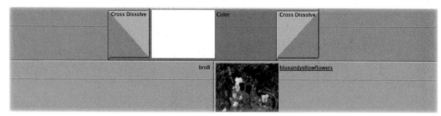

- **Use a Plugin:** There are several manufacturers that have flash transition plugins. The one we like the best is from Too Much Too Soon (http://mattias. nu/plugins/). The Flashframe transition is great and allows you to easily control the brightness and blur of the flash. Best of all, the whole package is free!

More Control

When it comes to transitions, two controls that confuse a lot of people are the start and end controls for a transition when it's loaded in the Viewer.

❶ To understand these controls a bit better, load the Star Iris transition into the Viewer, which can be found in the Effects tab of the Browser > Video Transitions > Iris > Star Iris.

❷ Drag the border control for the Star Iris up to something like 15 and change the default black to something that's a little easier to see.

❸ Apply the transition to an edit in your sequence. Play back the transition to see how awesome it is! Umm, we're just kidding. Notice, though, that the star starts from nothing and expands up to the outer edges of the screen.

❹ Double-click on the transition from the sequence to load it back into the Viewer.

❺ Adjust the Start slider to something like 25% and now play back the sequence. This time you'll notice when the playhead hits the transition, the Star is already at 25% and then expands up to the outer edges of the screen.

❻ Now, adjust the End slider to something like 60% and play back the sequence. Now you should see the Star already at 25% when the playhead hits the transition and then the Star never really growing to the edges of the screen but stopping at 60%.

If this is hard to watch, simply frame through the transition so you can see it a bit more clearly. By adjusting the Start and End sliders for a transition, you now have a lot more creative flexibility for your transitions.

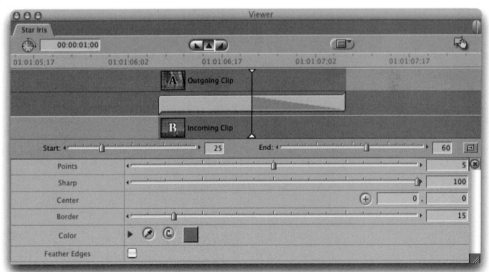

ON THE SPOT

CHAPTER 5

Fixing It in Post
Using Color Correction … You Need It!

Lots of folks open the Color Corrector effect, play for a few minutes, get confused by the scopes, and run. Well, after this chapter, the color corrector will be your best friend.

Use color correction as an opportunity to improve your show. It's the polish that really makes a show stand out. Every shot can be tweaked and improved; too little contrast, the wrong color balance, too much saturation, the whites too hot—the list of problems can go on forever. Here's the best part: With the three-way color corrector and its friends, you can often fix these problems in less than a minute!

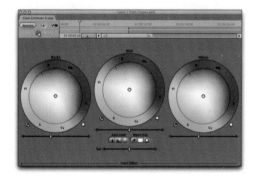

Read on, and in no time you'll master the three-way color corrector—and start making it do some pretty slick tricks. Pretty soon you'll even know about using composite modes such as Add, Multiply, and Soft Light. This may all seem pretty scary to an editor ("But I'm not a colorist!"), but hang on, we'll get you there. Plus we'll even dip our toes into Color, the new professional color-grading application from Apple.

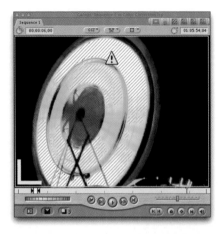

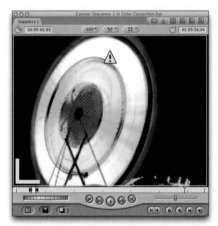

Photo credit Time Image (http://www.timeimage.com/)

Why Is There an Exclamation Point on My Monitor? (Or, Do Zebra Bars Really Grow in My NLE System?)

For those of you in a hurry—and we suspect most of you are—here's a "quick" way to spot problems. Use the Range Check command (View > Range Check). An exclamation point means you have a problem, as do red stripes. Green stripes just mean areas close to the legal limit.

Excess Luma (Control + Z)

If your image is too bright, you'll have problems in a broadcasting environment (and even in nonbroadcast situations too). Be sure your whites don't exceed their limits. Simply apply a Color Corrector 3-way filter and pull the Whites slider to the left until the exclamation point goes away. Although the Broadcast Safe filter may fix the luminance problem, most video can afford a few tweaks to the color balance and saturation. That's where the Color Corrector 3-way filter really shines.

Excess Chroma

If your image is too saturated, you'll often have colors that bleed (or spread) across the screen. Reds and yellows often have this problem. You can use a Color Corrector 3-way, the Broadcast Safe filter, or the new RGB Limit filter to fix this problem. Simply desaturate or clamp the illegal colors. If you have a really oversaturated image, the Broadcast Safe filter won't do the job on its own; be sure to use the RGB Limit filter or Color Corrector 3-way for tough images.

Both

This is how we usually work. We want Final Cut Pro to warn us if there's a problem by popping up the exclamation point. A little work with color correction usually solves the issue. If we have a hard time spotting the trouble area (luminance versus saturation), we'll just switch to one of the specialized views.

Color Corrector 3-way: Yeah, It's That Easy

The Color Corrector 3-way filter can solve many problems (and it's fast!). Most people get overwhelmed by the interface, but the key is to use one slider at a time. We usually work in this order to fix a "typical" shot that's not broadcast safe. Make sure your range check is on for both luminance and saturation, and view things on a broadcast monitor if possible.

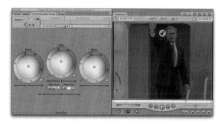

Photo credit Time Image (http://www.timeimage.com/)

❶ If needed, rebalance the image by sampling with the eyedropper. You may want to turn Range Check off temporarily so you can get a better selection.

❷ Move to the Mids slider to adjust the exposure of the image. To the right brightens, to the left darkens.

❸ Adjust the Whites slider. Slide it slowly to the left until your red zebra stripes disappear.

❹ Roll the Blacks slider to the left to restore contrast.

❺ Readjust the Whites slider and then the Mids slider if needed.

❻ Roll a little saturation in (or out) to taste. Be sure to check the image on scopes to ensure your saturation levels are safe.

Calibrate

If your broadcast monitor isn't calibrated, your color correction is worthless. We freely admit that monitor calibration isn't a forte, and if we wait too long to do it, we usually have to pull out a cheat sheet to remember all the steps. So we'll share this wonderful bit of knowledge with you.

You already own a step-by-step tutorial. It's buried in the *Final Cut Pro User Manual*, Volume III, page 540. Follow the steps—it works!

Photo credit iStockphoto (http://www.istockphoto.com/)

75

A Simple Clean Up for Digital Video Footage Captured In Low Light

Photo credit Time Image (http://www.timeimage.com/)

Most people will shoot their video cameras in any type of light, but unfortunately that doesn't always provide the best type of image. Single-chip video cameras were just not made to handle low-light recording, but that doesn't mean you can't use the imagery. So try a trick that digital still photographers use: Run a one- or two-pixel Gaussian Blur filter on just the Blue Video channel. Don't do too much more, or the footage will start to "bloom" or soften in color.

By Gary Adcock, Studio 37, Founder of the Chicago FCP User Group

Playhead Sync

Photo credit Time Image (http://www.timeimage.com/)

You've applied color correction to a clip in your Timeline and want to access the controls. You double-click the clip, make some adjustments, and go to the next clip. Somewhere along the way you forget to load the clip that you had wanted to work on. Only after several clicks do you discover that you've messed up a shot by color correcting the wrong item. The Viewer can keep up with what you're doing in the Timeline automatically. In the Viewer, there's a drop-down menu for playhead sync. Setting the Viewer to Open will automatically open the shot at which you're looking at in the Timeline. This is very useful for color correction or other effects work.

Quick Adjustments: Gear Up

Most of the time, holding down the Command key slows down your sliders. In the Color Corrector 3-way filter, it sometimes has the opposite effect. If you're trying to remove colorcast or quickly roll the hue, hold down the Command key to make quick adjustments in the color wheel areas. In other areas of this filter, it serves as a Gear Down command and will slow the dragging of the handles.

Using Eyedroppers: You'll Poke Your Eye Out

Inside the Color Corrector 3-way, you'll see three eyedroppers in the upper area. These are useful for fixing color balance. Think of this as white balancing in post; we've even fixed video shot on the wrong camera preset.

❶ Use the Whites eyedropper to click on something that should be white. Don't go for the whites of someone's eyes; go with a large area such as a wall.

❷ Use the Blacks eyedropper to click something that should be black.

❸ The Mids eyedropper really only works when using a chip chart or something with 50-percent gray.

❹ If the color balancing is overcompensated, you may need to drag back toward the center in the color wheel.

Photo credit Time Image (http://www.timeimage.com/)

Taking Something Away

Here's a way you can make finely shot footage look aged. In the early days of film, many of the film stocks weren't very saturated with color, and more often the footage had the look of a hand-colored black and white film. Final Cut Pro lets you to get this look in another one of the real-time Color Correction filters.

Select Filters > Color Correction> Desaturate (Highlights or Lows)—Highlights and Lows are actually the same filter, so don't be confused.

This filter is used to desaturate (or remove) the color in an image higher or lower than the 50-percent luminance threshold. This can create some useful visual transitions if you're coming out from black and white footage or a still image into moving video. Ramping the effects of this filter as part of the transition will give your finished piece a more filmic look.

By Gary Adcock, Studio 37, Founder of the Chicago FCP User Group

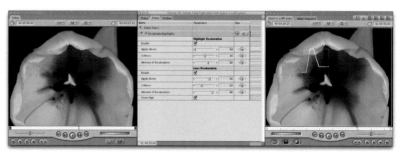

Photo credit Time Image (http://www.timeimage.com/)

Backwards Thinking

When color correcting, you'll often need to see the difference between where you started and where you are. Fortunately, Final Cut Pro allows you to compare your current frame to others in the Timeline.

❶ Switch to color correction arrangement. (Layout > Arrange > Color Correction).

❷ Underneath the scopes is the Frame Viewer tab; switch to it.

❸ The Frame Viewer's default is a vertical split. On the left is the current frame (green control handles), and on the right is the current frame without any filters.

❹ Switch one of the sides to see the previous frame. Now you can compare your color correction to the previous shot. The popup list provides other comparison options that you might find useful as well.

By Jeff I. Greenberg, Principal Instructor, Future Media Concepts

Composite Modes: Add It Up

Dark video? That never happens to us, of course, but we hear this is a good fix. If you have a shot that's really dark, you can use the screen mode to lift the details out.

❶ Place a cloned copy of the dark shot above itself (Option + drag and then hold down the Shift key).

❷ Contextual-click and change the composite mode. Add works well to combine the lightest elements.

❸ If it's too light, reduce the opacity of the top clip. If it's too dark, clone an additional copy on a third track.

This works great on surveillance/security video, as well.

Photo credit Time Image (http://www.timeimage.com/)

Your Color Is Garbage (Matte, That Is)

By using two (or possibly three) effects, you can create striking areas of focus. Darkening, brightening, and/or color correcting selective parts of a frame will do this. Essentially, we're using an Eight-Point Garbage Matte effect to create a portion of a clip on top of itself. By using soft edging, it'll blend from the effected area to the unaffected area.

❶ Clone a copy of the clip above itself in the Timeline. Select the clip with the Selection Tool, and then drag straight up while holding the Option and the Shift keys.

❷ On the top clip, add two effects, an Eight Point Garbage Matte (Effects > Video Filters > Matte > Eight-Point Garbage Matte), and a Color Corrector 3-way filter.

❸ Load the upper clip in the Viewer, and access the Filters controls.

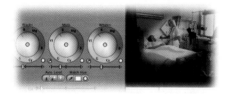

❹ Click each of the plus signs after each point (point 1, point 2, and so on), and work your way around the area in the image. Once you click a plus sign, go over to the Canvas, and click and drag until the dot is where you want it to be. You don't have to drag the dot from its initial position—you can just click and hold, and the dot will jump to where you're clicking. It takes a moment as you drag for the screen to update.

❺ Go down the Filter parameters, and feather and smooth the effect. If you solo the track (V2 in our case), you'll see that only part of the clip is now visible, and it has soft edges.

❻ Deciding that we're happy with the area, we wanted to darken everything else. We selected the Invert checkbox on the Eight-Point Garbage Matte filter, which left us with just the background.

❼ Before you leave the Eight-Point Garbage Matte effect, make sure to go to the Preview pull-down menu, and select Final.

❽ Go to the Color Corrector 3-way filter, reduce the saturation, and reduce the Black slider and the Mid slider, making a darker background surrounding a "hole" that shows through to V1.

By Jeff I. Greenberg, Principal Instructor, Future Media Concepts

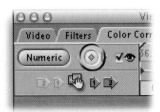

Photo credit Time Image (http://www.timeimage.com/)

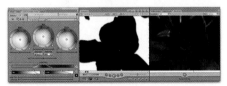

Photo credit Time Image (http://www.timeimage.com/)

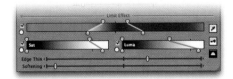

Keyframing

Sometimes problems in a shot just pop in and out (like relatives). Or maybe the color issue changes over time. Don't worry; you can keyframe the Color Correction effects to make gradual fixes. In the upper-left corner of the visual interface of the effect is an Insert/Delete keyframe button. By clicking this you'll add a keyframe for all properties. This can be useful if you want to adjust the midtones and saturation to simulate lighting effects over time. In fact, you can even pull off a "time lapse" effect with lighting sources.

A Spot of Color

You can use this specialty effect to add dramatic emphasis to a shot by leaving only one color and stripping the rest. To pull this effect off, you'll need to use the Color Corrector 3-way filter. This effect works best on clip with a dominant color region.

❶ Apply the Color Corrector 3-way filter, and access the filter's visual controls.

❷ Using the Select Color eyedropper in the Limit Effect controls, select the desired color you'd like to keep.

❸ Click the key icon to view the matte. Use the Select Color eyedropper while holding down the Shift key to add to the matte.

❹ Finesse the matte by adjusting the Width and Softness sliders for the Chroma, Saturation, and Luma values in the Limit Effect controls. When the desired color is clearly selected, there will be no holes in your matte.

❺ Click the key icon twice to toggle back to View Final.

❻ Slide the Saturation slider to the left to desaturate the clip.

❼ At the bottom are controls to tweak the effect. Check the Invert box at the bottom of the parameters list. Adjust the Thin/Spread and Softening sliders to enhance the effect.

A Frame with a View

There's even more to love about the Frame Viewer:

- The border between the green/handles allows you to change the area where you're splitting the frame.

- The three buttons on the bottom are great:

  - V-Split allows you to vertically split the frame.

  - Swap allows you to swap sides.

  - H-Split allows you to horizontally split the frame.

- The pull-down menus permit you to look at shots ahead or behind your current location in a number of different ways to compare the clip you're correcting. This is great for continuity with skin tones.

By Jeff I. Greenberg, Principal Instructor, Future Media Concepts

Photo credit Time Image (http://www.timeimage.com/)

One Hot Spot

Have a problem in just part of your image? There are two approaches worth taking:

- **Color Corrector 3-way filter:** The best method is to select the hot spot with the Limit Effect command. Base your selection solely on the luminance (ignoring saturation and hue). Be sure to feather your selection significantly. Now your adjustments to the Mids and Whites sliders will be much more gentle.

- **Broadcast Safe filter:** This filter will clamp most illegal levels and knock them into place. It can sometimes lead to banding, but it's fast and easy to apply.

Photo credit Time Image (http://www.timeimage.com/)

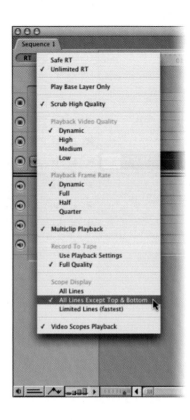

Video Scopes ... Seeing Your Whole Picture

As you do more color correction and grading in FCP you'll quickly become best friends with the scopes. One thing to know about is that you can change your scopes to adjust how accurate (or not) they are when analyzing your picture.

❶   Make sure you open the scopes by choosing Tools > Video Scopes or Option + 9.

❷   In the Timeline choose the RT pull-down in the upper left-hand corner.

❸   Under Scope Display, choose whether the scopes will be analyzing All Lines, All Lines Except Top and Bottom or Limited Lines (fastest).

Confused about the differences between these modes? Here's what's going on.

- **All Lines:** Every scan line is analyzed and then displayed in the scopes.

- **All Lines Except Top and Bottom:** Analyzes and displays all lines except for the top and bottom nine lines. These lines are ignored because information like sync and closed captioning are present in these lines.

- **Limited Lines (fastest):** Final Cut Pro scans 32 lines distributed evenly across the entire footage, which most of the time is good enough to get an idea of what's going on with the footage.

The catch about these different modes is that during playback only Limited Lines (fastest) is used. If you have selected another option only when paused or while scrubbing will FCP display the more accurate scopes.

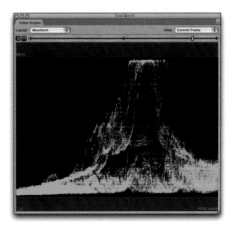

IRE versus Percentage

When talking about video scopes you often hear people describe video levels in IRE (Institute of Radio Engineers) units and also in percentages. What's the difference? Put simply IRE units measure analog video, while digital video is measured in percentages.

Which one you use depends on where you're measuring the video. If you measured the video on a digital scale (like in FCP) you'd be measuring in percentage. If you measured on an analog scale (like a Hardware CRT scope) you'd be measuring IRE. Don't worry, though, if properly setup, 100% equals 100 IRE and 0% equals 0 IRE.

The Scoop on Scopes

You've probably heard from various people that if you're going to do any serious amount of color correcting or grading, that it's wise not to rely on software scopes but to invest in a "real" set of scopes. Well, what does that mean?

To understand this, let's take a look at the three categories of scopes so you can choose the one that best matches your needs.

- **Hardware (CRT):** These are the scopes that people are generally referring to when they talk about hardware scopes. Found in millions of edit suites, these scopes can be SD or HD or both, and can offer a wide range of input options. These scopes use CRT tubes (yep, just like your old TV) to draw the image on their screen. These scopes, if properly calibrated and maintained, can be extremely accurate. Accuracy comes with a price—literally! These scopes (especially for HD versions) are very pricey! Lastly, different types of scopes like parade, vectroscope, etc., often have to be purchased separately as individual units, thus adding to the overall cost.

- **Hardware (Rasterizers):** This type of scope is becoming very popular and generally is more customizable and flexible than a CRT-based scope. These scopes work by having a hardware component (cards in a computer) process incoming video and audio signals and then display information on a computer monitor. Because functions are controlled via software, these scopes can easily be calibrated and updated as needed. While still expensive basic units are not nearly as expensive as CRT-based scopes. Additionally, rasterizers often include a wider variety of scope types than the CRT-based scopes.

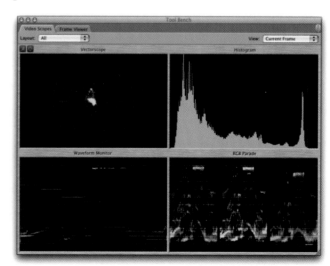

- **Software Scopes:** These scopes are built into the software program you're using (FCP, Color, etc). This type of scope often gets a bad wrap for not being accurate, but this isn't always true. The scopes in FCP, for example, can read every pixel on every line of video—now that's accurate! Another big plus of software scopes is that they don't require an additional expense as they are bundled with the software.

Photo credit Time Image (http://www.timeimage.com/)

Make Your Gray Skies Blue

It's not unusual for your skies to be washed out. This is often a problem, because video doesn't offer the same dynamic range as film (the difference between darks and highlights). Fortunately, Final Cut Pro allows you to isolate the color correction, so you can achieve a fix just to the problem area.

❶ Apply the Color Corrector 3-way filter, and access the filter's visual controls.

❷ Using the Select Color eyedropper in the Limit Effect controls, select the desired color you'd like to keep.

❸ Click the key icon to view the matte. Use the Select Color eyedropper while holding down the Shift key to add to the matte. You can click in the Viewer or Canvas window.

❹ Finesse the matte by adjusting the Width and Softness sliders for the Chroma, Saturation, and Luma values in the Limit Effect controls. When the desired color is clearly selected, there will be no holes in your matte. Also, adjust the Softening slider to improve the matte. You may get a better matte by using fewer limiting ranges.

❺ Click the key icon twice to toggle back to View Final.

❻ Adjust the color balance wheels and saturation of the shot.

You may need to add a second color corrector to finesse the scene or isolate another problem area.

Photo credit Time Image (http://www.timeimage.com/)

The Ultimate Full-Color Spread

We're about to make your entire screen a mess (it'd be much better at this point to have that Cinema Display or a second screen.) Now that you understand what is possibile with the Frame Viewer, you can have more than one Frame Viewer. To build an entire layout dedicated to color correction, follow these steps:

❶ Move your Viewer down to the lower-left corner (more on that later).

❷ Add scopes and move them to the upper-left corner.

❸ Tearing off the Frame Viewer, move it to the top row of windows (upper-right corner).

❹ In our screen capture we've already added a Color Correction effect to the shot. We've changed the Frame Viewer to show Next Edit and Previous Edit. This way we can maintain a "look" from shot to shot.

❺ Rearrange your Viewer on top of the Browser, making sure to just leave a little space to mouse over the Browser if necessary.

❻ Position the Timeline to sit in the bottom right.

❼ Use the up and down keys to go from shot to shot.

❽ The Color Corrector controls are directly under your scopes—making them easy to glance up at.

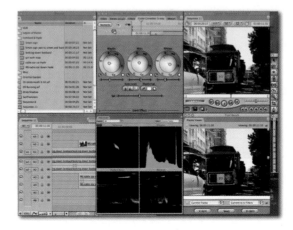

❾ Is this cramped? Absolutely. Go get a second monitor (or a nice 20-inch, 23-inch, or 30-inch Cinema Display). Most editors swear by having a two-monitor system (and others swear by just a one-monitor system).

> Note: An alternate approach to setting up your windows is also suggested by author Tom Wolsky and is shown in the lower figure. Be sure to experiment and find a layout that works well for you.

By Jeff I. Greenberg, Principal Instructor, Future Media Concepts

85

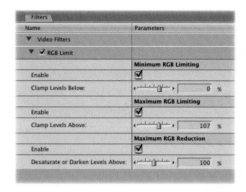

Go Ahead—Limit that RGB

One area that many people don't understand when color correcting and grading their footage is maintaining legal RGB levels. RGB? I thought most digital video was $Y'C_BC_R$, you're probably thinking (if you're a geek like us!).

Well, you're right, but at some point, it's a pretty safe bet your footage will be displayed on an RGB device. Also, some conservative broadcasters might reject a master tape with illegal RGB values. Both are reasons to maintain legal RGB values.

Fortunately there is help! Final Cut Pro 6 includes a filter called RGB Limit. You can apply it to ensure legal RGB levels. Here's how the controls work:

- **Minimum RGB Limiting:** Here, you can choose whether to activate clamping at a certain percentage using the Clamp Levels Below control. RGB values that fall below the percentage you define will be clamped or brought up to the percentage you define. Its default is 0%.

Photo credit Artbeats (http://www.artbeats.com)

- **Maximum RGB Limiting:** As the name suggests, these control the maximum RGB values for your video. Using the Clamp Levels Above control, you define the percentage where clamping will take place, meaning that RGB values above the percentage you define will be clamped or brought down. Its default value is 107%. Our feeling is that this is probably okay for most broadcasters, but if you want to be extra safe, a value of 100% would be best.

- **Maximum RGB Reduction:** Here you control at what percentage portions of the signal will be desaturated or darkened (in that order). In other words, after clamping has been applied any part of the signal that is above the percentage you set with the Desaturated or Darken will be desaturated or darkened. Its default is 100%.

Power Windows: Simple Vignettes

When color correcting and grading a show, we use vignettes all the time. Vignettes are a simple way to draw a Viewer's attention subtly to a person's face or some other object on screen. Here is an easy way to create a customizable vignette in Final Cut Pro.

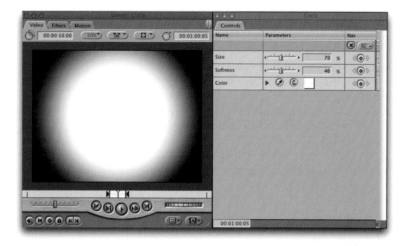

❶ Using the Video Generators pull-down in the Viewer (or in the Effects tab of the Browser), choose Shapes and then the shape you want. Circles and ovals work well.

❷ Edit that shape onto the Timeline one track above the video you want to effect. Make sure it's the same length as the clip below.

❸ Right-click on the shape and choose Composite Mode > Multiply.

❹ You should see your video displayed inside of the shape you created. Not quite what you were thinking? Don't worry, let's customize it.

❺ Turn on your clip overlays and drop the opacity of the shape layer down to something like 30%.

❻ Double-click on the shape to load it back into your Viewer. Click on the Controls tab and adjust the size and softness of the shape. Higher softness values will make the vignette less noticeable, but don't push it too far or you'll lose the effect.

A Bigger Box of Crayons—FCP Plugins

If color correction and grading is important to you (we're certified junkies) then you should really check out some of the great third-party tools that are on the market. There is some overlap between these three manufacturers, so be sure to download the demos and try things out.

- **Nattress Productions:** This manufacturer offers several powerful tools for processing video; in the color correction and grading space there are a few standouts. The **Film Effects** package offers great control over 3:2 pull-down, 24p conversion, and de-interlacing. Plus it has a great library of preset looks, proper film-style dissolves, sharpening, and gamma control. Another option is their **Big Box of Tricks**, which offers several filters (more than 70). The package includes several plugins that fix specific image problems such as noise and flicker. Plus the package offers great control over levels, curves, and image stylization effects. (http://www.nattress.com)

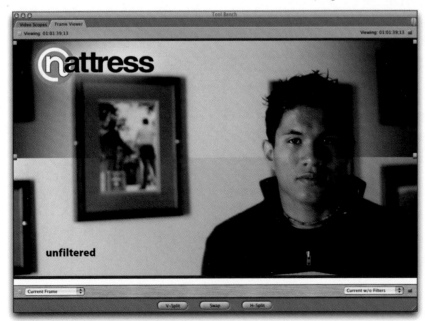

- **Magic Bullet:** The latest version of Magic Bullet is a suite of products that consists of three different products. **Magic Bullet Looks** allows for the creation of special looks that process your image. There are several presets as well as great options to customize. **Magic Bullet Frames** offers conversion from interlaced material to 24p. **Magic Bullet Colorista** allows for powerful color correction. (http://www.redgiantsoftware.com)

- **Noise Industries:** The **Editing Pack** offers several useful tools for improving video images. A strong collection of blurs is complemented by a Dewrinkler filter for improving skin. The Vignette and Matte Generator also offers several options for creating interesting power window effects. (http://noiseindustries.com)

Photo credit Artbeats (http://www.artbeats.com)

Help! My Scopes Are Hard to See

By default, the scopes in Final Cut Pro use light lines to signify their results. That's fine and all, but that doesn't mean you have to like it. Simply contextual-click a scope, and you can access several different display options that may help you see your results more clearly (such as making them green).

Plus, in Final Cut Pro 6, there are two buttons at the top of each scope that let you adjust the brightness of the scales and display data.

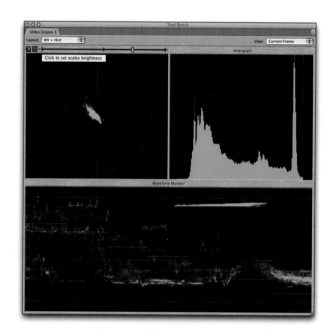

Help! My Scopes Are Too Small

Oftentimes you may want to see multiple scopes at once. You had this option before, because Final Cut Pro allowed you to view groupings of scopes. Now, however, you can have more than one scope window. In fact, you can have up to six (which is more windows than unique scopes—go figure). Simply choose Tools > Video Scopes (Option + 9) repeated times to add scopes.

Pandora's Box

When the Color Corrector 3-way filter was introduced, there was a lot of confusion. Everyone seemed to be drawn to the controls at the bottom of the screen. They wanted to tweak and fiddle, and pretty soon people started complaining they couldn't get consistent results.

Those controls are for limiting the effect. This is called secondary color correction and is for isolating your touchup to specific areas. Unless that's what you want, don't touch! Fortunately, these are now in a hidden area of the interface of Final Cut Pro.

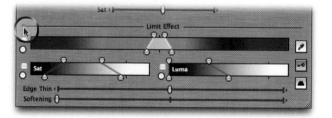

A Helping Hand

When Color was first introduced, any sort of color correction that was done in FCP was ignored when the sequence was brought into Color. This was a bummer because many people wanted to use Color's toolset to expand upon their initial corrections in Final Cut Pro. This changed in version 6.01 of Final Cut Pro and Color 1.0.1. Corrections that were done in Final Cut Pro can now be brought into Color.

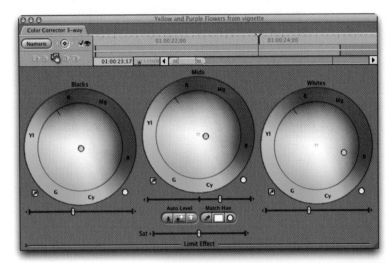

There is a catch, well, two catches (actually):

- First, only the Color Corrector 3-way will come into Color. It's translated as a correction in the Primary In room.

- Second, because FCP operates in $Y'C_BC_R$ color space and Color operates in RGB, the Color Corrector 3-way will have to be translated, which could result in some shift of the correction.

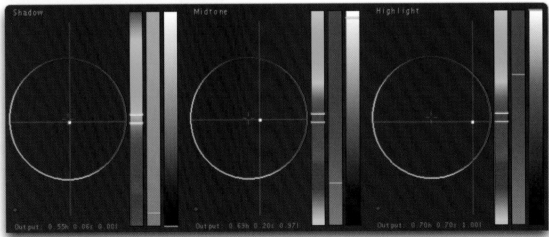

Joy in Repetition

Although "Joy in Repetition" is a great song (look it up!), the same can't be said for color correction in Final Cut Pro. Let's see, you've color corrected one interview (and it looks great!). At some point, that person is going to pop back into your show.

Let's see:

- Same person
- Same location
- Same camera
- Same lighting

We bet you can use the same color corrector. Simply drag the effect icon off to a bin. Name the effect so you can easily find it. Now you can drag the effect preset onto your new clip. Unless something dramatically changed, the effect should work. If you do need to tweak, you're at least five steps closer to "done."

It's a Wash

Need to put some life into washed-out video? Composite modes can be used to increase saturation and contrast. Simply place a cloned copy of a clip on the track above itself, and change its composite mode. Be sure to experiment with the several different modes to get alternative looks.

Photo credit Artbeats (http://www.artbeats.com)

Choosing Final Cut Pro or Color

One conundrum that Color poses is you now have another choice besides Final Cut Pro for color correction and grading, so how do you decide which one you should use? Unfortunately, there is no simple answer for that.

In general, we have found projects that require more grading than simple correction, benefit immensely from Color, while many corporate communication and lower budget broadcast pieces can be corrected more efficiently using Final Cut Pro. With that said, however, the choice is ultimately dependent on your workflow. Here is some food for thought:

Consider Using Color for color correction and grading if:

- your primary role is that of a colorist. Color will provide you with most of the tools required to excel in that role.

- you require much finer control over your image using features exclusive to Color, like curves, multiple secondary color corrections, and scan and pan.

- you must meet strict broadcast standards. We have found Color's broadcast safe controls to be more exact than Final Cut Pro's.

Consider using Final Cut Pro for color correction and grading if:

- color correction and grading are among many tasks that you need to complete. Final Cut Pro is multifaceted while Color pretty much excels only at correction and grading.

- if speed is your primary concern, use Final Cut Pro. Because you never have to leave the Final Cut Pro interface, your workflow should be faster than going to Color, where you will have to render and possibly render again when coming back to Final Cut Pro.

- the project is still in an intensive editing phase, but for some reason you want to do some color correction now. Since the Color Correction filters travel with the clip inside FCP, minimal effort is required for adjustments.

- you need to color correct and grade stills, Motion and LiveType projects, text and other generators. These items will not appear in Color.

- you don't have the time to learn Color and are already proficient with the color correction and grading toolset inside of Final Cut Pro, and that toolset meets your needs.

Lastly, if you do plan a Color workflow, it is a good idea to consider at what point you should send the project to Color. It can be very frustrating and sometimes technically complex if you've started correcting a project and then half of the show gets re-ordered. For that reason, it's generally a good idea to wait until the picture lock has been achieved on the project before sending it to Color for correction and grading.

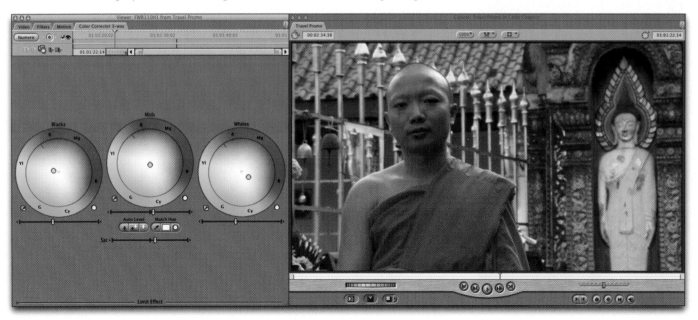

Photo credit Artbeats (http://www.artbeats.com)

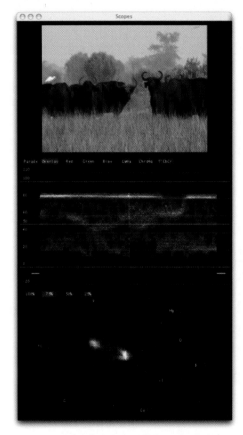

Photo credit Artbeats (http://www.artbeats.com)

Get It In—Color, That Is

We love Color! Finally, we have a professional-level color correction and grading tool. It is important to know, however, that when you send a sequence to Color, there are limitations. And depending on your project, some of these limitations can be important.

- Most filters that you have applied in Final Cut Pro will not be previewed or rendered by Color. Once you have rendered and sent your project back to Final Cut Pro from Color, the filters you've applied will once again take effect. This is especially important for Color Correction or Image Control filters (with the exception of the Color Corrector 3-way which is translated as a correction in the Primary Room in Color). Prior to sending to Color, it's a good idea to remove those filters, as you might get weird results when your project has returned to Final Cut Pro and those filters are again active. In general, you want to choose either Color or Final Cut Pro to do your color correction and grading work, and not mix the two.

- Track layering will be maintained in Color, however Opacity and composite modes will not be previewed or rendered out of Color. Instead, this information is maintained and rendered in Final Cut Pro.

- Like filters, transitions are not previewed or rendered by Color, instead, the transitions are rendered when the project returns to Final Cut Pro.

- Speed effects are maintained and previewed by Color (although variable speed effects do not play properly in Color). They aren't, however, rendered by Color; instead, Final Cut Pro renders them.

- Generators like text and shapes, still frames, Motion and LiveType Project files that are in your sequence are ignored by Color and will not be previewed. Their position on the Timeline is maintained and when the project is sent back to Final Cut Pro, they will relink and be displayed again.

- If you do need to color correct or grade generators or graphics material, you will need to render them out of Final Cut Pro as self-contained QuickTime files and reedit them back into your sequence.

Still Store It

One of the challenges of color correcting and grading a show is making sure that your color and "looks" that you've applied to shots are consistent over the course of the entire show.

Most of the time, trusting your memory about what a previous shot looked like is a bad idea. Also, always having to flip-flop back and forth on the Timeline is a pain. Color has a great tool called Still Store for helping with these problems. Here's how it works:

❶ Find a shot you want to store. Choose Still Store > Store (Control + I).

❷ Move your playhead in the Timeline to another clip.

❸ Choose the Still Store Room (Command + 7).

❹ Notice the clip that you just saved (along with previously saved clips) appear in the room.

❺ Select the thumbnail of the shot you saved and click the Load button in the bottom right-hand corner of the room.

❻ In the upper right-hand corner of the room, check the radio button next to Display Loaded Still (Control + U).

❼ In the Preview display you should now see a side-by-side comparison of the clip you're currently on and the loaded one from Still Store.

❽ Using the Transition and Angle controls in the Still Store Room you can adjust how the images are being split. Using the radio buttons below these controls, the Preview window will snap to presets as labeled (left to right, right to left, etc.).

The Quick Copy in Color

Oftentimes when color correcting and grading you'll find the need to copy corrections and grades from one clip to another. For example, maybe an angle of a character appears multiple times throughout a sequence. Instead of redoing the correction, which can lead to consistency issues, copy the grade. A quick way of doing that is simply by dragging.

❶ Grade the first shot to your liking.

❷ You'll notice that after you move your playhead off of that first clip the grade appears under the clip as a bar labeled P1 (P stands for primary). You can have up to four primary grades (P1, P2, etc.) and eight secondary grades (S1, S2, etc.).

❸ To copy a grade from that first clip simply select the P1 bar (or P2, etc.) and drag it to your new clip. The new grade has been applied to the clip.

If you're more of a keyboard or menu person you can also copy grades from the currently selected clip by choosing Grade > Copy Grade. Notice you can actually "store" five different grades and if you want, use keyboard shortcuts. To paste a grade, simply go back to the Grade Menu > Paste Grade and choose the number that you had previously saved to.

The only catch is when you copy a grade using this method, it's not storing an individual grade but rather all of the grades (both primary and secondary) for that clip. So when you paste the grade, all of the primary and secondary grades will be pasted.

Note: The words grading and color correcting are often used interchangeably. In the strict sense, correcting would be just that; "correcting" a shot that has problems, where grading refers to giving the shot a "look."

Photo credit Artbeats (http://www.artbeats.com)

Using Color for Broadcast Safe

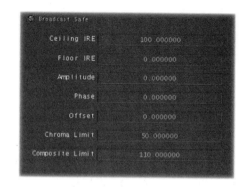

Have you been getting varying results from Final Cut Pro's Broadcast Safe filter? When you have to be sure that every pixel in your footage is legal, you need a hardware legalizer! Don't have thousands of dollars for one? Here is another option.

Color has very robust Broadcast Safe options. We've found using Color for broadcast safe is a safer option than using FCP's Broadcast Safe filter. Even if you don't do any corrections, you can still take advantage of Color's broadcast safe features.

❶ Send your sequence to Color by choosing File > Send To > Color.

❷ In Color, choose the Setup Room (Command+1) and select the Project Settings tab.

❸ In the upper right-hand corner of the room you'll notice the Broadcast Safe category. Make sure this option is checked.

❹ You can adjust the controls here as you see fit (check the Color user manual for a description of each control).

❺ After you're done with your corrections (or not, depending on if you want to use Color simply for broadcast safe) choose Render Queue > Add All and then Render Queue > Start Render. Your footage will render.

❻ Then Choose File > Send To > Final Cut Pro.

❼ Back in FCP open up the new sequence (noted with (from color) at the end) and check out the results.

Photo credit Artbeats (http://www.artbeats.com)

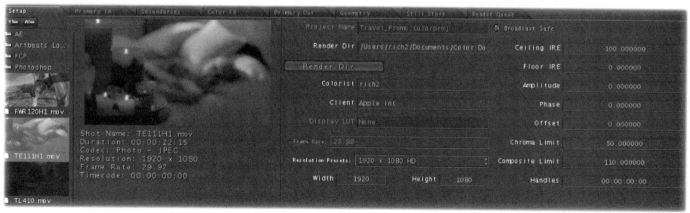

ON THE SPOT

Living Large
Working in an HD World

It seems like everywhere you go these days you're bombarded by high-definition. Of course, a lot of this has to do with television, but we've even seen ads for high-definition bottled water and makeup, seriously!

The simple fact is that production and post-production is moving to high-definition faster than you can blink. New technology comes out seemingly every day that pushes HD to new limits. The great thing is that as technology keeps progressing, cost of admittance into the HD world keeps getting lower.

It seems like many people we talk to are intimidated by working in HD. This is understandable as there are lots of new terms and numbers to keep track of. With that said, however, the beautiful thing about Final Cut Pro is that working with HD is just about as easy as working with, say, DV.

In this chapter we'll focus on a lot of big picture HD issues and techniques to help make your move to HD an easy one (and you'd better move quick!).

Frame Rate or Field Rate

Sometimes we miss the good old days where choosing a frame rate was an either/or decision. When it comes to HD, one area of confusion that we get asked about a lot is the difference between frame rate and field rate.

It's common to see numbers like 720p60 or 1080i60 as part of a description.

- The first part describes the vertical resolution.

- The P or I describes whether the footage is progressive or interlaced.

- The last part describes its frame or field rate.

In HD video, frame rate and field rate are often used interchangeably and it can be hard to tell what someone is talking about. Here is an easy way to think of it.

- When an HD format is interlaced, the number generally describes field rate (1080i60 would describe 60 fields per second).

- When an HD format is progressive, the number generally describes frame rate (720p60 would be 60 frames per second).

Image courtesy Panasonic

The interesting thing is that field can describe frame too! This is because field rates are double that of frame rates. So 1080i60 footage has a frame rate of 30fps. Got it? Well, it's not that simple. Most of the time numbers like 60 or 30 really represent fractional field rates (59.94) or frame rates (29.97) for backward compatibility with NTSC television. Math—oh, how we hate you.

Offline For HD

HD video, is of course, really big; not just the frame size, but the data rates are large as well. It's common in many HD workflows to get the most out of the footage by working uncompressed.

The question then becomes, how do you deal with dozens of hours of pristine uncompressed HD footage? Go buy a 30 TB Xsan system, of course! Didn't plan for that in the budget? No worries. Simply digitize your footage in an "offline" codec and save tons of space.

Here are some options:

- **DVCPRO HD:** An HD codec for offline? Yep! Since DVCPRO HD has a very low data rate you can save a ton more footage than you can uncompressed and it will look wonderful.

- **ProRes 422:** Apple's brand spanking new codec was designed to deliver SD data rates for HD and it's so good you can even use it as a mastering codec.

- **DV:** Using the DV codec for offline has become common in many uncompressed SD workflows, but it can also work for HD workflows. Because DV is heavily compressed and because its frame size is SD, you'll have plenty of headroom for large amounts of HD footage (you'll have to choose how your HD footage is scaled, i.e., letter box, edge crop, etc.).

- **Offline RT (Photo JPEG):** The old standby works for HD footage as well. In fact, there are even easy setups for Offline RT HD inside of FCP.

Image courtesy G-Technology Inc.

Like other offline workflows, when you've reached picture lock, simply use the Media Manager to create an offline version of the project and recapture just the footage you need in uncompressed HD space.

Apple ProRes 422 1440x1080 25p 48 kHz
Apple ProRes 422 1440x1080 30p 48 kHz
Apple ProRes 422 1440x1080 50i 48 kHz
Apple ProRes 422 1440x1080 60i 48 kHz
Apple ProRes 422 1920x1080 24p 48 kHz
Apple ProRes 422 1920x1080 25p 48 kHz
Apple ProRes 422 1920x1080 30p 48 kHz
Apple ProRes 422 1920x1080 50i 48 kHz
Apple ProRes 422 1920x1080 60i 48 kHz
Apple ProRes 422 8-bit 1440x1080 50i 48 kHz
Apple ProRes 422 8-bit 1440x1080 60i 48 kHz
Apple ProRes 422 NTSC 48 kHz
Apple ProRes 422 PAL 48 kHz

Putting the Pro in Resolution

One of the biggest new features in Final Cut Pro 6 is the ProRes 422 codec. The idea behind the codec is to give HD quality at SD data rates. And it works! Comparing ProRes 422 footage side-by-side with uncompressed HD, it's almost impossible to tell the difference. As an added benefit, it was designed with real-time performance in mind.

The codec is available in two modes—the standard ProRes 4:2:2 and ProRes 4:2:2 (HQ), which stands for high quality. The codec can be used for both SD and HD footage, though most of the time you'll use it solely for HD footage. Pro Res 4:2:2 is currently one of the best alternatives to an uncompressed SD or HD workflow.

There are a number of ways to work with ProRes 422 in FCP.

- Capture and edit in ProRes 422 using capture and sequence presets.

- Transcode your video to ProRes 422 using the Media Manager or Compressor.

- Render to ProRes 422. Sequences that use either native HDV or XDCAM HD and that use long-GOP MPEG-2 can see significant increases in RT performance by rendering to ProRes 422. To do this, choose Sequence > Settings or Command + 0 and then Render Control. In the Render section, choose ProRes 422 in the codec pull-down.

HDV—HD for the Masses

We've been working with HD for a while and have gotten used to the five- to six-figure prices of HD equipment. A few years ago when HDV burst onto the scene, we were initially excited that HD was finally going to be accessible to more modest budgets.

HDV brings about a lot of issues, however, and here are some you should be aware of:

- HDV uses Long GOP MPEG 2 compression. This is how all that HD footage can get on that little HDV tape. The problem is that MPEG-2 only has "real" frames every 15 frames (for NTSC). If you edit native HDV, Final Cut Pro has to do a tremendous amount of processing to display the video.

- Because of the "real" frames issue, frame-accurate capture, output and recapturing can be difficult.

- HDV also uses 4:2:0 chroma subsampling. This means that tasks like chroma keying and color correction are made much more difficult because of the lack of color information in the video. (Most pro formats are 4:2:2.)

Don't get us wrong, we love HDV, but for some projects, especially those that require lots of chroma keying and color correction, we tend to avoid it.

Intermediate for Happiness

Okay, so now you know that HDV uses MPEG-2 compression and that means that not every frame is a "real" frame. Editing native HDV puts a lot of strain on your system. By transcoding your HDV footage to another codec on capture like the Apple Intermediate codec, you can make your editing experience much smoother.

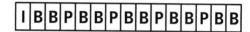

The Apple Intermediate codec was designed to be used in HDV workflows and therefore matches HDV in some technical ways such as bit depth (8 bit) and chroma subsampling (4:2:0).

Another option, if you want to keep a native HDV sequence, is to render to the new Apple ProRes 422 codec. The ProRes 422 codec is a super efficient codec and, therefore, by rendering to it you will see dramatic increases in real-time performance.

Note: If you have an XDCAM HD sequence you can also render to ProRes 422 because it also has a Long GOP MPEG-2.

Open Access

Open format Timelines is one of our favorite features in Final Cut Pro 6. They become particularly useful when you need to integrate SD footage into an HD show. However, you need to make sure a couple of options are set up correctly.

❶ Open up User Preferences by pressing Option + Q.

❷ Choose the Editing tab and in the lower right-hand corner make sure Always scale clips to sequence size is checked. With this box checked, Final Cut Pro will scale your SD footage to the HD frame but it will not distort the aspect ratio. The result will be a blown up pillar boxed image.

❸ Open up your sequence settings by choosing Sequence > Settings or Command + 0 and choose the Video Processing tab.

❹ Change the Motion Filtering Quality pull-down to Best. This ensures Final Cut Pro will scale your SD clip using the highest quality. Click OK.

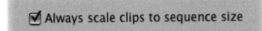

If, for whatever reason, you did not have the Always scale clips to sequence size checked in your User Preferences you would have ended up with your SD image centered in the HD frame as a small box. Don't worry though, you can fix this.

❶ Select the SD clip you want to scale.

❷ Choose Modify > Scale to Sequence.

❸ The clip's scale has automatically been adjusted to fit the HD frame size.

While the scale to sequence method can be very helpful in working with SD footage in HD projects, scaling is happening (potentially a lot) so expect some degradation of the footage.

> Note: Be wary of the Conform to Sequence command also found in the Modify menu. This command will adjust not only scale, but also aspect ratio possibly resulting in a stretched SD image if you conformed to an HD sequence. Conform to Sequence will also adjust field dominance by applying a Shift Fields filter if needed.

Playing with the Big Boys

So, the studio just called to let you know they've increased the funding for your latest blockbuster to 200 million dollars! OK, pinch yourself, Steven Spielberg!

In all seriousness, a very exciting development over the past few years has been the emergence of 4:4:4 R'G'B' HD video. What's that, you ask?

Well, most SD and HD video is 4:2:2, meaning that color information is thrown out and sampled at half the amount of brightness. Because our eyes are far more sensitive to brightness, most people can't tell.

Additionally, most SD and HD digital video is encoded $Y'C_BC_R$. This is a technical way of getting RGB color (how we see the world) to fit in the bandwidth (space) requirements of most digital video tape formats. Taken together, these two aspects of most digital video act as compression schemes, i.e., a way of getting a lot of video onto small tapes.

So 4:4:4 R'G'B' HD video records the full amount of color and doesn't convert it to video color space. The result is unbelievable quality that has been used for some very popular feature films. The technology is still very expensive but we should expect to see the prices come down in coming years.

Quality comes with some overhead. To work with 4:4:4 R'G'B' video in Final Cut Pro you must have the following:

- Dual Link SDI capture card. The signal is so big it takes two SDI cables to carry the information from a 4:4:4 R'G'B' deck to the capture card.

- 4:4:4 capable codec. Capture card manufacturers like AJA have their own.

- Extremely fast hard drives to support the data rate of 4:4:4 R'G'B' video.

NOTE: Sony's HDCAM SR is an example of a 4:4:4 R'G'B' capable format.

Monitoring Down

When monitoring HD video, it's just as important as it is with SD video to do so on a calibrated monitor, but there is another important consideration when monitoring HD video: Watch it as SD. What? Watch it as SD? Are you crazy? Well, that's debatable, but watching HD footage as SD has one large advantage.

Many programs at some point will still be watched as SD. A broadcast piece might be shown on a network's HD channel and at the same time be shown on their normal SD channel. By only monitoring HD, you might miss important things like SD action and title safe. Plus, like many other aspects of post-production, viewing HD on an SD monitor is a way of viewing your HD program in the "worst case" scenario.

So how do you monitor HD on SD monitors? Here are a few options:

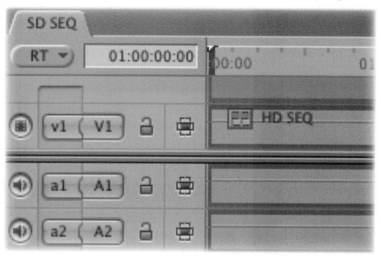

- Many hardware capture cards support downconvert on output in real-time. Both AJA and Blackmagic Design have products that support this real-time downconvert.

- If you don't have a capture card capable of real-time downconvert, you can still view your program on an SD monitor. Simply nest your HD show in an SD Timeline. Final Cut Pro will automatically letter box the footage. You could also blow up the image (performing an edge crop). You might have to render but this is an easy way to check an SD version of your show.

Fancy Flat Screen

So you've just spent more money than you'd like to think about on a huge new LCD or Plasma television. You better put that TV to work! One way to do this is by setting up that fancy new set in your edit suite and using it to impress your clients! Also, monitoring on one of these sets is a great way to monitor what your audience will probably be using in their homes. (LCD and Plasma sales are through the roof.)

Both AJA and Blackmagic Design make products capable of converting SDI to HDMI, which is the best connection type on most sets. The cool thing is that these converters can also process audio, so you get a one-stop solution for video and audio monitoring.

If you don't have the budget for an LCD or Plasma set plus an SDI converter, another way of monitoring HD is by using an LCD flat panel connected to your computer. Just make sure the monitor is capable of displaying HD (1920×1080 or at a minimum 1280×720).

❶ Connect a second LCD to your computer.

❷ In Final Cut Pro choose View > Video Playback > Digital Cinema Desktop Preview.

❸ Then choose View > External Video > All Frames.

Now you're monitoring HD!

> Note: When using an external display you might notice your video is not in sync with what is being displayed on the computer monitor. To adjust this latency, choose Final Cut Pro > System Settings and then click the Playback Control tab. Adjust the frame offset between 0 and 30 to fix the problem.

None
Digital Cinema Desktop Preview – Main
Digital Cinema Desktop Preview
✓ Digital Cinema Desktop Preview – Full Screen
Digital Cinema Desktop Preview – Raw

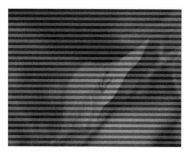

Interlaced

Progressive

HD Progressive or Interlaced—Pick Your Poison

One question we get asked a lot is, when working in HD, is progressive or interlaced better? The question is not as simple as it might seem. Here is some food for thought:

Consider progressive if:

- you might possibly be going back to film.

- you might have to create additional versions of the show. It's easier to create interlaced versions from a progressive master than the other way around.

- you have a lot of motion. Progressive footage tends to look "smoother."

Consider interlaced if:

- compatibility with existing NTSC interlaced television is a must. Not having to convert from progressive reduces the possibility of introducing artifacts.

- you have a lot of detail. Interlaced footage tends to look "sharper" when compared to progressive footage.

Pull It Down

> Long Frames ▶
> Remove Advanced Pulldown
> Synchronize with Cinema Tools

Are you a 24p addict just like us? Don't worry, there is nothing to be ashamed of! Some cameras, like Panasonic's Varicam can record 24p (really 23.98) within a 720p60 signal. It does this by duplicating frames. To get back to 24p you can remove what is known as Advanced Pulldown to get the footage back to 24fps. You can do this on capture from a FireWire source (like Panasonic's AJ HD1400).

❶ Open your capture presets (Final Cut Pro > Audio Video Settings and choose the Capture Presets tab) and select a DVCPRO HD preset to edit.

❷ Make sure the Remove Advanced Pulldown and/or Duplicate Frames from FireWire sources is checked.

If you forgot to do this you can always remove the duplicate frames after the fact.

❸ Select your clip in the Timeline and choose Tools > Remove Advanced Pulldown.

Ahhh, 24p! Love it!

Crank It! (Using Variable Frame Rates)

One of the things we love about HD cameras, including Panasonic's Varicam, is the ability to shoot variable frame rates. These allow you to create "over-cranked" and "under-cranked" speed effects in-camera, similar to that of traditional techniques used in film cameras.

The catch is that the Varicam always records at 60fps. When you choose a different frame rate (between 4–59fps), the camera inserts duplicate frames which are marked for removal later on. So, for example, if you shoot at 12 frames per second, the camera will mark the duplicate frames. Then, inside Final Cut Pro using the DVCPRO HD Frame Rate Converter, you can select your target frame rate (what your sequence is using) and process the clip. The result will be an over-cranked or under-cranked effect.

① Set up your capture by making sure you're using the 720p60 codec and that the frame rate is 59.94 or 50fps.

② Also, if using a FireWire-capable deck, make sure you don't choose to remove Advanced Pulldown and or Duplicate Frames (you choose this when editing a capture preset).

③ Ingest the clip.

④ Select the clip and choose Tools > DVCPRO HD Frame Rate Converter.

⑤ In the dialog that pops up, choose the frame rate that matches that of your sequence. Make sure you Remove Duplicate Frames by checking that box.

⑥ Choose whether to make a new self-contained QuickTime. If this box is unchecked, Final Cut Pro will create a reference file.

⑦ Check Import Result into Final Cut Pro to have the file automatically brought back into Final Cut Pro after processing.

⑧ After clicking OK, choose a destination and name for the processed media.

> Note: Panasonic's popular HVX200 P2 camera can also record different frame rates, but because it is not tape-based, no frame duplication is needed and these clips can be brought in at their native frame rate.

Create Master Clips
DVCPRO HD Frame Rate Converter...
Long Frames ▶

Image courtesy Panasonic

Hard Drives—Gimme Some Speed!

One of the biggest challenges in working with HD is getting enough speed out of your hard drives to be able to play back multiple streams of HD. While compressed formats are generally no problem for modern drives to play back, when you get into uncompressed HD, drive speed is of the utmost importance. Just one stream of uncompressed 10 bit 1080i at 29.97fps is 165MB/s!

When working with uncompressed HD, RAIDs are a must and interfacing with those RAIDS becomes your biggest option. Let's take a look at the choices.

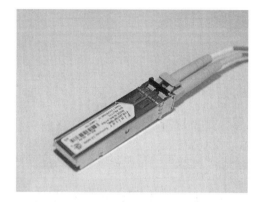

- **SATA:** Serial ATA is the new kid on the block. With speeds up to 300 MB/s it is extremely fast and well suited for uncompressed HD applications. Originally designed as an interface for internal (inside a computer) applications, in recent years SATA has found a place in external drives and RAIDS. When attached to an external device it is known as eSATA (external Serial ATA).

- **Fibre Channel:** The holy grail of interfaces these days, and if you've ever looked into purchasing a fibre channel device, you might have thought these devices were made of gold! Available in throughputs of 100, 200 or 400MB/s, fibre channel devices are very fast and are often used in super high-performance RAIDs like Apple's Xserve RAID. When absolute stability and speed is needed for your HD projects, think Fibre.

- **SCSI:** Yes! People still use SCSI (Small Computer Systems Interface). In fact, SCSI is still quite popular for RAID systems. With throughputs of over 300 MB/s it provides enough speed for uncompressed HD, but many will favor SATA over SCSI for ease of setting up and also for cost.

P2—You Too?

We admit it, we're addicts. Tapeless acquisition addicts, that is. OK, well, there is that Twinkie and Diet Coke addiction too ....

Panasonic's P2 format is an amazingly flexible format that lets you shoot DV and both 720 and 1080 DVCPRO HD with different frame rates. The cool thing is that it does this without using tape!

Footage is recorded directly onto solid-state memory cards called P2 Cards. The benefit of using this (or other tapeless formats) is that instead of capturing the footage you literally transfer it from the card as you would any other electronic file.

The catch is that Final Cut Pro can't natively use the files from a P2 card. The media files are wrapped in another file called an MXF (Material eXchange Format) file. For Final Cut Pro to use this file it must be unwrapped.

Apple designed a new feature in FCP 6 called Log and Transfer for transferring P2 footage (it does work with other tapeless formats).

❶ Mount your P2 card(s).

❷ Inside FCP choose File > Log and Transfer (Shft + Command + 8).

❸ When the window opens up you'll see your mounted card in the Browse area. Click on a clip contained on that card to load it into the Preview area. (There are two views—one called flat and the other called hierarchal.)

❹ Use the Preview and Logging area like you would if you were using the Log and Capture window.

❺ After you've logged your footage, simply click the Add Clip to Queue button.

❻ The clip will be added to the transfer queue and transferred to your Logging bin in your project (the media goes to your scratch disk).

> Note: If you have spanned clips (clips that are spanned across multiple P2 cards) all the cards must be mounted and you must use flat view to see the spanned clips. For more information on spanned clips and P2 in general, check out the HD and Broadcast Formats PDF found in the Help menu in Final Cut Pro.

XDCAM—Yes Ma'am!

Another format that we've been using a lot recently is Sony's XDCAM HD. XDCAM records HD onto a Blu-ray DVD dubbed Sony Professional Disc. These discs come in sizes up to 50 GB! Like P2, the main benefit of shooting XDCAM HD is not having to capture the footage, but rather just transfer it. Unlike formats like P2, Final Cut Pro does not have any built-in support for the format (yet).

Have no fear though, Sony was nice enough to provide a free (amazing—I know!) piece of software to allow you to transfer footage from an XDCAM HD professional disc. To download the software, simply go to: http://bssc.sel.sony.com/BroadcastandBusiness/markets/10014/xdcam_info.shtml.

Once you've installed the software, mount your XDCAM HD disc and do the following:

1 Choose File > Import > Sony XDCAM.

2 This will launch the Sony XDCAM transfer software.

3 Your disc will show up on the right-hand side of the screen in the Source view.

4 With a disc selected, the clips will be displayed in the Clip Image view in the middle of the window.

5 Clicking on a clip will load it into the clip player. From here you can use the player to set In and Out points and view metadata in the adjacent Info view.

6 To import the clip, choose the project you'd like to import into using the Send Clip to Final Cut Pro Project pull-down and make sure the checkbox is checked.

7 Click Import. The file will be imported to your selected project.

4×3—Still Gotta Be

While we kind of wish that the entire world was HD, the sad fact is that it's not. Don't worry, it will be soon! In the meantime, however, for at least the next few years we will probably have to plan on still having 4×3 outputs of our projects.

This can be challenging because you probably want to shoot and post in HD (16×9) and may even be delivering an HD version of your show but you also have to make a 4×3 version. So what to do? Well, it starts in the field.

- Many cameras have a 4×3 safe mode that will display 4×3 overlays in the view finder or LCD.

- If you're using an external monitor, some have the same overlay features but you can also take a less technical approach and simply tape off the 4×3 area on-screen.

- Make sure that everyone on the production knows that 4×3 safe has to be maintained.

In post, the same rules for masking or displaying 4×3 safe zones apply. In addition:

- Make sure everyone involved in post knows that 4×3 safe has to be maintained.

- Text and other graphic elements should be created with 4×3 safe in mind.

- During editing, make sure that you respect 4×3 action safe when selecting shots.

- Before doing your final outputs, watch the show on a 4×3 monitor not a 16×9 monitor. You may have missed something, and watching on a 4×3 monitor will make your mistakes clear.

Uprez Me, Please

We edit a lot of documentaries and on most, the footage (interviews, recreations, etc.) is shot in HD, but often there is also a lot of 4×3 archival footage. So, how do you integrate the 4×3 footage into your HD show? Well, one option is to uprez the footage to 16×9 HD!

In the past, this often meant using very expensive hardware-based standards converters at a big post house. Sure, the footage looked great, but with our budgets on most docs, we can't afford to do this.

Fortunately, manufacturers like AJA (www.aja.com) have capture cards that support the ability to upconvert SD footage to HD. We've had great results using these cards to change resolution as well as aspect ratio of our SD footage.

> Note: There are a lot of software solutions out there as well. Hardware is a worthwhile investment, but if you're in a pinch you can try a software solution out.

Creatively Using SD in HD Projects

Once people start working on HD projects, they seem to start hating SD. Well, we don't blame them. Why would you ever want to go back to SD? Well, unfortunately SD will be with us for a bit longer.

Instead of simply hating it, one thing to consider about SD is how to integrate it creatively in your HD projects. You don't always have to uprez it to use it!

A simple method is to use SD footage as part of a layered composite. Because SD footage is much smaller than HD, you can fit several SD frames into one HD frame and conversely you can create some interesting looks by stretching and distorting the SD footage. Several uses of this include:

- Create the effect of a video wall by framing several SD clips in their full resolution.

- Create abstract backgrounds by scaling, distorting and then blurring or otherwise effecting the SD footage.

- Keep the SD footage at its native frame size. This can add to the feeling that the SD footage is old or archival (this is perfect for many documentaries).

HD-DVD—Whoop! Whoop!

So you've shot and edited your HD masterpiece. Now what?

One option you have is to author a high-def DVD. Just keep in mind that HD DVD and Blu-ray DVD are still in their infancy as formats and not many people have the players to support playback.

❶ Select your sequence in the Browser and Choose File > Export > Using Compressor.

❷ Compressor will launch automatically, adding your sequence to the batch.

❸ In the Settings window, choose Apple > DVD > HD DVD: H.264 60 minutes (or you could choose the 90 minute group if needed.)

❹ Drag that settings group (folder) onto your sequence in the Batch window. Choose a destination and click Submit.

❺ After your video is done encoding, launch DVD Studio Pro.

❻ In the disc inspector, change your project to HD DVD.

❼ Import your pre-encoded files into DVD Studio Pro.

❽ Author the disc as you normally would.

❾ Build the disc and test it in Apple DVD player.

❿ To burn the disc, you'll need an HD DVD or Blu-ray DVD burner (these are available but still quite expensive).

Note: You could, of course, create your own H.264 preset. Also, HD DVDs can use MPEG-2 (at much higher bit rates than SD DVDs). You can use the existing Apple MPEG-2 preset for HD DVD or create your own.

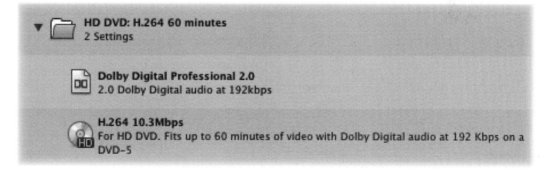

HD DVD: H.264 60 minutes
2 Settings

Dolby Digital Professional 2.0
2.0 Dolby Digital audio at 192kbps

H.264 10.3Mbps
For HD DVD. Fits up to 60 minutes of video with Dolby Digital audio at 192 Kbps on a DVD-5

```
✓ NTSC DV
  NTSC DV Widescreen
  NTSC D1
  NTSC D1 Widescreen
  NTSC D1 Square Pixel
  NTSC D1 Widescreen Square Pixel
  PAL D1/DV
  PAL D1/DV Widescreen
  PAL D1/DV Square Pixel
  PAL D1/DV Widescreen Square Pixel

  HDV/HDTV 720p/29.97
  HDV 1080p/29.97
  DVCPRO HD 720p/29.97
  DVCPRO HD 1080p/29.97
  HDTV 1080p/29.97
```

Graphically Speaking

One area that we get a lot of questions about is prepping graphics for use in HD.

The first rule you should always follow is to create your graphics in the size of your final output. We've seen more headaches caused by designers making graphics during offline editing when the image size might be smaller, and then having to recreate them again when the project moves to online editing.

Otherwise, creating graphics for HD projects you should follow these rules:

Format	Size	Pixel Aspect Ratio
720p (Including 720 HDV)	1280×720	1.0
720p (DVCPRO HD)	960×720	1.33
1080	1920×1080	1.0
1080 HDV	1440×1080	1.33
1080 DVCPRO HD	1280×1080	1.5

Note: Not the best at remembering details?
No worries, Photoshop CS3 has presets for all common HD frame sizes.

Master of All Masters

You've probably heard a lot about shooting and posting in 24p. Besides being cool marketing speak, 24p, specifically the 1080p24 master could be considered the ultimate master, or as its often known in the biz, the universal master.

Here's why:

- 24fps is the same frame rate as film, so doing a film output requires no frame rate conversion.

- Converting to 25fps is a simple telecine process, speeding up the footage (about 4%).

- Converting to 29.97fps is also a simple telecine process (3:2 pulldown).

- Allows for easy creation of 24fps SD DVD and HD DVD.

- Because 1080p is currently the best that HD gets, it's easy to convert it down to 720p.

- The universal master can easily downconvert to SD frame sizes either by letterboxing, edge crop or squeezing (anamorphic).

ON THE SPOT

CHAPTER 7

Type-Oh!
Creating Titles That "Work"

"Just slap on a title and get it out the door." These aren't the words that make for a good show. Titles can make or break a show. They're just another one of those "attention to detail" pieces that set you above the pack. We've come to rely on lower-thirds, informational graphics, and title slates to help communicate our messages.

If your text flickers, buzzes, or looks like ants marching across the screen, you need this chapter. If "just put some white letters on the screen, and use that cool Courier font," sounds good to you, then you really need this chapter. A lot of considerations go into choosing the right font, making it readable, and making it fit into your show. And what if you want more? Don't worry; in this chapter, we tackle some of the top issues with Adobe Photoshop, Apple LiveType and Motion. We'll get you up and running and on your way to better titles that will make your clients happy.

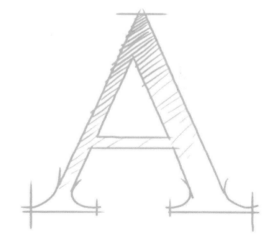

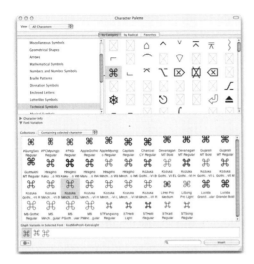

Lose That Umlaut (Symbolically Speaking, Of Course)

Need special characters but can't remember where they live on the keyboard? OS X has a great feature for this—the Character Palette.

❶ Go to System Preferences > International > Input Menu, and enable the Character Palette.

❷ Notice the new icon in your menu bar (likely a flag that matches the language). When needed, simply click it and choose Show or Hide Character Palette.

❸ The palette automatically floats above your active application.

❹ Be sure to check that you're using the same font in the text generator or other application.

❺ Double-click or drag to use the special character.

You're Glowing

Making a graphic or text generator "glow" is a nice way to soften its look. This can help reduce the computer-generated "hardness" of the graphic.

❶ Edit the title generator or graphics into your Timeline.

❷ Under the Motion tab, apply the Drop Shadow and access its controls.

❸ Set the Offset to 0 to center the glow.

❹ Change the Color to match your element, or pick a different color as your light source.

❺ Adjust the Softness and Opacity to taste until the desired effect is achieved.

Templates Are Your Friends

By using a template, you can quickly build repetitive titles with a consistent style. The goal here is to get it right the first time.

❶ Pick a title that's representative of those you'll need. It's a good idea to select the longest title so your template can accommodate all your needs.

❷ Create a new title using a text generator.

❸ When satisfied, drag the title from the Viewer to your bin. Be sure to name the clip.

❹ Re-edit the template into the Timeline, and then modify each one.

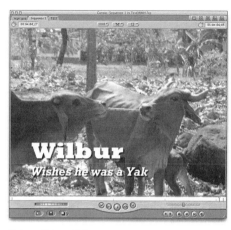

Photo credit James Ball

Better Drop Shadows

When placing type against a moving background, a contrasting edge is a necessity. This is often accomplished by using a drop shadow. But sometimes a drop shadow isn't enough.

❶ Use Outline Text from the Generators well.

❷ Set the line width to a narrower setting (somewhere between 10–25).

❸ Crank the line softness up (40 or higher).

❹ Combine with a Drop Shadow from the Motion tab.

❺ Reduce the Offset value so the shadow is tighter. Increase the Opacity and Softness to taste.

121

Mostly There (Softening CG Elements)

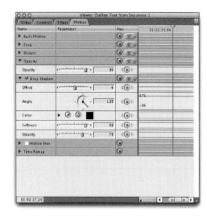

CG Elements tend to look ... computer generated. One way to improve your look when mixing lower-thirds and your video is to reduce the graphic's opacity. Try setting your graphics between 90-percent and 95-percent opacity. This will slightly soften your look and improve readability.

Save Everything

LiveType will not cover you automatically with an Autosave feature. So, be sure to frequently save your work. While on the topic of saving, is your client going to ask for a change? Always save your LiveType project, and you'll be able to go back and change the font, the text you may have misspelled, or the person who has been promoted.

By Jeff I. Greenberg, Principal Instructor, Future Media Concepts

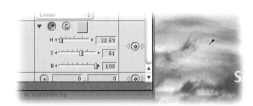

Paint with Your Scene

Trying to decide which color to use for your type? Consider using the eyedropper tool to sample color. In the Text Color parameter, you can grab an eyedropper and then pick a color from within your scene. Consider using one of the lighter elements of your scene for white. The color will likely have a small colorcast to it, and that's a good thing. This persistence of color will help tie the graphic and background together.

Just be sure to add a contrasting edge with a dropshadow or stroke for maximum readability.

Black and White Vision

Need to test your graphics for proper contrast? Most designers forget to strip their color away when testing for readability. This is important because several color combinations don't differ significantly when comparing luminance.

❶ Position your playhead over the questionable graphic.

❷ Press Shift + N to create a freeze frame in the Viewer.

❸ Select the Viewer.

❹ Strip all color away using Effects > Video Filters > Image Control > Desaturate.

❺ Analyze the graphic for proper readability. Be sure to stand at least 10 feet away from the screen.

Carve It (A Better Bevel)

Looking to create a beveled edge? The built-in bevel filter doesn't work on text. Instead, you'll need to use the channels to create the edge.

❶ Choose Effect > Video Filters > Channel > Channel Offset.

❷ Switch the Channel to move only the Alpha Channel.

❸ Offset the Channel to taste, usually a value of three to ten pixels for the X and Y axis will work, but you may need to vary this based on the size of your graphic.

❹ Experiment with the Edges settings to refine your look.

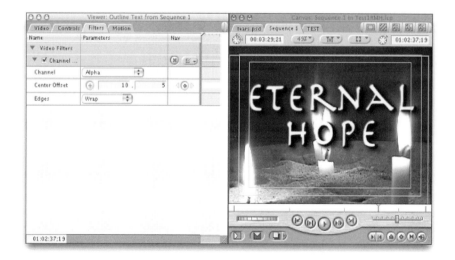

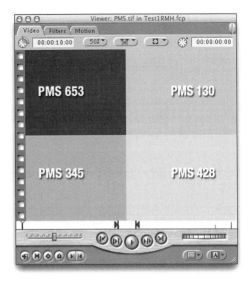

An Approved Color Palette

Need to use certain colors in your show? Make a color strip. In Photoshop, you can create an RGB document that contains blocks of color. By using the Custom Color Picker, you can fill those blocks with Pantone colors. You can also convert from CMYK colors (because most style guides never bother with RGB values). Save this as a single graphic and import into Final Cut Pro. You can now use your eyedropper tool to select colors for use in graphics and generators. If you aren't sure what colors you need, check at the PANTONE Color Cue. This handheld device lets you measure color quickly (and affordably) from physical objects. Keeep in mind Pantone only works accurately in the print world, but this is as close as you can get.

You Must Be in the Back Row

Remember when your mom used to yell at you for sitting too close to the TV? Now look at you, just inches from your edit system's screen all day long. When designing video graphics, you'll likely use type that's entirely too small. Remember, use a larger font and get some distance between you and your monitor. Send the signal out to an external monitor, then get up, and sit on the client's couch or stand in the back of the room for a while. Review your graphics from a more reasonable vantage point.

A Good Argument for Larger Type

Your computer monitor likely displays 1,000–2,000 lines of resolution. A VHS tape can reproduce about 200 lines of resolution. With such a significant loss of quality, be sure to start out with larger type.

LiveType Giving You RAM Envy

Setting your Canvas to Draft quality will improve the speed at which LiveType creates a RAM-based render. This will degrade the quality of the look only for the preview, but it allows LiveType to preview faster because it has to calculate fewer pixels. To access the setting, choose Edit > Project Properties. If you're performing text alignment or kerning, switch to a higher-quality setting.

By Jeff I. Greenberg, Principal Instructor, Future Media Concepts

Codecs For Clarity

One question we get a lot is "why does my text look so soft?" While there are few answers to this question, the most common reason is the codec that is being used for the sequence the text resides in. Compression heavy codecs like DV and HDV tend to make text look soft.

Consider "up-rezing" to an uncompressed sequence when you're done with your show to help with the text and graphics. If you're going back to tape you'll need pretty fast hard drives to play this sequence back, but if you're outputting to DVD or QuickTime you don't need to worry if your drives can play this back.

To "uprez" your sequence use the following steps:

1. Duplicate your final sequence so you can have a back up.

2. Open the duplicate sequence and go the Sequence Menu > Sequence Settings (Command + 0).

3. From the compressor pull-down choose 8- or 10-bit uncompressed (10-bit will create bigger render files compared to 8-bit).

4. Click OK.

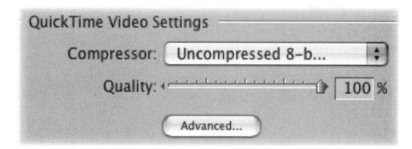

5. You will have to re-render your sequence but your text and graphics will thank you for it!

125

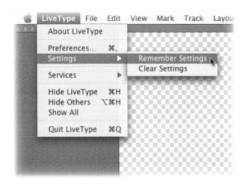

A Permanent Change: Remembering LiveType Settings

If you've changed your LiveType settings, make this "semipermanent." Choose LiveType > Settings > Remember Settings. Now that you've done this, every future LiveType project starts up the same way.

By Jeff I. Greenberg, Principal Instructor, Future Media Concepts

Stop Wasting Time

When working in LiveType, make sure your duration is the duration of the effect. Drag your In and Out points (or use the keyboard equivalents I and O) to mark the length

of time for which you want to preview your effect and create your effect. Only create the time you need!

Make sure, though, that you reset your In and Out points, or your render by default will only cover that preview section.

By Jeff I. Greenberg, Principal Instructor, Future Media Concepts

Move Beyond LiveType

Looking for cooler text animation? Then be sure to put the time in and learn Apple Motion. There are numerous text behaviors that allow you to do everything that LiveType can do and much more. Plus, it comes with more LiveFonts as well. Perhaps the biggest bonus is that it runs much faster, often previewing in real-time. Before taking the leap, though, be sure to see if your machine can handle this cutting-edge software. Be sure to check the tech specs on Apple's website and be sure that you get a powerful graphics card.

How to Get High "Marks"

You've probably heard that art directors always look for true quote marks (" "). The same holds true for apostrophes or single quotes (' '). But how do you access these when all you have is an engineering-style keyboard? After all, you probably knew that the key next to the Return key was for indicating feet and inches (they look like this, 6' 3").

You access the true quote marks by pressing the following:

Option + [	for	"
Option + Shift + [	for	"
Option +]	for	'
Option + Shift +]	for	'

Important Symbolism

When building screen graphics, there will be several special symbols you'll need. The following table shows a few of the symbols clients ask for most. These are on a standard U.S. keyboard, so if you can't find something, fire open KeyCaps from your Utilities folder. And remember, not all fonts have full character sets (especially the cheap sets).

Symbol	Key Combination	Name
●	Option + 8	Bullet
TM	Option + 2	Trademark
¢	Option + 4	Cents
°	Option + Shift + 8	Degrees
´	Option + E + Letter	Accent
®	Option + R	Registered
©	Option + G	Copyright
√	Option + V	Check Mark
	Option + Shift + K	Apple

"Hello"
He's
6'3"

127

Side-by-Side Credit Roll

We've seen people jump through some amazing hoops to perform side-by-side credit rolls. They do one credit roll for the tile justified right, then move left, and do another credit roll with the name justified left, and then move right. Then aligned...and the horror continues.

Actually, it's very easy. Open the Scrolling Text Option under Text in the generator's tab or Effect tab. Simply type the person's title, then an asterisk (*) with no spaces, and then the person's name. You'll see that your list has them right and left justified to each other. And that mysterious "gap width" slider now does something. (This only works with center-justified scrolling text.)

Powerful Text Effects Made Easy

A great new tool came across our desks recently called FxFactory. This cool package harnesses the power of FxPlug which allows for incredible effects, high bit-depths, and fast rendering. One of the nicest features is that the effects work in both Motion and Final Cut Pro. While the package is not just about text (there are a lot of great filters) here are a few of our text-oriented favorites:

- **3D Text Cloud & 3D Text Grid:** These two are amazing— hundreds of words moving in 3D space with tons of control and no effort.

- **Particle System:** A very flexible particle system that you can use right inside of FCP. Great for creating textures and you can even make a logo or text into a particle.

- **RSS World News:** Plug in an RSS feed (such as a news page) to quickly generate new text.

- **NI Blurs and Glows:** These filters go a long way to creating impressive text effects and transitions—several times better than the bundled filters.

Curious? Don't be; you can try it free for 15 days! FxFactory is a free download which gets you unlimited access to free plug-ins and a chance to try all other plug-ins and locked features for 15 days. (http://www.noiseindustries.com).

Blur Me

Blurs are useful for all sorts of things and text is no exception. Our three favorite blurs for text are Gaussian, Radial, and Wind Blur. Let's take a look at each one to create a cool transition effect for your text.

Gaussian

❶ Load your text into the Viewer and apply a Gaussian Blur filter (Effects > Video Filters > Blur > Gaussian Blur).

❷ Select the Filters tab in the Viewer and make a keyframe for the Radius parameter at the beginning of the clip; make the value something like 50.

❸ Go 10 or 15 frames into the clip and adjust the Radius value down to 0 (a new keyframe is added automatically).

Radial

❶ Load your text into the Viewer and apply a Radial Blur filter (Effects > Video Filters > Blur > Radial Blur).

❷ Select the Filters tab in the Viewer and make keyframes for the Angle and Steps parameters at the beginning of the clip; make the values something like 90 and 10.

❸ Go 10 or 15 frames into the clip and change the Angle and Steps parameters back to 0 and 0 (a new keyframe is added automatically).

Wind Blur

❶ Load your text into the Viewer and apply a Wind Blur Filter (Effects > Video Filters > Blur > Wind Blur).

❷ Select the Filters tab in the Viewer and make keyframes for the Direction, Radius and Steps parameters at the beginning of the clip; make the values something like 90, 100 and 10.

❸ Go 10 or 15 frames into the clip and adjust all three parameters back down to 0 (a new keyframe is added automatically).

Adding a fade in/out or cross dissolve transition of 5–7 frames at the start of each clip can help soften the effect in each method.

Watch the Decimals

Here is another tip to help sharpen up text. Often editors and designers place text wherever it looks good. Well yeah! That makes sense! Many times though, the clarity of the text is sacrificed by this method.

The problem is that often the center point for the piece of text is on a coordinates like 100,60.3, where 100 is the X position on screen and 60.3 is the Y position.

The Y position directly impacts text clarity, because scan lines are drawn top to bottom. Additionally, there are no sub-pixels, meaning that in our example, because the text exists on a value of 60.3 Final Cut Pro has to "share" parts of the text with neighboring pixels thus making the text soft.

To fix this, simply load the piece of text into the Viewer.

❶ Click on the Motion tab.

❷ In the center point boxes (the first one is the X coordinate, the second is they Y coordinate) make sure the Y coordinate is a whole pixel. When you make the change the difference in many cases will be subtle but if you look hard the text is sharper.

If you have a large group of titles that have this problem, like a group of lower 3rds, fix the first one, copy the clip (Command + C) select the other titles and paste attributes (Option + V). Make sure you only have the Basic Motion text box checked.

Watch the Y-Axis

On a related note, keep an eye on the Y value. If you've cut video or field-rendered animation into your show, you need to keep the Y value even (literally). The number needs to end in 0, 2, 4, 6, or 8, otherwise the field order will be reversed and the video or animation will strobe.

Create Texture for Your Text

"Can you make the text look...better?"

If we've heard it once we've heard it a million times. Fact is, plain text is just that—plain. Of course there are lots of things we can do to jazz up our text but using composite modes combined with text color and opacity is among the easiest.

❶ To experiment with composite modes and text, place your text on the layer above your video.

❷ Right-click (Control + click) on the text and choose Composite Modes. From here choose the composite mode you like best.

❸ Changing text color and opacity are two more ways to adjust these effects.

Another very cool way to add texture is to use travel mattes. This works in the same way as described above, but the layer order is just opposite. Your text is on the bottom layer and your video on the top layer.

❶ Select your video layer and right-click.

❷ Choose Composite Mode Luma.

❸ Your video will now play inside of the text. You can reposition your text over the video to get the best overall look.

Need some textures to get you started?

- http://www.rhedpixel.com/soulmates/ interior/soul_text.sit

- http://www.photoshopforvideo.com/ resources/

Political Glow

We've all seen a political ad where at the end of the spot the candidate's name or message glows up and down. This effective method of highlighting text is easy to accomplish in FCP with the Outer Glow filter.

1 Load your text into the Viewer.

2 Choose Effects > Video Filters > Glow > Outer Glow.

3 Click on the Filters tab.

4 For the Inner and Outer color parameters choose the colors you'd like in the glow. Yellows and off-whites tend to work the best. Making these colors similar but slightly different also works well.

5 Set a keyframe for the Radius and Brightness parameters at the start of the clip and enter a value of 0.

6 Go slightly into the clip (one second is good) and change the Radius and Brightness parameters to higher values (10 and 5 work well).

7 Go forward another second or so and adjust the Radius and Brightness parameters back down to 0.

You can use the other parameters to adjust the glow to taste. Saving this effect as a favorite is a good idea. Trust us; you'll be using it all the time.

Pick a Font Fast

You've probably been in a situation with a client trying to choose a font for a title. This can sometimes be frustrating and a time-consuming process. Luckily, Motion has a real easy way to preview font changes in real-time.

1 Create your title in Motion.

2 Make sure your HUD is open (F7).

3 Select your text, and then in the HUD, choose the Font pull-down.

4 Hold your mouse button down and scroll through the various fonts. You'll notice your text dynamically updates.

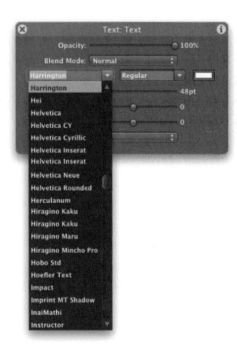

Text Now in 3D

One of the coolest new features in Motion 3 is the ability to transform objects in 3D space, including text. Not only is placing text in 3D space cool, it also gives you many more creative Options for placing the text in your composition.

Putting your text into 3D space is pretty straightforward.

❶ Create a new piece of text.

❷ With your text still selected click the Adjust 3D transform tool (Q).

❸ Make sure the HUD is active (F7).

❹ Use the controls in the HUD or in the Canvas window to position and transform your text in 3D space.

Want to take it up a notch? By starting playback and turning on recording (A), changes that you make will automatically be recorded. This is a very cool way to quickly animate your text in 3D space.

Lights, Camera, Really Cool Text!

If putting your text in 3D space in Motion wasn't cool enough, now in Motion 3 you can also add lights and cameras to create really interesting effects like spotlights and fly overs.

- To add a light, choose the Object Menu > New Light (Shift + Command + L)

- To add a camera choose the Object menu > New Camera (Option +Command + C)

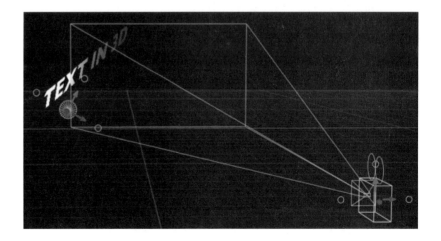

The really neat thing is that both lights and cameras will accept behaviors with cameras even having its own dedicated category. This makes it even easier to jazz up your text.

ON THE SPOT

CHAPTER 8

One-Click Wonders

Buttons and Keyboard Shortcuts

Time is money, and we all like money! This chapter shows you how to save time, even a few seconds here and a minute there. Nothing impresses a client more than the sound of keys banging and buttons clicking when they request a change or an effect.

If a client sees you using pull-down windows, they assume you're hunting (and that anyone can edit). Heck, anyone can use a pull-down window! Clients completely forget there's skill and art involved with editing.

With the advent of a mappable keyboard and the ability to create custom buttons, Final Cut Pro has become the uber-editing application we all want. In this chapter, we'll show you some of the best secrets for increasing your productivity, impressing your clients, and making a few extra bucks. Hey, if these tips make you 2 percent faster, you'll save an hour a week. That's more than 50 hours a year, an extra week of vacation. So, where are we going?

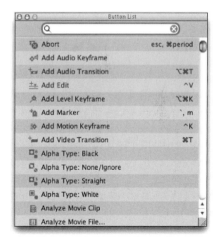

Place Your Hands "Here"

When editing on a desktop system, it's important to think ergonomically. Proper hand position improves your speed and cuts down on work-related pain. When editing, try placing your hands in the following position.

❶ Place the mouse in your preferred hand.

❷ Offset the keyboard so the J-K-L keys fall directly under your opposite hand.

Why? Well, you can access 90 percent of the edit commands from this position.

J	Play Reverse. Tap J to go faster.
K	Pause. Hold K down while using J or L to play in slow-motion.
L	Play Forward. Tap L to go faster.
I	In
O	Out
F9	Insert
F10	Overwrite

Add the Shift, Option, and Command keys for several additional Options that speed up editing. In fact, the neighboring keys all hold key commands by default; this is definitely "prime real estate" in the editing world.

Just a Little Bit—How to Trim

Trim commands are at your fingertips, as well. You can perform single frame trims by tapping the following keys:

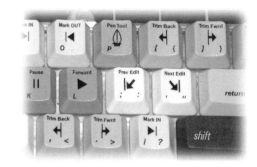

, or [	Trim Minus One Frame
. or]	Trim Plus One Frame
Shift + , or [	Trim Minus Many Frames
Shift + . or]	Trim Plus Many Frames

In Final Cut Pro, you can set the Multi-Frame Trim Size to be up to 99 frames. We find that using a 10-frame or 15-frame trim size is the most useful for NTSC projects. These work because they translate to 1/3- and 1/2-second trims. So if you're working in PAL (25 frames per second), or film (24 frames per second), you may want to adjust accordingly.

Jump Around

Need to give your other fingers something to do? When your fingers are on the J-K-L keys, your pinky (or pointer) can hit the semicolon (;) and quote (') keys to jump to the previous and next edits, respectively.

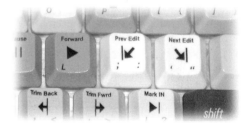

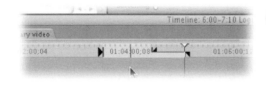

Inside Out (Marks You Need)

A fundamental keyboard shortcut is using I to mark an In point and O to mark an Out point. In fact, three-point editing is the key to quickly (and accurately) assembling your rough cut. Want to really speed your way through the Viewer and Canvas? Try the following advanced keyboard options.

Modifier Key	I	O	Purpose
Shift	Go to In	Go to Out	Quickly jump to the set mark. Useful for checking points before making an edit.
Option	Clear In	Clear Out	Quickly clear a mark to change an edit. You don't need to clear a mark if you're going to make a new mark.
Control	Set video In point	Set video Out point	Useful for performing a split edit. Only visible if a separate audio In point is set.
Command + Option	Set audio In point	Set audio Out point	Allows you to make a split edit where the audio and picture change at different points.

Modding the Keyboard

Keyboard shortcuts are great, and they're even better if you actually learn them. We find color-coded keys to be a plus, and lots of manufacturers make great keyboards for Final Cut Pro and other applications. But chances are you have a perfectly fine keyboard that came with your computer.

Instead of buying a new keyboard, check out Logic Keyboard. They sell a do-it-yourself kit (complete with a key ripper). It's an easy swap and they have keys for both types of recent Apple keyboards. Plus it's far cheaper than buying a whole new keyboard. Installation takes about 10 minutes. But here's an important tip: take one key off at a time and replace; the first time we tried it we had trouble remembering where every key went.

Giving Thanks

Thanks to the customizable keyboard, you can create keyboard shortcuts where none existed before. And thanks to the new button creation tool, you can create quick button shortcuts on the Timeline of your favorite keyboard shortcuts.

Best Place to Start

Two keyboard shortcuts to learn before moving forward in this chapter are Option + H to open the Customize Keyboard Layout window and Option + J to open the Button List window. Of course, your first exercise could be to make buttons for both of these commands.

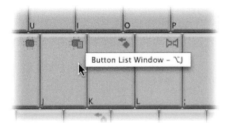

Filters and Motion Path Buttons... Now This is Cool

So you want your favorite filter to be a one-click button? A single click to add a Color corrector, that special fly-by, or even that custom Star Wipe. Impossible, some may say. Not, we say.

Here's the trick. Create an effect, transition, or motion favorite. Once created you can go into the open the "button list" (Command J) and type in **favorites**. Check out the list. Now you can drag the button icon that corresponds to your newly created "favorite" into your button bar. Pretty cool.

139

Selective Zoom

Suppose you want to zoom in to just a few clips. Simply highlight them (Shift + select or lasso them), and then press Option + Shift + Z. Boom—you zoom into just those clips in your Timeline.

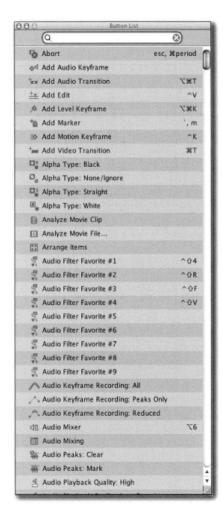

I Am the Keymaster

Want to know all the keyboard shortcuts? Call up the Custom Keyboard Layout window. On each tab, you can roll over each key and learn what that key can do. When you've memorized all those (call us if you do), switch to the button list and start on those. By then, version 7 will be out.

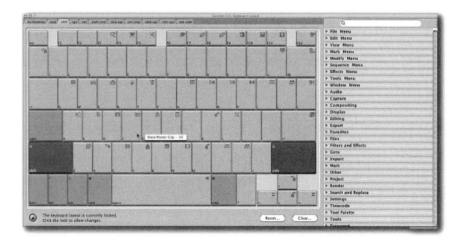

Time on Your Side

Apple chose to bury the Time Remap tool in the toolbar with the Slip and Slide tools.

We think it's a lot more convenient to have the Time Remap Tool button right on our Timelines, so we just put one there. Go to Tools > Button List to open the button dialog box. Type the word **time**, grab the Time Remap Tool button, and drag it to the Timeline. While you're there, grab the Time Code Overlay button, the Zoom In to Timeline button, and the Zoom Out of Timeline buttons. These work beautifully on your Timeline window, as well.

Buttons on the Move

A lot of folks know how to bring a button to a button bar and can readily move them from bar to bar, but they don't realize you can copy a button from one bar to another by Option + dragging it to the new bar.

Browsing Buttons (Making a Better Browser)

Our favorite buttons to put on the Browser bar are Long Frames: Mark and Analyze Movie. Using these, you can quickly highlight one or a group of clips and see if you've dropped frames or have other problems, all with one click.

Saving Window Layouts

When we present Final Cut Pro, we tend to drag windows all over the place. As a matter of fact, we do it when we edit, too. Our desktop becomes a real mess! It's nice to be able to quickly revert to a nice clean layout. Final Cut Pro allows you to save your window layouts simply and quickly by going to Window > Arrange > Save Window Layout. But there's no keyboard shortcut, so assign one. We use Shift + Command + U. We like this combination because it works well with the restore layout combination Shift + Option + U. Of course, to be really efficient, we make a button to save the window layout right on our Timeline bar.

Now the fun begins. Create buttons for all your custom window layouts. You can be as messy as you want and with one click—instant maid service—you'll have a nice, clean layout. If only we could create a button like this for our kitchens!

Miss the Power Button?

For those of you longing for your old keyboard, here are a few good shortcuts that work from the Finder:

Sleep, Restart, Shutdown dialog box	Control + Eject
Restart	Command + Control + Eject
Sleep	Command + Option + Eject
Shutdown	Command + Control + Option + Eject

Gary Adcock, Studio 37, Founder of the Chicago FCP User Group

Button, Button

Want to create a button for your favorite keyboard shortcut, but you can't remember its name? No worries—you can search the button list by typing the keyboard shortcut into the search field. You can now simply drag the button to the button bar of your choice.

The Terminator

Does contextual-clicking to remove a button seem too slow? Just drag the button off the bar. Poof—up in smoke.

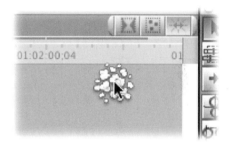

Gone Button Crazy

You can tell by now that we're pretty giddy over the Option to create lots and lots of buttons. Well, here's a tip to manage them: You can contextual-click any button, change its color, and even put spacers between them. (Psst—you can even give a color label to the spacers.)

Here's the kicker: You can save and reload button sets. This allows you to create one set for basic editing, one for finessing your edit, one for color correction, one for audio mixing, one for well, you get the picture.

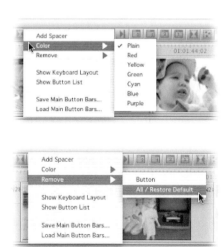

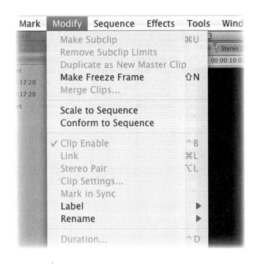

Come On Over to My Pad

All of these button and keyboard shortcuts work well for us, but we realize each editor is unique. Here's a tip about how to customize Final Cut Pro to meet your workflow: Keep a pad of paper next to your computer. Any color will do—we like yellow. Use the application heavily for about a week. Now, every time you go to a pull-down menu, write it down. Then add a check mark each time you return to that menu action. After a good 40 hours of use, you'll have a real good idea of what buttons and shortcuts will work for you.

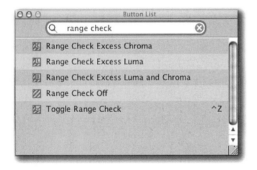

Is It Safe?

The Range Check tool, which was added in version 3, is great to make sure your shots are broadcast safe. We always thought it'd be nice to be able to quickly toggle "range check" on and off for Excess Luma and Chroma. With the buttons in Final Cut Pro we can. Search for "range check" in the button list, and drag the set of three buttons to the bar above the Canvas. While you're in the Customize Button window, type **title safe**, and drag that button next to the excess luma and chroma buttons. Now you'll know when it's safe during your editing marathons ... Man!

Startup Commands

Need to get things off to a good start?

Force Mac OS X startup	Hold down X during startup
Select a hard drive to boot from	Hold down Option during startup
Startup from a CD (with a System Folder)	Hold down C during startup
Startup in FireWire Target Disk Mode	Hold down T during startup
Startup from a network server	Hold down N during startup

Gary Adcock, Studio 37, Founder of the Chicago FCP User Group

The Entire Picture: No More, No Less

Want to see the entire picture—no more, no less? Press Shift + Z while working in the Canvas or Viewer, and the video will Fit to Window. Try this in the Timeline, and you can see your entire program. This tip works in the Viewer and the Canvas because if the picture isn't sized to the window (or smaller), you won't get proper playback.

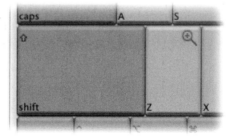

Minimize	⌘M
Send Behind	
Arrange	▶
✓ Tool Palette	
✓ Viewer	⌘1
✓ Canvas	⌘2
Tool Bench	⌥5
✓ Timeline	⌘3
✓ Audio Meters	⌥4
✓ Browser	⌘4
Effects	⌘5
Favorites	⌘6
Export Queue	
Viewer: Slug	
Browser	

Quick Switcheroo

Do you like carpal tunnel? Stop clicking on each window in FCP when you want to use it and start using keyboard shortcuts! With a little practice, you'll be flying around the different windows without clicking.

- Command 1 = Viewer

- Command 2 = Canvas

- Command 3 = Timeline

- Command 4 = Browser

- Command 5 = Effects Tab in the Browser

- Command 6 = Favorites Bin in new Window

- Command 7 = Trim Edit

- Command 8 = Log and Capture Window

- Shift Command 8 = Log and Transfer Window

Quick Duplicate

There are a lot of ways to duplicate things but this is one of the easiest.

- In the Browser click on a clip and while holding down the Option key drag the clip into a new bin to duplicate it.

- In the Timeline, click on a clip and while holding down the Option key drag the clip to a new spot in the Timeline. If you let go of the Option key you will be doing an overwrite edit of the duplicate, and if you keep holding the Option key you will be doing an insert edit.

Navigate Your Markers

We're big fans of markers. Besides doing lots of cool things like acting as chapter and scoring markers, they're a great tool for doing things like marking beats in an audio track or noting problems.

They're kind of hard to navigate just by dragging the playhead in the Timeline or the scrubber bar in the Viewer.

To navigate markers quickly:

- Press Shift + Down Arrow to navigate to the next marker.

- Press Shift + Up Arrow to navigate to the previous marker.

Print the Keyboard

While the ability to map your keyboard has been around for several versions of Final Cut Pro, when the feature first came out we were quick to map every possible combination and possibility that we could think of. The problem was that we quickly forgot how we mapped the keyboard.

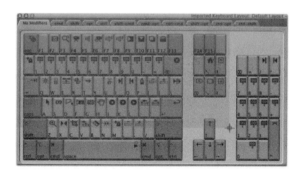

An easy way to help you remember your mapping is to take a print of the keyboard.

❶ Choose Tools > Keyboard Layout > Customize (Option + H).

❷ Map your keyboard as you see fit.

❸ Press Command + Shift + 4. This will turn your cursor into a crosshair.

❹ Draw a marquee around the keyboard window and let go of the mouse (you'll hear a camera snap).

❺ This will put a file called Picture 1 (assuming it's the first one you've taken) on your Desktop.

❻ Print this out and mark it up with notes to yourself about your keyboard shortcuts. Pretty soon you will find that you have mastered even the most complex of keyboard layouts.

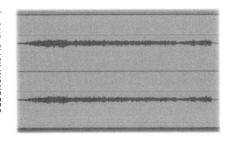

Wild Waveforms

Using audio waveforms on the Timeline is a great way to quickly be able to view your audio. The option to toggle waveforms on is kind of hidden, so why not use a keyboard shortcut! You can toggle audio waveforms by using Option + Command + W.

Don't Use A ... in Motion

One of the first keyboard shortcuts that people learn in Final Cut Pro is A for the selection tool. While this is a great keyboard shortcut to know, diving into Motion using A for the selection tool can *quickly* cause lots of problems.

In Motion, A is the keyboard shortcut to toggle recording on and off. To activate the selection tool in Motion use Shift + S.

Subclip Without a Mouse

It's often helpful to subclip a larger clip into more manageable chunks. Oftentimes you can subclip a long interview into shorter responses or a long B-Roll clip into specific shots. In all cases, this is nondestructive editing, thus leaving the larger original clip untouched. Follow these steps:

1 While viewing a clip in the Viewer, you can use J-K-L to navigate.

2 Mark In and Out points using the I and O keys.

3 When you have the desired region, press Command + U to create a subclip.

4 The clip is automatically selected in the Browser. Name it, and then press Enter.

5 Press Command + 1 to return to the Viewer, or press Command + 2 to return to the Canvas.

Dynamically Zoom in Motion

This is a really cool way to zoom in and out on the Canvas in Motion.

By using Command + Space bar and dragging the mouse you can dynamically zoom in and out on the Canvas. This method is very advantageous for quickly zooming in and out but there is a catch.

By default Command + Space bar is the OS X command to activate the Spotlight search box. Don't worry, though; there is a quick fix.

❶ Open up System Preferences and choose Spotlight.

❷ At the bottom notice that Command + Space is the default. While you can assign function keys, these might get in the way of other FCP functions.

❸ The best bet is to change this to Command + Option + Space (it's one more key, but you get the best of both).

Fill the Screen

Giving a demo or just want to make an area bigger to show the client what you're working on? Under OS X you have a Zoom feature that's part of Universal Access. Designed to help those visually impaired, it's quite useful for focusing on small elements or taking the Canvas monitor full-screen:

- Press Command + Option + 8 to enable the feature or go to the Universal Access System Preferences pane. Be patient because it takes a few seconds to launch.

- Press Command + Option + + (the plus sign) to zoom in.

- Press Command + Option + - (the minus sign) to zoom out.

- Press Command + Option + 8 to disable the feature when you're done.

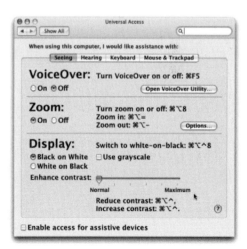

Power Log

Did you realize you can log faster than real-time? Try these three tips to get your footage in fast:

- Simply tap the L button multiple times to play the tape faster. With practice you can ramp your playback speed up and still understand the dialogue. All of your logging controls still work.

- Better yet, log while viewing. Tap I to mark an In point, and then press F2 to simultaneously add the Out point and log the clip.

- Uncheck the prompt box in the logging window. After you name the first clip, all subsequent clips will be progressively numbered or lettered.

Bar None? No, Bar All!

You've built a great button bar and have all the tools you need within one mouse click. Now idiot-proof it, and save that bar. Contextual-click the bar, and choose Save All Button Bars.... All of your button bars are stored in one setting in your User Preferences folder.

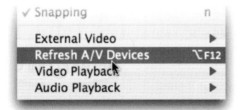

Refresh AV Devices

Ever plug in a deck or camera after launching Final Cut Pro HD, and the system just can't see it? Then give it a little "kick." Choose View > Refresh A/V Devices or press Option + F12. The device should now be seen. If not, then check cables, quit, and relaunch.

Shortcut to Set Logging Bin

Your logging bin is important, as it's where all clips get moved to after you've logged them in the Log and Capture Window. But setting the Logging bin could be a little easier. We suggest (big surprise here) a button.

❶ Call up your button list by pressing Option + J.

❷ Type logging in the search window.

❸ Drag the Set Logging Bin button to the Browser or another convenient location.

❹ Highlight the bin in question and just click the button. Problem solved.

Using Ink and Motion

Looking for a bunch of Motion shortcuts? Then get a tablet! If you've got a tablet then you can use Gestures to quickly access some of the most useful commands. You can't use Gestures unless you have a tablet attached and the Handwriting Recognition is turned on in the Ink preferences in System Preferences.

To set up Motion Gesture Preferences:

❶ Launch System Preferences and turn on Handwriting Recognition in the Ink Preferences area.

❷ In Motion, choose Motion > Preferences (or press Command + ,).

❸ Click Gestures.

❹ For "Gestures are," ensure that On is selected and select an Input Method.

Not sure which shortcuts to use? Just print out this handy reference guide and slip it under the clear tracing mat on your tablet.

http://manuals.info.apple.com/en/Motion_2_Gestures_Reference.pdf

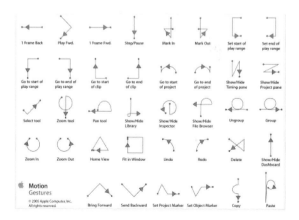

151

ON THE SPOT

Telephone Effect

Hum Remover

I Can't Hear You ...

A Little Louder Please

Hey, They Panned My Show!

Audio Insurance Is the Best Policy

Capture Settings

Toggle Audio Keyframing

Got to Split Your Tracks

Audio Hijack Pro/Line In

Pop Killer

Dangers of Unlabeled Tape

High Pass vs. Low Pass

Where To? (Getting the Right Mix)

Reverb or Echo?

Compressor/Limiter and the Peak Limiter

It All Adds Up

That Music is HOT ... Too Hot!

Your Professional Music Tool

Get the Drop on Digital Audio

CDs Get Converted

Force Fitting Audio

Don't Have a Hissy

Making a Record of Peaks

A Better Musical Bed

WOW 99 Sliders Audio Mixer

Copy Paste Attributes

Record Audio Keyframes

Making Waves

Audio Playback Quality Preference

Save Your Hard Work in Soundtrack Pro

How to Edit an Audio Track Destructively

How to Edit an Audio Track Nondestructively

Fixing Levels Without Thinking (Much)

Seeing Red ... Boxes, That Is

Don't Want to See Red?

Sync Two Clips Using Audio

When the Mics are Off

Quiet Down! Reducing Noise in Your Clip

Hearing What You Don't Want

A Quick Way to Better Audio

"Give Him a Boost"—Fixing a Thin Male Voice

Prepping for the Ultimate Gain

Get Into Podcasting

The HUD Can Help with Position

Multipoint Video HUD On the Fly

Timecode for your Wave

Assigning Audio Outputs

Submixes—Part One and Two

Helping Your Case

What to Export

Creating a Script

After Export—The End of the Audio Road

Now in Surround Sound

Sounds Good
Enhancing and Troubleshooting Audio

Audio provides more than 70 percent of the experience when watching a video or movie. If the picture is less than perfect but the audio is clear, people will watch. Conversely, if the audio is poor and the picture is great, they'll get weary of fighting to hear and give up.

In this chapter, we'll show you how to clean up poor audio, make sure your levels are balanced, and teach you how to build a soundstage with the panning controls.

The biggest mistake for first-time filmmakers and directors is a flat, uninteresting audio bed. The richer your audio mix, the more professional your finished show will feel. So go ahead, take advantage of some of those 99 audio layers, keyframe the pan and volume sliders, and of course, enjoy those real-time audio filters. We're listening!

153

3 Band Equalizer
Band Pass Filter
Compressor/Limiter
DC Notch
Echo
Expander/Noise Gate
Gain
High Pass Filter
High Shelf Filter
Hum Remover
Low Pass Filter
Low Shelf Filter
Notch Filter
Parametric Equalizer
Reverberation
Vocal DeEsser
Vocal DePopper

Telephone Effect

So you need to make it sound as if someone is talking on the telephone? The filter you want is the High Pass filter. It only lets the high-frequency sounds pass through, get it? Some folks like to use the Band Pass filter for this effect. It allows you to modify a single-frequency band. By choosing its center frequency, you can modify the boost or cut level.

The best thing about Final Cut Pro is that you can play your clip and adjust the filter in real-time until it sounds just like a telephone. This trick is also useful if you've aged your video to look like an old film, and you want to pull out some bass so the audio matches the "age" of the pictures.

3 Band Equalizer
Band Pass Filter
Compressor/Limiter
DC Notch
Echo
Expander/Noise Gate
Gain
High Pass Filter
High Shelf Filter
Hum Remover
Low Pass Filter
Low Shelf Filter
Notch Filter
Parametric Equalizer
Reverberation
Vocal DeEsser
Vocal DePopper

Hum Remover

This is a great little filter to remove AC noise from a track. Usually this happens because a power line was running parallel (as opposed to perpendicular) to your audio cable when you recorded your scene.

- Leave the frequency set to 60 (as in 60 cycles) if you were shooting in the U.S. or set it to 50 if you were shooting in a country where the power is 50 cycles.

- Q adjusts the filter resonance. Higher values result in a narrower but stronger resonance, which limits the frequencies affected by the filter.

- Gain is essentially the sound pressure level (a.k.a. how loud the audio is).

What about all those harmonics? Think of them as reflections or echoes of the original 60-cycle hum. Use only the harmonics you need because you may start removing frequencies you want in your audio.

I Can't Hear You

A clip is low, so you bring the gain up. But you can only do so +12db. What's a frustrated editor to do? Well, you have two choices:

- Mix the track to +12db.

- Duplicate the track by placing a copy of the clip(s) immediately below it. Select the desired clip, and then hold down Option + Shift. Drag directly below the currently selected clip.

This additive method will essentially "double" the sound. If it's now too "hot," then lower the levels on one of the tracks.

Want to try a different approach? You can use the Gain filter in Final Cut Pro 6. Just choose Effects > Audio Filters > Final Cut Pro > Gain.

A Little Louder Please...

Need to tweak the mix a little? You can quickly change the volume of a highlighted track from the keyboard. Use the following keyboard combinations to perfect the mix:

Gain –3db	Control [
Gain –1db	Control –
Gain +1db	Control +
Gain +3db	Control]

155

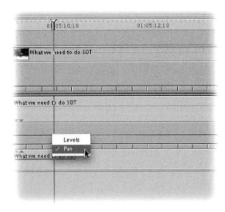

Hey, They Panned My Show!

Sound provides dimension to your project. By panning audio you can create a sound space that can envelop your Viewer. Cars can scream by left to right in your chase scenes. Stereo music from a band can become more centered as the camera pulls back from the stage, and you can have the audio follow your actors as they walk around in the shot. You can pan your audio in three places in Final Cut Pro:

- In the audio tab of the Viewer. (It's the dark purple line.)

- In the Timeline. You need to toggle on the "clip overlays" feature in the Timeline. (Control + click in the blank area once you see the keyframe area. Again, it's the dark purple line.)

- In the Audio Mixer tab of the Tool Bench window (the horizontal sliders below the headphone and speaker icons in each column).

Audio Insurance Is the Best Policy

Here's a recording trick we use in the field: If we're recording an interview or speaker from a single mic, we run the same feed into both audio channels. On the second channel, we reduce the recording levels by 3 db. This way, if the speaker gets too enthusiastic and spikes their audio past 0 db on channel one, we have a –3 db insurance policy on channel two.

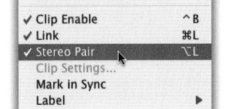

Capture Settings

When you capture audio from DV, you can choose to capture mono or stereo tracks. But don't panic if you picked the wrong setting. Because DV is all 0s and 1s, these settings determine how Final Cut Pro will interpret the audio. So you brought the clip in as stereo and you want discrete channels—just uncheck Stereo Pair under the Modify menu. And, of course, you link your discrete channels back together using the same modifier.

Toggle Audio Keyframing

We love being able to keyframe audio on the fly, but have been burned a lot by accidentally keyframing our audio filters. (You did know you can keyframe audio filters... didn't you?) Also when we are in the Audio tab of the Viewer window, it is a real pain to have to open up the Preferences or Audio Mixer window just to toggle Record Audio Keyframes on or off. So use the keyboard shortcut (Shift + Command + K) or why not make a button and put it in your Canvas's button bar. Click on – click off – Click on – click off – you get the idea.

Got to Split Your Tracks

If you recorded your audio in stereo and want to pan your tracks individually, then use the Modify pull-down menu to split the tracks (uncheck Stereo Pair under the Modify menu or press Option + L) and pan them to the center (Modify > Audio> Pan Center (Control + period)). Now you're ready to go.

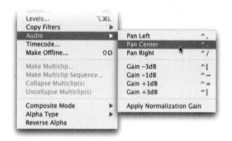

Audio Hijack Pro/Line In

Need to import a SWF file with audio? Good luck! While QuickTime can read a Flash version 5 file, it can't read the audio. We've had the same problem with other multimedia projects where the assets are locked, and the client can't find the original sources (but do own the rights to these materials!).

There are three great shareware applications to the rescue. Check out Audio Hijack and Audio Hijack Pro from Rogue Amoeba (what a great name!). There's also Line In, a shareware application from Ambrosia Software that's pretty good (and free) as well. These apps come in real handy when you have a tough audio file to capture. They essentially reduce the steps of hooking up an audio record device to your line out, recording, logging, and capturing down to to one software app. Definitely a time saver!

Audio Hijack Pro
Your Ears Will Thank You!
© Rogue Amoeba Software, LLC

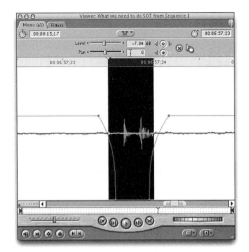

Pop Killer

For one reason or another you may get an audio pop at the edit point or even within a clip. Most video applications allow you to edit video at the frame level. Final Cut Pro goes way beyond this by allowing audio edits as small as 1/100th of a frame.

❶ Open the clip in the Viewer by double-clicking, and choose the Audio tab.

❷ Place the playhead over the click.

❸ Zoom in as far as possible by pressing Command + =. When zoomed in all the way, you'll see a highlighted region that's one frame wide.

❹ Hold the Shift key down, and drag the playhead. Park over the exact place where the pop appears.

❺ Use the Pen tool to add four keyframes in a row. The center two keyframes should straddle the audio problem. The outer keyframes are placed a few 100ths of a frame from the pop.

❻ Drag the inner keyframes down to –60 db. The unwanted noise should now be inaudible. The rest of the clip should sound unaltered.

Dangers of Unlabeled Tape

Always label your tapes in the field when you shoot them. Be sure to mark down microphone information, as well as the audio format that you shot in. Why? Because if you don't, it will haunt you.

We once got tapes Fed-Exed in for a project and things weren't labeled. The audio sounded awful, like the microphone was only the shotgun mic on the camera. It turns out that the interview was shot in 4-channel mode at 32 kHz. So both of the mic tracks bled together until we changed our capture settings.

The problem—first, why would you shoot a single interview in 4-channel mode when there are only two mics to begin with. Of course if the tape were labeled, we would have known this. To top it off, the DP didn't put his business card or contact information with the tape either. The moral of the story: Always label your tapes in the field when you shoot them.

High Pass vs. Low Pass

High pass was what our parents expected of us in college—low pass was what we did to eke by. When it comes to filters, these guys are opposite sides of the same coin.

The High Pass filter is designed to reduce low frequencies, leaving high frequencies alone. It's useful for reducing traffic rumble or airplane noise in a clip.

The Low Pass filter is designed to reduce high frequencies, leaving low frequencies alone. It's great for toning down a sound that's too "bright" and reducing things like tape hiss and machine noise from a clip.

AUBandpass
AUDelay
AUDynamicsProcessor
AUFilter
AUGraphicEQ
AUHighShelfFilter
AUHipass
AULowpass
AULowShelfFilter
AUMultibandCompressor
AUNetSend
AUParametricEQ
AUPeakLimiter
AUPitch
AUSampleDelay

Where To? (Getting the Right Mix)

There's a lot of confusion when looking at the Audio Meter. Unlike the analog world, you DO NOT want to mix to 0 db. What this means is that you'll likely need to adjust audio per clip.

- For a digital mix, you want to be near −12 dbfs when your output is videotape in a nonbroadcast environment.

- Many broadcasting environments request −20 dbfs is reference with peaks up to −10 dbfs.

- If you're going to the Internet, you can mix it hotter for playback on computer speakers.

- If you're "seeing red" in your audio meters, your audio is distorted.

- Even though your individual tracks may be at proper levels, when you combine tracks in the Timeline, the overall volume "adds up." Keep a careful eye (and ear) on your final mix.

Reverb or Echo?

So what's the difference between the Reverb filter and the Echo filter? Reverb takes place inside a space, such as in a room (with walls and such). Echo takes place in the great outdoors— amphitheaters, grand canyons, and baseball stadiums –adiums-iums-ms-s. Well you get the idea. Be careful, because these filters can quickly go from effective to cheesy.

Compressor/Limiter and the AU Peak Limiter

Both the Compressor/Limiter filter and the AU Peak Limiter filter are designed to smooth out inconsistencies in volume levels, consistently across all frequencies. Compression of volume reduces the dynamic range so that it doesn't become too loud. The attack and decay settings specify how fast this effect should adjust the volume levels.

The Compressor/Limiter filter has Threshold and Preserve Volume options. After making settings, use the Preserve Volume option to keep the overall level close to the original. The Threshold setting specifies the level at which the effect will be triggered.

It All Adds Up

You can test this yourself by taking bars and tone and putting them on A1 and A2; you'll find that it reads –12 digitally. If you add a second instance of bars and tone so the tone is also on A3 and A4, you'll find your audio is now –6 digitally, each instance adding –3.

This can be a serious problem; audio levels can combine and be louder summed than they are individually. Final Cut Pro's Mark Audio Peaks (Mark > Audio Peaks > Mark) is meant to point this out to you. It'll find all instances where a clip exceeds 0 and hence is adding distortion into your mix.

However, the feature doesn't work correctly. It marks an audio peak of a clip, but you need it to mark an audio peak of the sum of the clips to prevent peaking of the sequence. Any peak that occurs digitally will cause digital noise when played back out to tape. Follow these steps:

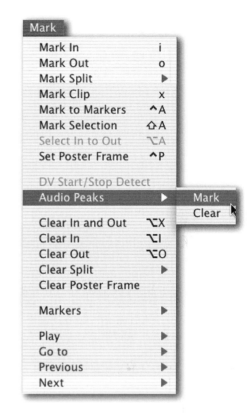

❶ Create a new sequence.

❷ Drag your existing master sequence into this new sequence.

❸ Go to Mark > Audio Peaks > Mark.

❹ Audio peaks are now detected on your Timeline. Be sure to visually note where the problem areas are.

❺ Double-click your master sequence now in your audio peaks sequence to open the original and make volume adjustments to repair the peaks.

❻ Return to the audio peaks sequence, go to Mark > Audio Peaks > Clear, and check for marks again.

Jeff I. Greenberg, Principal Instructor, Future Media Concepts

That Music is HOT ... Too Hot!

We talked about mixing to –12 db when you edit for nonbroadcast (–20 db for broadcast), but people often forget that music they convert and insert off music CDs is mixed to –0 db. (Yes, we meant to say the – before the zero. That's because music CDs are mixed and compressed so they sound nice and loud in your car and on your iPod; they peak right below 0 db.)

Remember, whenever you use music from a CD, pull its levels down so they hit the appropriate (–12 or –20 db) target levels of your show.

Your Professional Music Tool

The audio tool that sees the most use in our studios is iTunes (and not just because we're addicted to the iTunes Music Store). iTunes has several features that are useful to a video pro (and you can't beat the price!). Here are two great uses for this great application:

Create selects CDs: Use iTunes to create listening discs for your clients. This way, you can organize and deliver several tracks from stock music libraries or from Soundtrack Pro. Simply create a playlist of your tracks, and be sure to label each track clearly. Burn the playlist, and deliver it to your client in a format they can listen to in their car or at the gym. Now when they call to say they want you to use track 7, you're both on the same page.

Encode the rough cut: Client in a remote location (or producer "too busy" to come to the edit suite)? You can make an MP3 of the rough cut and email it. Often times, approval on the A-roll is really just a sign-off that the right sound bites are being used and the rough mix is acceptable. Simply create an AIFF file, and use iTunes to convert it to an MP3. The VBR encoding and Joint Stereo features (found on the Import tab of the iTunes preferences) offer superior file size.

Get the Drop on Digital Audio

Final Cut Pro can handle using different imported audio (almost always CDs or MP3s), but by converting it to the same rate as your project (DV would be 48kHz, 16-bit Stereo) it's possible not to use up any of Final Cut Pro's real-time audio abilities for the conversion. This will free up RAM for other purposes. Let's make a droplet, so all of this in the future becomes drag and drop.

1. Launch Compressor, and click the Presets icon.

2. Open the Settings palette.

3. Click the Settings button.

4. Open the Apple folder, then the Formats folder, then the Audio folder.

5. Choose the AIFF 48:16 preset.

6. Adjust the settings to no compression, 48 kHz, 16-bit, Stereo.

7. Click the Save Selection As Droplet (with the new converter selected).

8. Choose where you want the droplet to be saved and where you want its output to go on your drive.

9. Now just draw the files you need to convert onto the droplet, then click Submit.

Jeff I. Greenberg, Principal Instructor, Future Media Concepts

Audio 48 kHz

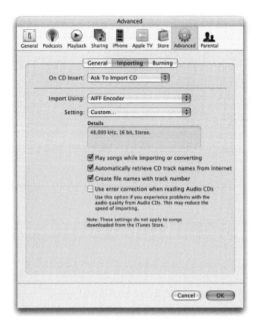

CDs Get Converted

Our favorite way to rip and up-convert music from stock music CDs is to use iTunes.

We all know music CDs are recorded at a sampling rate of 44.1 kHz. Final Cut Pro and digital video love to work at a sampling rate of 48 kHz. Yes, we know Final Cut Pro can up-sample on the fly, but why waste CPU power that could be going to your real-time video playback?

Here's all you need to do:

❶ Open iTunes.

❷ Open Preferences under the Edit menu.

❸ Click the Advanced icon in the toolbar then choose Importing.

❹ Under Import Using, select AIFF Encoder.

❺ Under Setting, select Custom.

❻ Another dialog box opens. Here, select a sample rate of 48.000 kHz. Click OK and then OK again.

❼ Now click the General button.

❽ Under iTunes Music Folder Location, change it to target your desktop. (This will make it real easy to find and move your newly ripped tracks.)

❾ Pop in your CD. If you're connected to the Internet, iTunes will go to the CDDB and grab the album name and track names. (Yes, it seem as if most of our library music is listed in the CDDB.) This is great because most of the work is done. Create a playlist of all the tracks you want to rip.

❿ Click Import, and you're done!

Once you've set up your preferences, just "rip and roll" every time you need to grab a music cut. Fast, easy, elegant...and of course...cool.

Force Fitting Audio

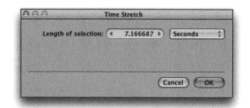

Your narration for your 30-second spot runs 32 seconds. No matter how you slice and dice it, you can't cut out one frame. Don't worry, Soundtrack Pro can help out.

❶ Send the narration file to Soundtrack Pro.

❷ Accurately select the region that needs to be retimed.

❸ Choose Process > Time Stretch.

❹ Change the Length of selection to measure in Seconds.

❺ Enter a new duration for the audio and click OK.

❻ Soundtrack Pro retimes the audio and attempts to keep the pitch identical to the original.

❼ Close and save the project to return the audio to Final Cut Pro.

> Note: This works great for picking up a little speed. But you can't force fit a :30 script into a :15 spot. Have reasonable expectations.

Don't Have a Hissy

Few people really understand the Vocal DeEsser or Vocal DePopper filters. Who are these guys, and why are they in my Audio Filters tab? These two filters are there to help your audio narrations. They literally do what they sound like they do. The Vocal DeEsser removes sibilance from your narrations...those hard "s" sounds that make your narrators sound "hissy." The Vocal DePopper controls and dampens the explosive ("p") sounds that result from bursts of air hitting the microphone when saying sentences such as "Peter Piper picked a peck of pickled peppers."

3 Band Equalizer
Band Pass Filter
Compressor/Limiter
DC Notch
Echo
Expander/Noise Gate
Gain
High Pass Filter
High Shelf Filter
Hum Remover
Low Pass Filter
Low Shelf Filter
Notch Filter
Parametric Equalizer
Reverberation
Vocal DeEsser
Vocal DePopper

Making a Record of Peaks

The audio meters in Final Cut Pro are a fairly good measure of your audio, but one issue we find a little frustrating with the audiometers in FCP is that there is no readout for peak levels. Sure, the meters themselves will hold on a peak for a second or so, but just by looking at the meters you have no idea if a peak occurred at −12, −11, or somewhere in between.

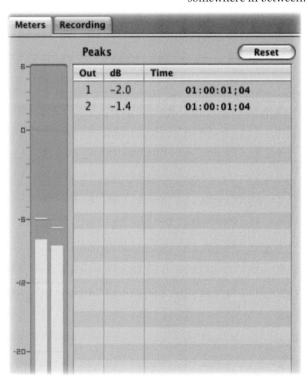

Why is this an issue? you ask. Well, if you're delivering a piece for broadcast, generally there are strict rules for what your average levels should be, as well as your peaks. Having peaks that exceed what the broadcaster requires is a sure way to have your tape rejected.

Fortunately, Soundtrack Pro has a great set of meters that give a numeric readout of your peaks. This makes identifying peaks a breeze. To use these meters simply send your sequence to Soundtrack Pro as a Multitrack Project and use the meters in Soundtrack Pro to measure your peaks (and while you're at it, mix your whole piece in Soundtrack Pro!).

If you discover peaks that are above your broadcaster's specs, simply adjust the levels in Soundtrack Pro for that given piece of audio.

A Better Musical Bed

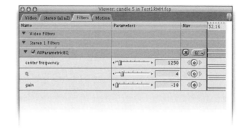

Because of timing or budget constraints, you can't involve an audio editor to "sweeten" your audio mix. Audio mixing is where almost all NLE editors are weakest. Sitting in front of your system, you use a general-level mix adjustment or keyframing to adjust the levels to "mix" the audio. The simplest example is narration or dialogue against music. You bring the music down to accommodate the voice.

A better idea is to lower the range of the music that interferes with the vocal spectrum.

The human voice (the important parts of it anyway) exists from around 500 hz through about 2000 hz (or 2 kHz.) You can lower the music to create a "pillow" for the vocal ranges to exist.

Why the music? If it's a large track, it's easy to make one adjustment rather than hundreds. It's still permissible to also use levels or keyframing on the music track.

Using a parametric equalizer, it's possible to dampen the music inside of the audio spectrum where the vocal ranges exist. A parametric equalizer has a Q value—a value that permits the effect to adjust a wider or narrower band of frequencies. With it set low, a wider set of frequencies are affected; with a Q set high, a very narrow band, or "notch," is affected.

First, select the track(s) on the Timeline you want to apply the Parametric EQ filter to (choose it from the Effects menu), double-click the track, and go to the Viewer to adjust the controls.

Adjust the frequency to be halfway between 500 and 2,000, setting it to 1250. You can then drop the gain of that selection of the sound spectrum down −18 decibels. With a little experimenting, we found that a Q setting of 4 was acceptable for us.

And there you go. You'll get music that's strong, along with vocal tracks that are intelligible. Would you prefer an experienced audio editor looking at your work? Absolutely! But when you're a one-man band or the budget isn't there, then a little bit of sweetening goes a long way.

Jeff I. Greenberg, Principal Instructor, Future Media Concepts

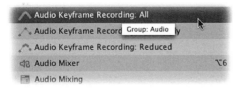

WOW 99 Sliders Audio Mixer—Gotchas and Shortcuts

Final Cut Pro has a great feature that lets you mix up to 99 tracks of audio using sliders. Here are some tricks to make it work faster and better:

- Remember to activate Record Audio Keyframes (Shift + Command + K).

- For a smoother mix, choose to record reduced keyframes only.

- If you haven't already done this, create a set of buttons (Audio Keyframe Recording Group in the audio mixer to let you toggle between All, Reduced, and Peaks Only).

- Create a button for "audio mixing" that automatically resets your windows for audio mixing. We put ours on the canvas of the Timeline.

- Create a button for "audio mixing" that just opens up the Tool Bench window with the Audio Mixing tab open.

Copy Paste Attributes

You can currently only record keyframes for one stereo pair or mono track at a time. If you want to map these keyframes onto another set of tracks, simply copy and then select Paste Attributes (under the Edit menu or press Option + V.) The trick is to uncheck the Scale Attribute Times option. This way your keyframes will match up whether the clip lengths are the same (assuming you had them both start at the same time).

Record Audio Keyframes

This one bears repeating: If your Record Audio Keyframes feature isn't on, all you do is change levels between keyframes, not create new keyframe points. Also, remember you can choose to adjust multiple tracks, but you can only manipulate one slider (or pair) with the mouse at a time.

Making Waves

Many editors find audio waveforms helpful when editing. You've likely noticed the waveforms in your Viewer menu. It's possible to view this same information directly in the Timeline:

❶ Highlight the Timeline or Canvas, and press Command + 0 to access the Timeline settings.

❷ Select the Timeline Options tab.

❸ Check the Show Audio Waveforms box.

❹ Make the desired tracks larger to see the audio waveform data in the Timeline.

Want quick access? Simply click the submenu at the bottom of the Timeline, and choose Show Audio Waveforms.

Better yet, press Command + Option + W to toggle waveforms on or off. Be sure to turn these off when not in use because they slow down the Timeline's ability to redraw.

Audio Playback Quality Preference

This can be a confusing preference setting (under User Preferences). Your first reaction may be to set this to High (versus the default of Low). However, the Low setting is what you want. This preference setting is only used while you're mixing sample rates in a Timeline. It'll give you a close but not perfect approximation of your mix.

If you switch it to High, guess what. You'll probably get those annoying little beeps, and your audio may need to be rendered to be heard (in that case, choose to mixdown your audio in advance).

When you're ready to print to tape or edit to tape, Final Cut Pro automatically renders your audio at full resolution. One word of warning, though. If you perform crash records directly from the Timeline, your audio may play back at low resolution.

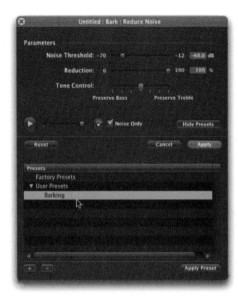

Save Your Hard Work in Soundtrack Pro

If you take the time to fix your audio, you might want to save your work. Chances are the problems in one clip will appear again in your show (for example, every time you use a particular interview). Fortunately you can save your Noise Reduction presets for later work.

1 In the Reduce Noise dialog click the Show Presets button.

2 The Presets drawer opens at the bottom of the window.

3 Click the + (plus) symbol to add a preset.

4 Name the preset so it is easy to locate.

To reuse a preset:

1 Choose a preset from the User Presets list.

2 Click Apply.

> Note: Presets are stored at the User level (not by project). If you want to delete presets for old jobs, click the name of the unwanted preset and click the – (minus) symbol.

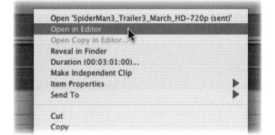

How to Edit an Audio Track Destructively

Why use a destructive edit? Perhaps you'd like to permanently fix an audio issue, or you have a file that you want to process for use outside of Final Cut Studio.

To open an audio file in its native format:

1 Select an independent audio clip in Final Cut Pro's Timeline (if a file is attached to video, you'll need to press Command + L to unlink the file).

2 Right-click and choose Open in Editor.

3 Soundtrack Pro launches and opens the audio file. If you open a stereo file, both channels load (the left channel will be on top).

4 Any edits you make to the file are 'destructive.' They are permanently applied when you close and save the file.

How to Edit an Audio Track Nondestructively

While you can edit an audio file directly in Soundtrack Pro, there are distinct benefits to creating a Soundtrack Pro project.

- Effects that you apply can be re-edited in the future.

- Edits to a clip are nondestructive.

- You can open a similar clip to check settings for use on another.

Fortunately, nondestructive editing is easy:

- In Final Cut Pro select a clip in the Timeline. Right-click and choose Send To > Soundtrack Pro Audio File Project.

- In Motion, select an audio track. Then choose Edit > Send Audio to Soundtrack Pro.

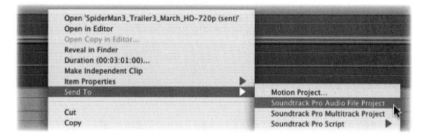

Fixing Levels Without Thinking (Much)

Seems that audio levels can't agree— get a bunch of audio clips in your Timeline and levels will vary. Fortunately, Final Cut Pro 6 makes it easier with the new Normalization Gain command. The command works by scanning the audio file for the loudest peak and then applies a Gain filter that raises the volume to the requested level. The command is nondestructive, so you can remove the effect if you choose.

To apply normalization gain to audio clips:

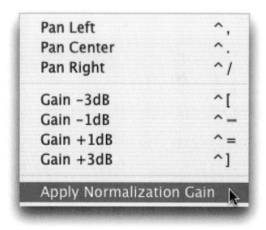

1. Select one or more audio clips in a sequence.

2. Choose Modify > Audio > Apply Normalization Gain. Final Cut Pro opens the Apply Normalization Gain dialog box.

3. In the Normalize to field, enter the value you want to raise each audio clip's peak value to, then click OK.

4. Final Cut Pro calculates the peak value for each clip.

5. A Gain filter is applied to each clip at the appropriate level.

Seeing Red ... Boxes, That Is

If you have little red boxes with small numbers in them on your Timeline, Final Cut Pro is telling you that your audio and video are out of sync. It's even telling you by how much. What we love about this feature is that to fix the problem all you need to do is Control + click the box (either in the video or audio track), and Final Cut Pro will do the math to slip or move your audio and video into sync. If you Control + click the red box in the video, Final Cut Pro will move or slip the video. And if you Control + click the audio, well, you guessed it—the audio moves or slips. If an option is grayed out, that means there would be a clip collision if the media were moved.

Don't Want to See Red?

Sometimes you want to resync your audio and rid yourself of those red boxes. For example, we were cutting together a thunder and lightning storm and guess what? The claps of thunder didn't match up with the flashes of lightning. (Hey, this is real, and sound travels way slower than light.) Of course, on TV we expect to see and hear these events simultaneously. So what did we do? We unlocked the tracks, slid the audio to match the video, and relocked the tracks. It looked great, except for those (now) annoying out-of-sync boxes. There's a simple solution: Highlight the track, and select Modify > Mark in Sync. The red boxes disappear!

Sync Two Clips Using Audio

One way to sync two clips in the Timeline is to listen to the audio while playing the clips. However, stopping playback, making a change, and then playing again is quite tedious and unnecessary.

Instead:

- Align the two clips in the Timeline as close as can be done quickly.

- Select one of the clips—the one with room to move in the Timeline.

- Hit S on the keyboard or select the Slip tool and make it active.

- Start playback.

- Use the < and > arrow keys to slip the selected clip one frame in the indicated direction.

Note: Actually, it's the ',' and '.' keys—pressing Shift to select < and > actually moves five frames each direction, or whatever you have selected for your multiframe jump.

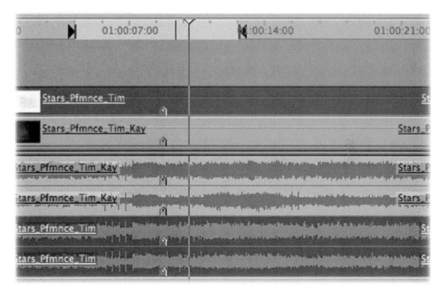

There's a short hiccup while Final Cut Pro repositions the clip, and then playback continues.

Set an In and Out point and activate Loop Playback from the View menu, or press Control + L on the keyboard. Use Shift + \ to start playback from In to Out. The result is a loop over the selected area so we can quickly synchronize the clips using a readily identifiable piece of audio.

Phil Hodgetts – http://www.digitalproductionbuzz.com/BuZZdex/

photo iStockphoto.com

When the Mics are Off—Equalizing Off-Mic Sound

No matter how simple it seems, eventually a microphone gets turned off or unplugged. Although there's not a whole lot that will help off-mic audio, or camera mic, shot in a big room with reverberation, skillful equalization can help.

Although the only real solution for bad audio is to get good audio in the first place, or to go back and re-shoot, that isn't always an available option. Equalization can help, but don't expect miracles.

Try this as a starting point:

1 Add a High Pass filter and set it to around 300 Hz—everything below that will be reduced.

2 Apply a Parametric Equalizer and set the Frequency to 2250 and the Q to 2 or 3. The goal is to boost the key voice frequencies between 1500 and 3 kHz.

3 A slight lift in the top voice frequencies of 6–8 kHz might also help—try adding another Parametric filter.

Compression might make the problem worse (so steer clear of the Compressor/ Limiter filter), but the Expander/Noise Gate filter might be helpful to kill the room tone between the words. If you do that you'll probably have to add room tone for consistency.

Phil Hodgetts – http://www.digitalproductionbuzz.com/BuZZdex/

Quiet Down! Reducing Noise in Your Clip

Background noise? Air conditioning rumble? Soundtrack Pro makes it easy to fix. By combining the Set Noise Print and Reduce Noise commands you can dramatically improve a clip.

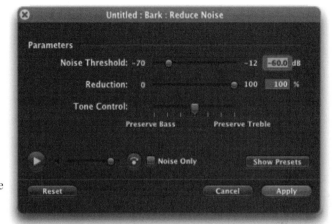

1. Select a clip in your Final Cut Pro Timeline.

2. Right-click and choose Send To > Soundtrack Pro Audio Project File. The audio moves from your Timeline into Soundtrack Pro.

3. Zoom into a part of your audio file that contains just the background noise that you'd like to remove. Select the audio in the Soundtrack Pro Timeline.

4. Choose Process > Noise Reduction > Set Noise Print. The noise print identifies the frequencies that you'd like to remove from the file.

5. Select the audio in the Timeline that you'd like to repair (this will usually be the entire Timeline).

6. Choose Process > Noise Reduction > Reduce Noise. The Reduce Noise dialog appears.

7. Click the Preview button (play icon) to hear the noise reduction previewed.

8. Drag the Noise Threshold slider left to lower the threshold, or drag it right to raise the threshold.

9. Drag the Reduction slider to the right to increase the amount of noise reduction.

10. Use the Tone Control slider left to preserve more of the bass or treble content.

11. To toggle a before and after state, click the Bypass button.

12. When satisfied, click the Apply button.

Hearing What You Don't Want

One way to hone in how much noise reduction to use is by harnessing the Select the Noise Only checkbox.

1 Click the Select the Noise Only checkbox. With this box checked, you'll only hear the information that is being removed.

2 Continue to make adjustments in noise reduction until you start to hear the voice or desired sound (if you go too far, the audio will sound like it is underwater).

3 Back off the Noise Reduction sliders until just noise is heard.

4 When satisfied, click Apply.

A Quick Way to Better Audio—Repeat Yourself

Soundtrack Pro 2 adds an important feature for speeding up audio design and repair. When working with a Multitrack Project you can easily copy properties from one clip to another. You can use the Lift tool to copy properties from one clip and then use the Stamp tool to apply the properties to other clips.

1 Click the Lift tool icon at the top of the Timeline (UU).

2 The Sound Palette opens to assist with Lifting and Stamping.

3 Move your pointer over the clip in your Timeline that you'd like to use as a template for other clips.

4 By default the Sound Palette will use both Equalization and Process effects. You can uncheck either to limit which properties are lifted.

5 Click the desired clip in the Timeline whose properties you want to lift. Soundtrack Pro creates a temporary template named Lifted Data (Track Name). The clip's properties appear in the Sound Palette HUD.

6 The pointer immediately changes from the Lift tool (an upward arrow) to the Stamp tool (a downward arrow).

7 Uncheck any items you don't want to stamp in the HUD.

8 Click on any desired clips to Stamp the effects.

"Give Him a Boost"—Fixing a Thin Male Voice

If a male voice lacks body or depth, quite separate from actual level, here are some tricks to improving the quality of the voice.

When dealing with a thin sounding male voice recording, particularly relative to other male voices in the project, one should first check:

1. Make sure there is no phase problem caused by two microphones in close proximity to the speaker (such as the mic from the speaker being near the mic from an interviewer or other performer also picking up the signal but slightly out of phase with the primary signal).

2. If this is the case, dropping the second channel from the mix should resolve the problem with the thin audio.

photo iStockphoto.com

Otherwise:

- Boost the frequencies around 100 Hz—you may want to play with the frequency.

- Apply a de-esser if necessary.

- Apply compression at about 3:1 with a threshold of about −20 dB so there's a bit of gain reduction; keep the attack around 2 ms and release at 100 ms.

You'll want to do A/B comparisons with the original to make sure you're not adding artifacts to the voice. If it's still not acceptable you may require Dialog replacement if there's nothing in the signal to bring up or out.

Phil Hodgetts – http://www.digitalproductionbuzz.com/BuZZdex/

Prepping for the Ultimate Gain

Before using the Normalization Gain command, you may need to prep your Timeline a bit. If a clip has dramatic volume changes, you can use the Razor Blade tool to divide the longer clip into shorter clips. Split the clip where the volume change occurs. The Normalization Gain will work more intelligently.

Get Into Podcasting

Are you a podcaster? Well if you've got Final Cut Studio 2, then you've got some great podcasting software. The combination of Soundtrack Pro 2 and Compressor makes it significantly easier to create a podcast.

You can create three types of podcasts with Soundtrack Pro 2:

- **Audio-only Podcasts:** With the ability to record directly to the Soundtrack Timeline, you can easily record a show.

- **Enhanced Podcasts:** You can enhance an audio podcast by adding images and web links that can be synchronized with the audio. Plus you can use chapter markers to allow jumps via an index.

- **Video Podcasts:** You can send your video from Final Cut Pro to Soundtrack Pro in order to make improvements or add a musical score. When finished, you can easily export to Compressor for optimizing for web-delivery.

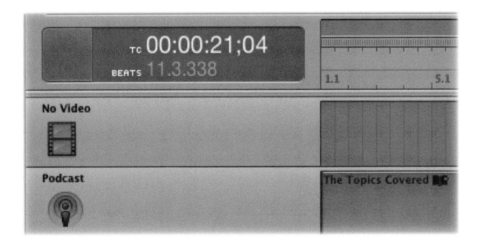

In order to access the podcasting options you'll need to make a view change:

1 Choose Show > Podcast Track from the Show popup menu in the upper-right corner of the Timeline. The podcast track opens near the top of the Timeline above the audio tracks.

2 Open the Details tab active by pressing Command + I.

The balance of podcast features are well described in the Soundtrack Pro manual. Be sure to check it out for new ideas.

The HUD Can Help with Position

With its bundled sound effects and design elements, Soundtrack Pro is an excellent tool for creating the perfect audio bed. But getting a sound effect perfectly synced can involve some trial and error. Fortunately, Soundtrack Pro 2 makes it easier with the new Multipoint Video Heads Up Display (HUD).

To view the Multipoint Video HUD choose Window > HUDs > Multipoint Video. You'll need to have a video clip in your project in order for the HUD to work. The HUD is useful for both selections and editing. It will adjust to show you the first, last, and middle frame of the affected area (with Timecode). As you make a selection or drag clips around, the HUD updates. This makes it much easier to precisely align effects to picture.

Multipoint Video HUD On the Fly

If you'd like to temporarily view the Multipoint Video HUD, just press the V key while dragging a clip. The Multipoint Video HUD will temporarily display until you release the clip. Once you release the clip, the Multipoint Video HUD will close automatically.

Timecode for your Wave

A great new feature in Final Cut Pro 6 is support for broadcast wave files (BWF). You've probably heard of WAVE files before, as they're the most common form of uncompressed audio files in the Windows world. The cool thing about broadcast wave files is that unlike regular WAVE files or even AIFFs, they support timecode.

Many on-location audio recording engineers working on films or other productions where audio is recorded separately, use broadcast wave files. When that audio gets into the post-production pipeline and imported into Final Cut Pro, the timecode comes with it and because most of the time this matches the video source, it is very easy to sync up video and audio.

In Final Cut Pro you can choose whether FCP uses drop frame or non-drop frame timecode by default. Choose a default in the Editing tab of User Preferences.

Assigning Audio Outputs

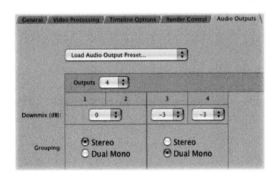

In the next few tips we are going to cover outputting a show to a professional deck (such as Digital Betacam). This format can support four channels of audio and the broadcaster for whom we're making the show requires that each channel on the tape contain a specific part of the mix. The first step is assigning audio outputs.

❶ Open your sequence settings (Command + 0).

❷ Select the last tab (Audio Outputs).

❸ From the outputs pull-down, choose the appropriate number of outputs to match your output device. In our example we are going to choose four to match our Digital Betacam deck.

❹ Our broadcaster requires that the first two channels be a stereo mix, channel 3 be all of our primary audio (narration, soundbites, etc.) and ch4 be music and effects. So, to meet this need make sure channels 1 and 2 are set to stereo with no down-mix and channels 3 and 4 to dual mono with -3 db down-mix on each channel. The down-mix is applied, because when stereo is mixed down to mono, the result will be louder; this control compensates for that.

> Note: It's always a good idea to check with your specific broadcaster about tape channel assignments.

Submixes—Part One

Chances are, you have a lot of tracks—don't worry—that's pretty normal. But how do you get sixteen (or more) tracks down to four? The simplest method is to create submixes based on the broadcaster's requirements. Our broadcaster wants a stereo mix on channels 1 and 2. Channel 3 should contain primary audio (narration, soundbites, etc.) and Channel 4 should contain music and sound effects.

❶ With all of your audio tracks active, choose File > Export > Using QuickTime Conversion. From the format pull-down, choose AIFF and then click options.

❷ A dialog box will pop up. Make sure under the channels pull-down you have Stereo (L R) selected. Remember, channels 1 and 2 on our tape will contain a stereo mix of the show.

❸ Make sure the sample rate and sample size pull-downs are set correctly (typically 48 kHz and 16-bit).

❹ Click OK and then give the file a name like MYSHOW_Ch1_2_STEREO_MIX.

❺ Click OK to export the file.

❻ In the Timeline, disable all tracks that are not primary audio. Don't just mute them—you need to disable them (the green audible button) or they'll be exported.

❼ Repeat step 1, but this time instead of choosing Stereo, choose Mono.

❽ Click OK and then give the file a name like MYSHOW_CH3_PRIMARY_AUDIO.

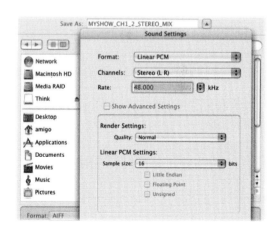

❾ Click OK to export the file.

❿ Now we simply need to repeat what we did for channel 3 for channel 4. Disable all tracks that are not music and effects.

⓫ Repeat step 1 but make sure you choose Mono for your export.

⓬ Click OK and then give the file a name like MYSHOW_CH4_MUSIC_EFFECTS.

⓭ Click OK to export the file.

> Note: If you have In and Out points set in the Timeline, only the clips in between will be exported. Also, any empty areas in the sequence will be exported as silence, including space you may have at the start of the sequence. Make sure your show starts right at the start of the Timeline and that you've cleared In and Out points.

Submixes—Part Two

After you've exported the three audio files, import them back into Final Cut Pro. There are just a few more steps to complete the submix process.

1 Duplicate your original Timeline, lock your video tracks, and delete all your audio tracks. Remember those audio output assignments we made earlier? Well, we are now going to assign tracks to those outputs.

2 Right-click on the track visibility icon for channel 1. From the popup, choose Audio Outputs > 1 & 2. Repeat the process for channel 2.

3 Right-click on the track visibility icon for channel 3. From the popup, choose Audio Outputs > 3.

4 Right-click on the track visibility icon for channel 4. From the popup, choose Audio Outputs > 4.

5 Next, edit each of the channels of the files you just imported into FCP on to the Timeline. So your Stereo Mix file goes on channels 1 and 2. Channel 3 Primary_ Audio goes on channel 3, and Music_Effects goes on channel 4. Pay special attention that you edit the submixes to the head of the sequence or they might be out of sync with the video.

Now you're ready to export your show back out to tape and have the correct audio assignments. Congrats!

Helping Your Case

So you've decided you're going to mix and sound design your show in Soundtrack Pro (good for you!). To make your life easier in Soundtrack Pro, there is one thing you can do in Final Cut Pro: create Scoring Markers.

Put simply, Scoring Markers are a way of getting a visual reference for when you want something to happen. That something could be a cue to add a sound effect at that location or to start a music sting or even that there is a problem at that location that you need to fix. To create Scoring Markers and get them into Soundtrack Pro, follow these steps.

1. Put the playhead at the place in your Timeline where you want to add the Scoring Markers. Make sure a clip is not selected (we want to add the marker as a Timeline marker).

2. Press the M key to add the marker. Type M again to open the Edit Marker dialog box.

3. Give the marker a name. Try to be specific; something like "Add Explosion Sound Effect Here."

4. Next, click the Add Scoring Marker button at the bottom of the dialog box. You'll notice that <SCORING> has been placed in the comment area.

5. Add additional Scoring Markers as needed.

6. When you're done, select the sequence in the Browser and choose File > Send To > Sound Track Pro Multitrack Project. Choose your export options and click save.

7. Soundtrack Pro will launch and you'll see your Scoring Markers.

What are you waiting for? Start building that mix!

What to Export

So you've created an award winning mix, but now what? Most of the time you'll need to get back to another application like Final Cut Pro. But what do you want to bring back to FCP—the whole mix? Individual channels or submixes? Well, in Soundtrack Pro, it's pretty easy to choose.

1 After you're done mixing choose File > Export.

2 A Save dialog will open. Choose the pull-down menu called Exported Items.

3 From here, you can choose to export the Master Mix, or combinations of busses and submixes or even individual tracks.

4 Next, choose the pull-down menu called File Type. Here, you can choose what type of file you will be outputting including AIFF, WAVE, and MP3.

5 Below this pull-down you can choose your bit depth and sample rate as well. If you mixed mono files in surround, you will need to export the individual files.

Note: If your going to be making the same type files over and over you can use the preset pull-down and create your own custom preset.

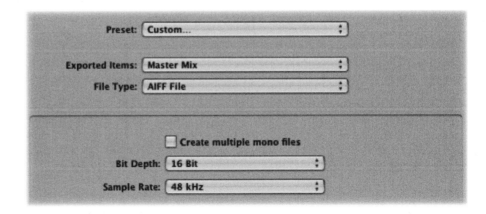

Creating a Script

If you find yourself doing repetitive tasks to your audio (and we all do), one easy way to automate that work is to create a Sound Track Pro Script. To do this, follow these easy steps:

1 Send the first offending piece of audio from Final Cut Pro to Soundtrack Pro by choosing File > Send To > Soundtrack Pro Audio File Project.

2 From within Soundtrack Pro apply analysis, effects, etc. to the clip as you see fit. As you apply these items notice that in the Actions tab in the left hand pane that they are stacking up in the order you applied them.

3 Once you're satisfied that the order of the actions is correct, choose File > Save As AppleScript.

4 A Save dialog box will open up asking you to give the script a name. Try to be descriptive. Also, be sure you don't save the script anywhere else except for its default location of User > Library > Scripts > Soundtrack Pro Scripts. Otherwise Final Cut Pro will not recognize the script. Save the script.

5 Back in Final Cut Pro, select the other clips you want to work with and go to File > Send To > Soundtrack Pro Script > NAME OF YOUR SCRIPT.

6 A dialog box will pop up to warn you that what you're about to do is destructive. Unless you are a glutten for punishment, make sure you click yes to convert the files into a Soundtrack Pro Audio File Project first. Choose a location and click save.

7 Soundtrack Pro will launch and will automatically apply the actions in the script to each file.

Hooray for automation!

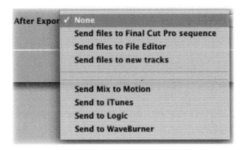

After Export—The End of the Audio Road

Ok, so you've mixed your show, chosen what you're going to export and what file type your export will be. Now what? Well, the last step in the output game is to decide what happens after the export is done. You have quite a few options, depending on what you're trying to do.

- **None:** The file(s) will be output with settings you've chosen and sent to the destination you chose. Nothing else will happen.

- **Send Files to Final Cut Pro Sequence:** This option will send the file(s) back to FCP in a new sequence. The cool thing is, if you had originally sent the project from FCP to Soundtrack Pro, your mix would be placed in a new FCP sequence that is identical to your original but with the file(s) located above the original audio with the original audio turned off.

- **Send Files to File Editor:** This option will open up the file(s) into the Soundtrack Pro File editor.

- **Send files to new tracks:** This option will automatically place the files you export into new tracks in Soundtrack Pro.

- **Send Mix to Motion:** Sends and opens your export to Motion.

- **Send to iTunes:** Sends and opens your export to iTunes.

- **Send to Logic:** Sends and opens your export in Logic.

- **Send to WaveBurner:** Sends and opens your export in WaveBurner (a CD mastering application bundled with Logic Pro).

One additional item that may appear here is if you have previously created scripts from Soundtrack Pro. Choosing the script will process the export using the actions in the script.

Now in Surround Sound

One of the best, and frankly, coolest new features in Soundtrack Pro 2 is the ability to mix and sound design in surround sound. Mixing in surround sound adds a gigantic amount of realism to your mixes and offers an amazing amount of creative control for your mixes.

If you're building your own mix, it is very easy to make your mix into a surround mix.

❶ Simply right-click your channel strips in the mixer or in the project pane and choose Use Surround Panner. This will enable you to pan in surround for that track.

❷ Next, make sure the default submix 1 is set up to output surround. To change this, simply choose Surround > 1–6 from the pop up menu in the track header, which is located either at the bottom of the submix 1 channel strip in the mixer or in the controls for submix 1 in the Timeline.

❸ To hear your surround sound mix, you need to make sure you have a multichannel audio interface and speakers set up. Otherwise, you will not be able to hear your mix in surround and Soundtrack Pro will mix down your mix to stereo.

After you've set up your Soundtrack Pro to mix in surround, the next step is to actually mix in surround! To do this you can use the mini surround panners located in each channel strip in the mixer and attached to each track in the Timeline. If you crave a little more control, you can use the surround panner HUD (heads up display). To launch the HUD, simply double-click on a mini surround panner.

For more explanation of the controls in the surround panner HUD check out page 300 in the Soundtrack Pro user manual.

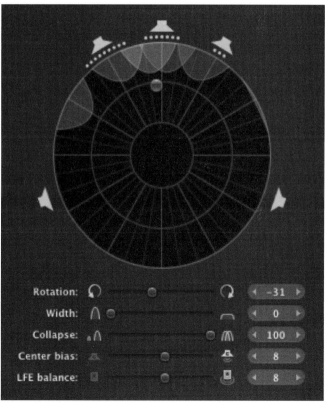

ON THE SPOT

Still Life
Designing and Importing Graphics

Wouldn't it be nice to just be an editor (sigh!) and only have to worry about editing the pictures? You could have a great post team with audio composers, graphic artists, and animators and, did we mention, you get an assistant editor, too?

Okay, wake up! The days of large post teams with leather couches and fresh-baked chocolate chip cookies are a thing of the past. You have to be able to do it all now. Your client's biggest expectation is good-looking graphics that work.

Don't worry; we've got your back. This chapter presents some great tips on prepping graphics. You'll find all sorts of information about working with Adobe Photoshop and Apple LiveType. We'll unlock the secrets of composite (blending) modes as well as working inside the safe title area. And when you're done, you'll never be afraid of an alpha channel again. As for the fresh-baked chocolate chip cookies, we suggest the slice-and-bake variety. Hey, we're all about saving time!

Feel a Change Coming On (Using External Editors)

By using Final Cut Pro's External Editors tab, you can assign Adobe Photoshop (or another graphics application) to be your graphics editor. This allows you greater flexibility in making changes.

1 Choose Final Cut Pro > System Settings.

2 Select the External Editors tab.

3 Click the Set button next to Still Image Files. Select your graphic editor of choice.

4 Now you can simply contextual-click on a graphic, and choose Open in External Editor.

The graphic will now open in the third-party application. Make any changes, and then close and save your document. As long as you don't add, subtract, or rename layers, the graphic will import correctly and update automatically in the Timeline.

> Note: Although you can set an external editor for audio files, it won't work if the audio is linked to a video clip.

Gimme Layers

Sometimes you'll want to import a layered Adobe Photoshop file. Final Cut Pro does a good job of this by importing as a composition and turning each layer into a track. To import the PSD file, do one of the following:

- Drag the files or a folder from the finder to a project tab or bin in the Browser.

- Choose Import from the File menu (Command + I). Select File or Folder from the submenu. Select a file or folder in the dialog box, and click Choose.

- Contextual-click in the Browser or a bin's window. Next, choose Import File or Import Folder from the popup menu. Select a file or folder; then click Choose.

Didn't I Ask for Layers?

We said Final Cut Pro did a good job of importing PSD files, but it doesn't do a perfect job. There are several features that can't be imported. Why? Well, two different companies make the products, and we're certain neither is fully willing to let all their secrets go.

Final Cut Pro   Adobe Photoshop CS3

You must do a little file preparation to make a smooth import. Be sure to work on a duplicate of the original PSD file. The following Adobe Photoshop features are problematic when importing layers:

- Blending Modes (partial support)
- Layer Effects
- Layer/Set Mask
- Adjustment Layers
- Grouped Layers (layers import, grouping ignored)

Keyable Movies

Want to create an Apple QuickTime movie that can be keyed through an alpha channel? It's doable if you know what options to pick.

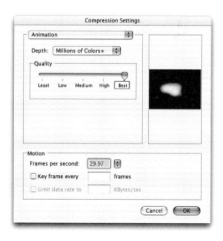

❶ Determine if your codec supports embedded alpha channels. Many uncompressed or low compression formats do. If you're using DV, however, you must choose Animation.

❷ Be sure to choose RGB + Alpha in the Output dialog box if it's an option.

❸ Specify Millions of Colors+ if you also want to embed an alpha.

❹ Render out your file or export it. As long as you've chosen a proper codec and specified to include the alpha, you'll get great results when keying your graphic.

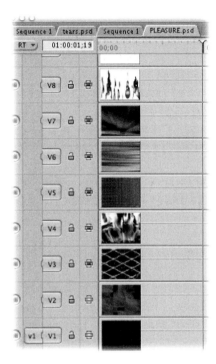

So, What Works?

Final Cut Pro's designers understand that many users will want to bring in layered files for compositing or animation. After all, Final Cut Pro does bill itself as a compositing application, giving users access to many of the commands traditionally associated with Adobe After Effects. Truth be told, about 85 percent of what After Effects imports, Final Cut Pro will bring over. In general, supported features include the following:

- **Layer order and layer name:** Be careful not to change them in your PSD file. Adding and deleting layers after import is also a no-no.

- **Opacity:** The imported layer's opacity becomes the Opacity control in the Motion tab. You can adjust the opacity within Final Cut Pro, as well.

- **Blending modes:** The following blend modes transfer correctly: Add, Subtract, Difference, Multiply, Screen, Overlay, Hard Light, Soft Light, Darken, and Lighten.

- **Layer group:** Layer grouping is ignored. However, all layers, including grouped layers, import as individual layers.

- **Layer set:** All layers within a layer set are imported to individual layers, but nesting is ignored.

- **Type layers:** Type is rasterized and can't be edited within Final Cut Pro. However, you can switch to Adobe Photoshop via the external editor, and make changes there that will update upon saving.

- **Solid solor fill layers:** Solid color fill layers are brought in as a graphic with a full-screen, opaque alpha channel.

- **Shape layers:** Shape layers are rasterized and import correctly.

- **Pattern fill layers:** Pattern fill layers import as the size of the composition.

- **Gradient fill layers:** Gradient fill layers are preserved upon import.

- **Smart Objects:** Smart Objects are rasterized upon import.

Give Me a Redeye, Pardner!

Editors often get redeye from their extraordinary social lives (or maybe it's those long edit sessions in dark rooms with bad delivery food). Photos often get redeye because the light bounces from the flash off the back of the eyeball (no, it has nothing to do with demonic possession).

Looking for an easy fix? Just open the pictures in iPhoto.

1. Select the photo in the iPhoto Browser.

2. Click the Edit button.

3. Marquee around just the eye area (do one eye at a time and try to avoid getting flesh tones).

4. Click the Red-Eye button to remove the color reflection.

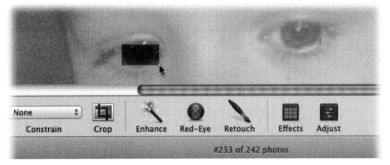

Layered TIFFs Save Time

While it's useful that you can import layered PSD files into Final Cut Pro, it's unfortunate that not all features carry over. On the other hand, when you need to change a graphic (such as a spelling mistake) it's very useful to have those layers ... Have your cake and eat it too ... hmm.

Okay, this is easy. In Photoshop, save your files as LAYERED TIFFs. Final Cut Pro will read it in as a flattened file, but you can make changes. Better yet, if you use the Open in Editor shortcut, you can open and modify the file. In fact you can add, delete, move, and rename layers with no ill effects (try that with a PSD file you've imported and watch what craziness breaks loose).

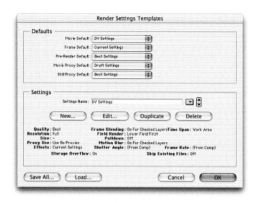

The Right Stuff (Rendering with Presets)

Need to output an Apple QuickTime movie from your motion graphics application? Most other compositing tools also support Output Templates. To get things right every time (without having to think), create templates. Each software package will handle things differently, but the results are the same.

For example, in Adobe After Effects, you can create both Render and Output Templates (Edit > Templates > Render Settings or Output Modules). Use the following settings when designing for NTSC DV video.

Render Settings

Quality	Best
Resolution	Full
Field Render	Lower Field First
Frame Rate	29.97

Output Template

Format	QuickTime Movie
Format Options/Codec	DV/DVCPRO – NTSC
Quality	Best
Channels	RGB
Depth	Millions of Colors
Color	Premultiplied
Audio	48.000kHz
Size	16 Bit
Channels	Stereo

Mobile Style

Layer Styles don't like to travel. This is a common problem because Apple applications do not correctly interpret Layer Styles. To import successfully, you need to flatten them. Using a technique called Targeted Flattening, you can create a merged layer and preserve an editable layer within the same document. This gives you the best of both worlds: proper imports and room for future revisions. Follow these steps:

1. Save your document under a different name by using File > Save As. This is an extra precaution against accidentally deleting your work. (We usually rename it **Document Name for FCP.psd**.)

2. Create a new (empty) layer, and link it to the stylized layer that needs processing. You can link two layers together by clicking in the space between a layers thumbnail and the visibility eyeball.

3. Leave the empty layer highlighted. While holding down the Option key, choose Merge Linked from the Layers Palette submenu. This merges the layers to the target layer but leaves the originals behind.

4. You should have a flattened copy on the target layer. Rename this flattened layer so you can easily locate it later. We recommend including the word flat in your layer name for ease of use.

Repeat these steps for all layers, and save your work. This method will produce a layered document, which will import properly into Final Cut Pro.

"Free" Backgrounds

LiveType has more than 150 different textures loaded. They all loop seamlessly, as well. If you're not happy with a default look, you can change the speed as well as the color. You can even get creative by taking a few of them into your Final Cut Pro Timeline and mixing them together using composite modes. All of these are royalty free because you've already bought them.

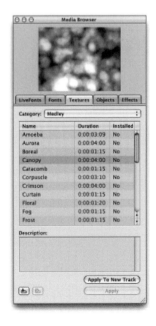

195

How to Update a Layer Style

You've imported a layer with a cool layer style applied, and now you need to make changes. If you've followed our advice so far, it's no problem. By using the External Editors shortcut, you can easily jump back to update a layer. In conjunction with targeted flattening, it's even easier to make changes.

❶ Contextual-click on the graphic in the Timeline, and choose Open in Editor.

❷ You'll automatically be switched to Adobe Photoshop if you've set your external editors up correctly.

❸ Select the flattened layer, choose Select All, and press Delete.

❹ Pick the original (unflattened) layer, and make your changes.

❺ Link the editable layer to the "recently" emptied layer. Highlight the empty layer.

❻ Repeat the targeted flattening procedure by holding down the Option key when you choose Merge Linked.

Close and save your document. When you switch back to Final Cut Pro, your changes will update automatically.

Templates for Menus

Need to create a DVD menu? Use LiveType. What? Use a type program to make a menu? Yup, there are some great templates for DVD menus (as well as bumper graphics) built right in. Simply choose File > Open Template (Shift + Command + O). You can use the Info and Promo categories to create graphics for DVD menus. Simply modify the templates, plug in your video, and change the type—instant motion menu backgrounds to use in iDVD or DVD Studio Pro.

It's easier to leave the text buttons off and add those during the DVD authoring stage.

How to Render Less

Would you rather render once or 300 times? The answer seems obvious, right? Yet so many people import graphics that are improperly sized into Final Cut Pro. Every graphic that isn't sized properly needs to be rendered.

The solution is to either work in a graphic application that supports nonsquare pixels or resize before you import. The following chart lists the "native" size your graphics should become.

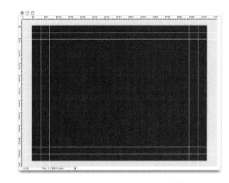

Format	Native Size	Square Pixel Size
601-NTSC 4:3	720×486	720×547
601-NTSC 16:9 Anamorphic	720×486	853×486
DV-NTSC 4:3	720×480	720×540
DV-NTSC 16:9 Anamorphic	720×480	853×480
601/DV-PAL 4:3	720×576	768×576
601/DV-PAL 16:9 Anamorphic	720×576	1024×576
1080i	1920×1080	1920×1080
720p	1280×720	1280×720

The above are the recommended settings from Apple's Final Cut Pro Group. Several other sources (including the DVD Studio Pro manual) say to use the following measurements. In our experience, both work just fine.

Format	Native Size	Square Pixel Size
NTSC 4:3	720×480	720×534
NTSC 16:9 Anamorphic	720×480	864×480
PAL 4:3	720×576	768×576
PAL 16:9 Anamorphic	720×576	1024×576

The best option, though, is to work with a graphics application that supports nonsquare pixels (such as Photoshop CS or later). This will cut down on your mathematical headaches.

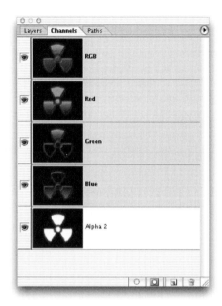

Alpha Channel (One Layer Graphic)

It's very important to get your alpha channel created correctly if you want to "key" a graphic on top of video tracks. An alpha channel contains the transparency of a document saved as the fourth channel in an RGB image. In Final Cut Pro, any area in the alpha channel that's black will allow video to pass through. Alpha channels also allow variable amounts of opacity because shades of gray in an alpha channel show areas of the graphic as partially transparent.

With something so fundamental to video, you'd think there'd be significantly less confusion as to how to create an alpha channel. Here's the fastest way for a single layer document:

1. A perfect alpha channel starts with an active selection loaded. To load a layer, Command + click on the layer's icon in the Layers palette until you see the marching ants. Note: If you have a layer style applied, you must flatten the layer style by merging it with a new empty layer.

2. Switch to the Channels palette, and click the Save Selection As Channel icon.

3. Save your native PSD file. Then pick Save As, and choose to save a PICT or TIFF file. Make sure the Alpha Channels box is checked.

How to Train Your Graphics Department

Graphic editing applications support many color modes. The two you want to use for video work are RGB and Grayscale. Be careful—many stock images and client logos come in the CMYK format. This is designed for print output and will not import correctly into Final Cut Pro. You can check a graphics format by looking at its title bar in Adobe Photoshop.

Alpha Channel (Multiple Layers)

If you have a multilayered document, things are a little trickier. But creating an alpha channel is still an essential part of cleanly keying graphics:

① Turn off the visibility icon for all layers that aren't part of the graphic you want to key.

② Create a new layer, and highlight it.

③ Hold down the Option key and choose Merge Visible from the Layers palette submenu. A new layer is created from the existing layers.

④ Command + click on the new layer's thumbnail icon to make an active selection. Then turn the visibility icon off for the merged copy.

⑤ Switch to the Channels palette, and Save the Selection as a Channel.

⑥ Save your file as a PICT or TIFF with an alpha channel using the previously described method.

Matte Settings

If you're using glows, drop shadows, or soft edges, you'll likely have a soft edge in your alpha channel. To get the best key possible, you want a clean glow or shadow. But this is difficult if you don't dig deeper into your import graphic settings.

By default, Adobe Photoshop creates a premultiplied alpha channel (an alpha channel that follows the edge exactly). This causes problems, however, because the background color will be visible around the edges of your graphic. If you do nothing, this will be a problem, because your glows will look "dirty," and partially transparent drop shadows will come through too strong.

In Final Cut Pro, it's important to identify what the graphic was on top of when the alpha channel was created. If you had a black background, choose Black. If you had a white background or the transparency grid, choose White.

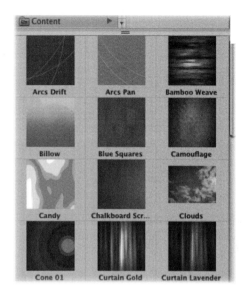

Free Stuff (Motion)

Looking for an easy to way add backgrounds, textures and other elements to your project without having to break the bank on expensive stock animation libraries? Fortunately the wonderful folks at Apple understand. Motion ships with tons of free content that you can use in your projects (all of it royalty-free).

1 To access this content from inside Motion choose the Library tab in the Utility pane (Command + 2).

2 Then choose the Content folder from the list.

Welcome to the world of free content!

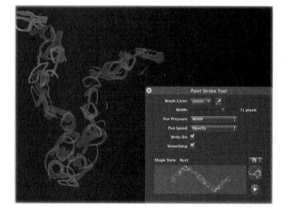

Write It

One of the coolest new features in Motion 3 is the ability to use the Paint Stroke tool to do a very cool write on effect. While there are lots of ways to customize this effect, let's take a look at the basics.

1 Select the Paint Stroke tool (P).

2 Make sure your HUD is active (F7). From here you can choose several options, such as brush color, width, pen pressure and pen speed (yes, this works with graphics tablets).

3 At the bottom of the HUD there is a pull-down for shape style. Here you can choose dozens of different pre-built shape styles for the Paint Stroke tool. Be sure to check out the very cool light strokes and organic elements.

4 To really get the effect right, make sure the checkbox for Write On is checked.

5 Draw your stroke.

6 Play back your Timeline and watch this ultra-cool effect.

Better Prep—Saturation

Sure, Final Cut Pro and Color have great toolsets for color correction and grading, but a little bit of prep on your images prior to using them in those applications can go a long way. One area that can really help is making sure that chroma in your images are broadcast safe.

To do this, try the following:

1 Open the image in Photoshop.

2 Choose Window > Actions.

3 Click on the submenu of the Actions palette and choose Video Actions.

4 Run the Broadcast Safe Saturation action.

This action is a better alternative, as it does not produce banding and posterization like the NTSC Colors action.

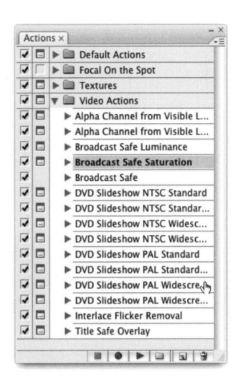

Better Prep—Luma Range

An astute reader might be wondering, what about luma in graphics? This is an often-debated question, with some resources suggesting changing your output levels to 16 and 235. While this used to be true, Final Cut Pro is now smart enough. It can map RGB images into video color space $Y'C_BC_R$ and doesn't need help from Photoshop.

How whites are handled is determined by a sequence setting. By choosing Sequence > Sequence Settings > Video Processing you can control how RGB white values are mapped to $Y'C_BC_R$. Using the Process Maximum White

and choosing White, Final Cut Pro will automatically map 255 to 100% luma which is perfectly broadcast legal! It's important to note that this setting may not be available for all codecs.

What about black levels and NTSC video, you might ask? Because you're dealing with digital video (and images for that matter), black level should be considered 0. Modern output devices will insert setup on output to analog devices.

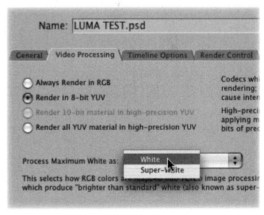

201

Want a Sprite?

No, not the refreshing soft drink. How about we create a sprite for use in a particle system in Motion? A sprite is one of the basic building blocks of a particle system and they are really easy to create in Photoshop. A sprite is really nothing more than a small grayscale image that can take the shape of say a raindrop or a snow flake.

Here are a couple of tips for creating a sprite that will work well in a particle system in Motion:

- Make sure the dimensions of the sprite are something like 64×64, or 128×128, or any other size that is easily divisible by 8. This so your computer can easily process it.

- Make sure the image uses the grayscale image mode.

- Make sure the image has an alpha channel.

After creating your sprite, simply import it into Motion and choose the Make Particle command.

Keep Me Layered

You might know that Final Cut Pro can use layered Photoshop files, but did you know Motion can too? This is a great way to create a motion menu for a DVD or put otherwise still graphics into... (wait for it) Motion!

1 To import a layered Photoshop file into Motion, choose the file in the File Browser tab (Command + 1).

2 Drag the file to either the Layers tab of the Project pane (Command + 4) or the Timeline tab of the Timing pane (Command + 7).

3 Don't let go of your mouse—a drop palette will open up. From here you can choose to import individual layers, merged layers, or all layers.

Video Actions Save Time

We've mentioned them once already in this chapter, but be sure to load the Video Actions that ship with Photoshop (starting with CS2). You'll find big timesavers like a one-click alpha channel and a DVD slideshow action.

The Interlace Flicker Removal action is a much better option for stills and graphics than a flicker filter in Final Cut Pro (no long render times and it only blurs the problem areas). Be sure to check the Video Actions out (just call up the Actions palette and pick the Video Actions in the submenu).

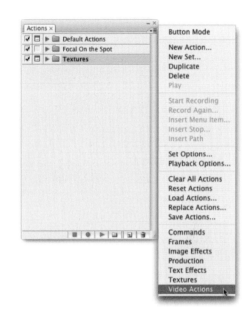

Use that Broadcast Monitor with Photoshop

Video graphics are meant to be seen on a video device, otherwise a whole slew of issues can't be seen. It is essential to check for color, interlace flicker, and readability on a television or video monitor.

In Photoshop (CS2 and later):

1. Make sure the DV video device is connected and powered on BEFORE launching Photoshop.

2. Choose File > Export > Video Preview... The popup window will present you with logical choices (you can roll over an item for a detailed description).

3. Click OK. For subsequent previews, just choose File > Export > Send Video Preview to Device.

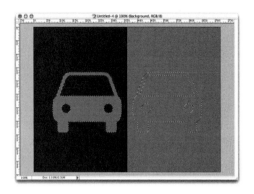

A Better Alpha

For best results, use a straight alpha channel. In this case, the background color should be the same color as your glow or drop shadow. This way, when the alpha channel is created, the edge has a consistent color (hence it's not premultiplied with a color that must later be removed). This is the preferred method of creating channels, but Adobe Photoshop doesn't work this way. You must place a solid color layer into the background that matches the glow, drop shadow, or soft edge. When creating a straight alpha channel, there's nothing different in the graphic (or fill) area. The essential difference is in the alpha channel area.

Going to LiveType—Part 1

Need to bring a logo into LiveType? It's no problem. LiveType recognizes graphics without layers. With this in mind, you can bring in a single-layered PSD file, and it will see the transparent area around the logo as an alpha channel. For more precision and support of styles, follow the aforementioned advice on creating an alpha channel. Choose Place (Command + I) to import. Using a PICT with alpha channel in RGB mode, you'll be on your way.

Going to LiveType—Part 2

No matter how much it would make your life easier, layered Adobe Photoshop files will not make it into LiveType. It's a good idea to save each layer out as a single graphic. Here's how ... the fast way: Adobe Evangelists is a GREAT website to find information about Adobe products such as Photoshop. In the Photoshop area is a collection of Actions. Download the Saving Out Layers action file at http://www.adobeevangelists. com/photoshop/actions.html.

A Better LiveType

By default, LiveType is likely not configured properly for your system. Be sure to call up Project Properties (Edit > Project Properties), and select the right preset for your tape format. While you're there, be sure to turn Render Fields on for smoother motion. Field rendering will increase your render times, but the quality is worth it. Also, for digital formats, you need to render LOWER field first.

Here's a bonus tip from Steve Martin of Ripple Training: Use Place Background Movie (Shift + Command + I), and bring in a video file. Check your preferences and you'll see the project has converted to the aspect ratio of the placed clip.

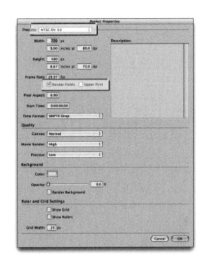

When Modes Collide

So you've discovered that some modes work and some do not—bummer. That's okay—you can still work around this limitation. You have two options to solve your problem.

Option 1: Pick a similar mode. Final Cut Pro recognizes most of the "original" blending modes. Subsequent versions of Adobe Photoshop have introduced additional modes. That's okay—they aren't that different.

ADOBE PHOTOSHOP	FINAL CUT PRO
Color Burn, Linear Burn	Use Darken or Multiply
Color Dodge, Linear Dodge	Use Lighten or Screen
Vivid Light, Linear Light, Pin Light	Use Hard Light or Overlay
Dissolve, Exclusion, Hue, Saturation, Color, and Luminosity	Must merge layers

Option 2: Merge the blended layers together. Link the two (or more) blended layers together. Choose Merged Linked from the Layers palette submenu.

Imported Still/Video Gamma Preferences

When you import graphics or video files created with non-Apple programs (such as Photoshop, After Effects, or Cinema 4D), their gamma often needs to be interpreted. The Editing tab of the User Preferences window offers control over the default interpretation (you can always adjust individual clips in the Browser). This Gamma Level property is used by Final Cut Pro to adjust for any gamma correction needed (this is most evident in the midtones of the image).

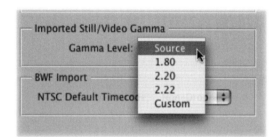

In general, Final Cut Pro assumes the following about your media:

- RGB-encoded media (such as TIFF or the Apple Animation codec) has a gamma of 1.8. This is correct for images created on a Mac.

- If the image file was created on a different platform (such as Windows), you may need to adjust the clip's Gamma Level property to 2.2.

- $Y'C_BC_R$ media has an implicit gamma of 2.2. You cannot adjust the gamma of $Y'C_BC_R$ clips.

Final Cut Pro supports gamma adjustment for the following types of media:

- Still images: JPEG, PNG, TIFF, layered or flattened Photoshop (PSD) files.

- QuickTime movie files: None or Animation codec.

Knowing when and how to manage color can be tricky. A common problem is the mixing of RGB graphics into a $Y'C_BC_R$ sequence. Final Cut Pro relies on QuickTime to import RGB media and always assumes that RGB media files have a gamma of 1.8.

When these clips are rendered, the image is brightened by an additional 1/1.22 to match the 2.2 gamma compensation required by the sequence. This is perfectly fine if the graphics material is created on a Macintosh computer. However, if the material was created elsewhere, you'll often encounter files where the gamma is already set to 2.2.

To set the default gamma value applied to imported files:

❶ Choose Final Cut Pro > User Preferences.

❷ Click the Editing tab.

❸ Choose one of the options from the Gamma Level pop-up menu:

- Source: Choose this option to ensure that clips appear the same as in previous versions. This option uses QuickTime to interpret the gamma of imported media files.

- 1.8: Choose this option if importing media files created with the Mac OS or created by an application in which you specified a gamma value of 1.8.

- 2.2: Choose this option if importing media files created with Windows systems or by an application in which you specified a gamma value of 2.2.

- Custom: This option is generally not needed.

When you adjust the gamma of a clip in Final Cut Pro, the original media file is not modified. Rather, only the clip in the project is affected. Remember, you can modify the gamma level of a clip after you import it in the Browser.

Photoshop for Video Podcast and Website

Forgive a little bit of self-promotion. If you are looking for more information on creating graphics with Photoshop, be sure to check out www.PhotoshopforVideo. com. You'll find a blog with lots of Apple news, plus a weekly podcast and lots of bonus articles for download. It's free—check it out.

ON THE SPOT

Master of Your Domain
Controlling the Timeline

The sun is shining, and you're driving down the Pacific Coast Highway in a cherry red convertible. You know every bend and curve in the road. Life is good. That's how you should feel about your Timeline. It's the window that gets your show from start to finish. The more you know about its nuances, the better your driving experience will be.

In this chapter, we'll show you how to get the most out of your Timeline, how to take advantage of its power, and how to do some tricks that will make, well, doing tricks easier.

The Timeline in Final Cut Pro has always been flexible. Lately it has become a contortionist, bending over backward to make your editing life easier. Once you get comfortable with nesting, stacking, resizing, and—well, you get the picture— you'll be the envy of every other driver, um, editor on the road.

Got Snaps?

Sometimes you want things to quickly jump into their proper place. Final Cut Pro refers to this as snapping. When turned on, items will snap directly to the playhead, an edit point, markers, keyframes, or In and Out points. This makes it easier to align clips (especially when keying graphics on a higher track).

Look for a small gray arrow that appears above or below the point that indicates the item has snapped into place. But what if snapping is getting in the way of your edit or composite? Turn it off!

You can turn snapping on or off at any time, even as you're dragging a clip. Simply press the N key to disable snapping. You'll notice the snapping icon change on the right edge of the Timeline.

Snapping affects several areas besides the Timeline. You may want to turn it off when scrubbing, trimming, or using motion controls. Even the Viewer and Canvas can be affected.

Tighten Up Your Timeline

A clean tight Timeline is a happy Timeline. Here are some quick cleanup tips:

Delete unused tracks: Select Sequence > Delete Tracks. Check both the Video Tracks and Audio Tracks boxes, and then select All Empty Tracks.

Drag me down: Reduce your layers. If you have stacked clips upon clips on multiple video tracks, you can hold down the Shift key and drag them to overwrite the clips below them. The Shift key ensures that your clip doesn't move left or right as you move it down.

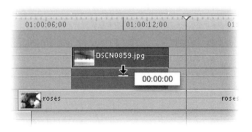

The Dividing Line—Part 1

When dragging tracks in the Timeline, *where* you drag is as important as *what* you drag. Careless dragging may result in an unintended overwrite edit when you intended an insert edit.

If you look closely at the Timeline, you'll notice that it's divided by a thin gray line. When dragging, look to see which region you enter to determine the edit type.

When dragging from the Viewer or a bin, use these tips:

- Dragging to the upper-third of the track results in an insert edit.

- Dragging to the lower two-thirds of the track results in an overwrite edit.

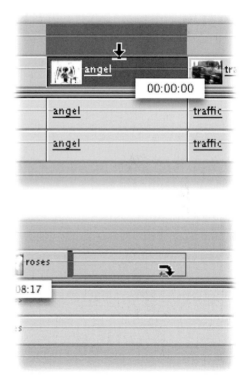

The Dividing Line—Part 2

Several different options are available when dragging within the Timeline.

When dragging in the Timeline, use these tips:

- Dragging in the Timeline horizontally results in an overwrite edit by default.

- Dragging in the Timeline horizontally results in an insert or swap edit when you hold down the Option key.

- Dragging in the Timeline vertically results in an overwrite edit by default.

- Dragging in the Timeline vertically results in an insert edit when you press the Option key after you start to drag.

- Pressing the Option key and then dragging in the Timeline vertically results in a cloned copy added to the Timeline via an insert edit.

- Pressing the Option and Shift keys and then dragging in the Timeline vertically results in a cloned copy added to the Timeline directly above the clip.

211

A Little Stability

Tired of scrolling up and down in the Timeline? Need to see audio tracks 1 and 2 so you can mix the music, but there are sound effects and natural sound living on tracks A3–A6? Sometimes it's just hard to see all the tracks you need.

It's easy, however, to create a static region in the middle of the Timeline. The static region can contain video tracks, audio tracks, or both. When you create a static region, you end up with three regions in the Timeline. The top video portion and bottom audio portion are scrollable. The middle portion can be resized and repositioned, but not scrolled. This style of Timeline makes it easy to constantly see your dialogue and A-Roll, while still having access to your other tracks.

To create the static region, drag the thumb tabs to set the number of tracks. Grab the central tab in the static region to move it up and down your Timeline. To eliminate the static region, drag the video tab downward and the audio tab upward.

Don't Drag and Drop

Professional editors edit from the keyboard. Don't believe us? Ever see a concert pianist use a mouse?

Mute, Solo, Audible: What's the Big Difference?

Here's a distilled overview of Mute, Solo, and Audible and when to use them.

Audible turns a track's sound on and off. If it's off, you can't hear it when you play back from the Timeline, and you won't hear it when you print to tape. This is very useful when doing multiple-language programs or news packages where you need a version with and without narration. Option + clicking an Audible button leaves that track live and silences all other tracks.

Mute and Solo are opposite sides of the same coin. The Mute button turns off audio playback for that track. The Solo button does the opposite—muting all tracks that don't also have Solo enabled. This is a great way to preview a specific group of audio tracks. Remember that you can mute or solo one or multiple audio tracks.

> Note: If you don't see all of these audio controls, be sure to click the Audio Controls button at the bottom of your Timeline.

Use the Solo Item(s) Command

A more advanced solo command is Solo Item(s). Follow these steps:

❶ Select the item(s) you want to solo.

❷ Press Control + S to invoke the Solo Item(s) command.

❸ All nonselected clips (above or below) have their visibility disabled.

❹ Press Control + S to disengage soloed items.

The key advantage to this method is that you'll only lose render files in the soloed and adjacent clips.

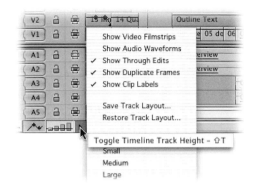

There's a New Triangle in Town

In Final Cut Pro a drop-down triangle appears to the right of the Toggle Timeline Track Height button called the Timeline Layout popup. It provides a quick and easy shortcut to several features, such as the following:

- Show Video Filmstrips
- Show Audio Waveforms
- Show Through Edits
- Show Duplicate Frames
- Show Clip Labels
- Save Track Layout
- Restore Track Layout

And it has shortcuts to the four default track heights:

- Reduced
- Small
- Medium
- Large

O, Solo Mio

Have eight layers visible but only want to see one? That's what soloing is for. It's possible to turn off all "other" layers to quickly refine your view. Simply hold down the Option key and click a track's visibility icon. All other tracks are made temporarily invisible. Option + click the soloed track to return to a normal view.

This will affect your render files, so this is most helpful when you're harnessing the power of RT Extreme. Once you get into heavy rendering, try not to turn track visibility on and off, or you'll lose video render files.

Let It Roll: Scrolling in the Timeline

Too many tracks in your Timeline, and you want to scroll up and down quickly? No need to grab the scroll bar on the right edge if you have a three-button mouse. Put the cursor over the Timeline, and use the third button to scroll up and down. It gets better; hold down the Shift key and you can scroll left and right (if you're using an Apple Mighty Mouse, just scroll). Don't stop now—place the cursor over the Viewer or Canvas, and you can scrub backward and forward. If you aren't impressed yet by Apple's thoughtful engineers, go try these shortcuts in a bin, on effect sliders, and even in the audio mixer.

Slippin ...

Advanced editors know that true power lies in trimming (those minor adjustments made to shots that perfect the edit). Slipping a shot involves changing what portion of the shot is seen while the duration in the Timeline remains constant. Many editors know about the Slip Item Tool (S) but don't know about the ability to slip within the Viewer. Follow these steps:

❶ Double-click a clip to load it in the Viewer.

❷ Hold down the Shift key, and click the In or Out point.

❸ Drag left or right to adjust the shot. The changes update in the Timeline automatically.

Getting Loopy

Need to analyze a shot? Sometimes you want to keep looping an item. Final Cut Pro gives you two options:

Loop Playback (Control + L) will jump back to the beginning of a clip or sequence when it reaches the end.

Loop Current Marker (Control + Option + 7) will create a playback loop between the two markers you are closest to.

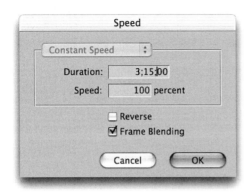

Give Me a Beat: How to Edit to Music

Have you got rhythm? Can you tap to the beat of a song with your foot? How about a finger? If so, you can quickly edit a montage to music:

❶ You may want to map the Add Edit command to a single keystroke without a modifier key. You can replace a key you don't use often for this new purpose. If not, the default combo is Control + V.

❷ In order to "cut" the beat, you need a solid layer in the Timeline. For this purpose you can use some Slug from the generator menu.

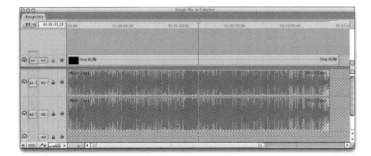

❸ Edit the Slug filler into the Timeline on an empty track, and lock all other tracks. Option + click the lock icon for the slug track to lock all other video tracks. Be sure to lock the audio tracks, as well.

❹ Slug duration is capped at 2:00:00, so you may need to change the speed of the slug. Highlight the track, press Command + J, and type in the new duration to match your music track. Changing the speed of the filler doesn't matter because you're going to replace it.

❺ Move your cursor to the start of the audio track and press Play.

❻ At each major beat or desired edit point, press the newly assigned key for Add Edit. The filler track will now be chopped up.

❼ Filling in the holes is simple. Load the desired source material, and place a single edit point to define the In or Out point.

❽ In the Timeline, press the X key to mark your In and Out point.

❾ Press F10 to perform an Overwrite edit.

❿ Repeat steps 7 and 8 until the end of the Slug is reached.

Close the Gap

This trick is particularly helpful when cutting down long interviews or closing gaps in a sound bite. When you find an area that needs to be exorcized, you can quickly make the cut from the keyboard (without having to switch tools). Simply load the entire clip into the Timeline, and then edit it down on the fly. Follow these steps:

1 When you hit the first gap, press I to mark an In point.

2 When you hit the end of the gap, press O to mark an Out point.

3 Press the Forward Delete key. On a PowerBook, press Shift + Delete.

4 Resume playing, and repeat the procedure for the next gap.

More Zoom Control

Zooming around your Timeline and want even more control? Try these two tips to speed up your navigation.

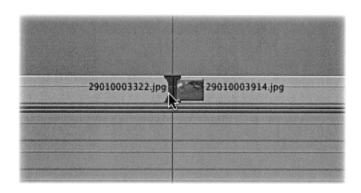

- Command and + or – will zoom in or out in the active window, whatever it may be.

- Option and + or – will zoom in only in the Timeline, regardless of which window is active.

Phil Hodgetts – http://www.digitalproductionbuzz.com/BuZZdex/

Timecode Gets You There Fast!

While click and dragging to navigate the Timeline is liberating for some, we find that it's kind of slow. One easy way to navigate the Timeline is by using timecode. To begin, make sure the Timeline is active and you don't have any clips selected—otherwise you will be moving the clips by timecode, not your playhead.

Simply type on the number pad the timecode you want to move to. For example, if you want to move to 5 seconds, type 500. Final Cut Pro will assume you're trying to move your playhead and place your entry in the current timecode box on the upper left-hand corner of the Timeline.

If you type:

- 1–2 numbers you're navigating by frames

- 3–4 numbers by seconds and frames

- 5–6 numbers by minutes, seconds and frames

- 7–8 numbers by hours, minutes, seconds and frames

Not so good with math? If you precede your entry with either a + or − you will navigate around your current playhead position. So let's assume you're at 5 seconds, typing in +213 will bring you to 7:13. Pretty simple but really fast!

Keeping Track of the Playhead When You Zoom

Although Final Cut Pro will zoom in around the Playhead by default, if there is a clip, clips or edit selected anywhere in the Timeline, the zoom will happen around the selection, not the Playhead. Instead of zooming back out, deselecting and going through the process again, try this:

- Click next frame, or previous frame on the keyboard, by default the left and right arrow keys.

- The Timeline will scroll to the Playhead position. Remember to press the opposite arrow key to return the Playhead to the frame it was previously on.

Phil Hodgetts — http://www.digitalproductionbuzz.com/BuZZdex/

Auto Conform Can Help You Make Up Your Mind

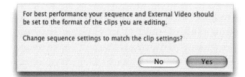

We first touched on the new Auto Conform options back in Chapter 2. Essentially, Final Cut Pro 6 tries to help you get your sequence settings right by changing the sequence settings to match the first clip edited into a Timeline. This can be a great timesaver as it allows you to get the sequence right without ever having to open the Sequence Settings window.

Sounds great, right? Just be sure to edit the proper format in first. Oh, and anamorphic clips need to be logged right ... and you might want to switch Motion Filtering to Best Quality ... and make sure you actually check which settings are being used ... I guess this feature isn't that useful.

Don't be lazy—you can use Auto Conform to get things right, or at least close to right. But never switch to full auto pilot mode. You'll always want to check and make sure your sequences are right. For more on Auto Conform options, see Chapter 2.

Get Your Scale On—Auto Scale Mixed Formats

In this day and age, it seems that mixed format Timelines are inevitable,whether it is HD and SD cohabitating, or a mixture of DV and D1 material. No one seems content to shoot and limit themselves to just one format exclusively. Infidels!

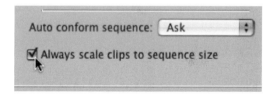

Fortunately, Final Cut Pro 6 can help you out. If you know a little mix and match is in your near future, you can tell Final Cut Pro to scale clips automatically.

- Clips whose frame size is larger than the sequence are always scaled down to fit in the sequence.

- You can choose how smaller clips are processed. Open the Editing tab of the User Preferences window and choose "Always scale clips to sequence size" if you want to force fit a clip.

- You can always adjust a clip in the Motion tab after the fact.

Nest Be Gone

In the old days, if you dragged one sequence from your Browser into another sequence in your Timeline, you'd simply have the nested sequence in your Timeline—not always what you wanted.

Now if you hold down the Command key while dragging the sequence into the Canvas or Timeline, all the individual clips will appear in your Timeline exactly as they appear in nested sequence from which they're sourced.

If you hold the Command key while dragging to the Timeline, Final Cut Pro will automatically add the needed tracks. If you're going to drag to the Canvas, however, it's very important to make sure you have enough tracks in your destination Timeline. Otherwise, only some of the tracks will come over.

Fly! (Trim on the Fly)

It's possible to trim on the fly. This way you can listen for an audio edit or look for a particular visual cue. Just make sure the Dynamic trimmimg checkbox is marked.

❶ Enter Trim Edit mode, and press the space bar to cycle your trim. The sequence will play around your edit point and loop. The pre-roll and post-roll are set in the Editing tab of User Preferences.

❷ When you reach the desired edit point, press the I key to move your In point.

❸ Press the up or down arrow to move through the Timeline to your next edit point.

Zoom ... Zoom ... Zoom

Want to see the entire Timeline from start to finish? Press Shift + Z to make the entire Timeline to Fit to Window. On the other hand, want to zoom in on just the selected area? Highlight one or more clips, and press Shift + Option + Z to Fit to Selection. These are valuable buttons that you should map to your Timeline window's button bar.

Where Do You Trim?

Sometimes you'll want to trim the incoming or outgoing side of an edit point. Instead of having to switch tools or hold down a modifier key, simply tap the U key. This will cycle your trim from centered at cut to incoming then to outgoing.

Using Transitions with Subclips

Subclips are a great way to zero in and permanently mark a section of a larger clip. You create them by marking an In and an Out, then pressing Command + U. This will create a subclip in the same bin that points to part of the larger media file. The problem is that you may have trimmed a subclip so tight that you can't add a transition.

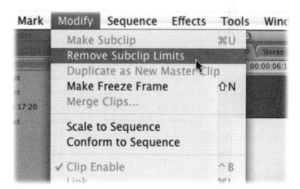

❶ Select the subclip in the bin or Timeline.

❷ Choose Modify > Remove Subclip Limits.

❸ You can now trim or use transitions beyond your original In or Out point.

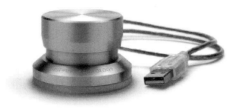

Silence, I Say!

So you're editing away and the phone rings. You take the call but want to continue editing. Wouldn't it be great if there were a really big mute button for your computer sitting on your desk that you could just smash and all would be quiet? Wouldn't it be even better if it glowed so you could find it in the dark? Get a Powermate from Griffin Technology. It can be programmed to be a great mute button, a volume controller, a jog shuttle or, truly, lots of things. Maybe program it to replicate Command F12 and jump Final Cut Pro to full screen playback a.k.a. Digital Desktop Preview. Now that will impress clients. And did we mention that it has really cool blue light ... oooh pretty.

We keep looking for USB ports to silence our kids during phone calls. Are you listening, Griffin?

Edit Markers (In)accurately

Markers are great, as they can store comments or compression information. They also can come in handy if you need to score music. The problem comes when you want to edit a marker. It used to be that you would have to get right on top of a marker and press MM to modify marker. Well, things are now a little easier.

1 Place your cursor on, or just after, the marker in question.

2 Press Command + Option + M to call up the Edit Marker dialog box.

3 Make your required changes.

4 Click OK.

Slug Fest

People who are new to editing often wonder what the purpose of a slug is. Slugs are not to be confused with the slimy gastropods found munching away in your garden but rather, they are useful black-only clips that can be used for a variety of editorial purposes. The term "slug" was employed by film editors to refer to the white leader that was used as a placeholder for takes or shots that had not come back from the lab. If you didn't have a needed shot, you would "slug in" some leader.

One way you can use slugs is to fill gaps to get a quick read on the gap duration. Control-click in any gap and choose "fill with slug" to fill the gap with a black-only slug. To get the duration of the gap, control-click on the slug and the duration will show up right in the contextual menu.

By Steve Martin – Ripple Training   www.rippletraining.com

Trim the Dynamic Trim

Final Cut Pro allows you to roll a trim point left or right from the keyboard. Double-click an edit point, and you switch to trim mode. You can now use J–K–L to roll the editing point dynamically:

❶ Enter trim mode by double-clicking between two clips with either the Selection Tool (A) or the Roll Edit Tool (R).

❷ Be sure to click Enable Dynamic trimming button at the bottom of the trim window.

❸ Trim left by pressing J or right by pressing L. You can hear the audio in real-time.

❹ Press K to make the trim.

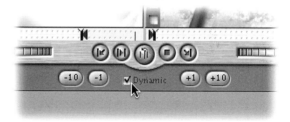

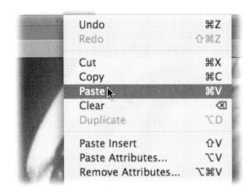

Undo	⌘Z
Redo	⇧⌘Z
Cut	⌘X
Copy	⌘C
Paste	⌘V
Clear	⌫
Duplicate	⌥D
Paste Insert	⇧V
Paste Attributes...	⌥V
Remove Attributes...	⌥⌘V

Copy + Paste = Change

It seems that copying and pasting clips in the Timeline is a bit of a moving target. We personally think it's a change for the better. Here's the new rule: If you copy something to your clipboard, it will paste into the same track, unless you change its target.

① Select your clip(s) in the Timeline.

② Press Command + C to copy the clip(s).

② Press Command + V to paste the clip(s) into the same track.

In order to copy and paste clips from one track in the Timeline to another, you use the Option key.

① Select your clip(s) in the Timeline.

② Press Command + C to copy the clip(s).

③ Option-click the lowest numbered Auto Select control to select the track you want to begin pasting into. If multiple tracks are selected they will paste to a higher track.

④ Press Command + V to paste the clip(s).

Slowly Trim the Dynamic Trim

But what if you want to roll the edit point more slowly? This tip will come in handy when trying to trim around syllables:

① Select the edit point with the Roll Edit Tool or Select Tool and double-click.

② Hold down the K key and use J or L to roll the edit point left or right at quarter speed.

③ When you find the edit point, release the keys to establish the new edit point.

Time Remap in the Timeline

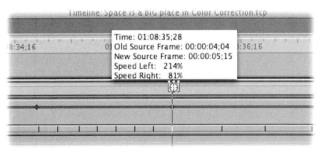

Final Cut Pro has some great time adjustment tools, replicating the similarly functioning TimeBender plug-in from Joe's Filters. It's also capable of allowing variable time adjustment without cutting or "blading" the track when changing speed. The advantage is that the clip length is no longer modified when using a variable adjustment.

The Time Remap Tool is behind the Slip and Slide Tools accessed by typing SSS on your keyboard. The icon appears as a small stopwatch, and it allows you to dynamically adjust your frame rate from the Timeline. To view the key-frame adjustment, make sure you select User Preferences > Timeline Options to check the "Speed Indicators" box and then turn on Clip Keyframes (Option + T or click the railroad tracks at the bottom left of the Timeline window).

Gary Adcock, Studio 37, Founder of the Chicago FCP User Group

Master of Time

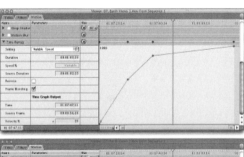

Need to change your playback speed? Easy, right? Just press Command + J. But what if you want the video to ramp up or slow down gradually? That's what time remapping is for. You'll need some practice with the tool to get the hang of it, but don't try to control it in the Timeline with the Time Remap feature. It's much easier to see your keyframes in the Viewer.

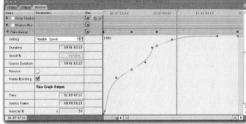

Follow these general guidelines:

- Keyframes indicate original video frames. If you add a keyframe at the 3:00 mark, then pull it forward to 1:15, the video will play back at double speed until that keyframe and then slow down afterward.

- Keyframes closer together create steeper slopes, which means faster playback.

- Keyframes further apart create gradual slopes, which means slower speeds.

- Make sure Frame Blending is turned on.

- Use the Smooth Point Tool (PPP) to improve the movement between keyframes. Bezier curves are your friend.

225

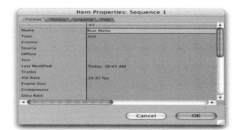

Labeling Generators in Final Cut Pro

The default label for generators in Final Cut Pro is the name of the generator. Renaming the clip in the Timeline makes it easier to find specific generators in the future.

When we create a Title 3D or Color Matte Generator in Final Cut Pro, the clip takes on the name of the generator. When there are a lot of titles or generators in the Timeline this can make it very confusing. Instead, rename the generator clip in the Timeline.

1 Select the clip in the Timeline.

2 Press Command + 9 to open the Item Properties, or open Item Properties from the contextual menu.

3 Rename the clip however you want; the color of the matte or the content of the title would be appropriate.

4 Press Return to exit Item Properties.

5 Now you can easily identify any title or generator and search for them.

Phil Hodgetts – http://www.digitalproductionbuzz.com/BuZZdex/

What You Want (Auto-Select)

The auto-select buttons help you work with only the tracks you want. Say you want to delete video from tracks 1, 2, and 5 but leave tracks 3 and 4 alone. Simply auto-select tracks 1, 2, and 5, mark an In and Out point in the Timeline, and delete. They're gone, and tracks 3 and 4 are untouched. Ripple delete works, too, but be careful. You may throw your Timeline out of sync.

Steal More (Attributes)

We stumbled across this trick while working on videos for a conference. In building the opening video, we had an effects-intensive piece cut to music. The client decided to edit a closing video with footage from the event. They wanted a "similar" look to both videos.

We simply duplicated the sequence and quickly re-edited the video. Here's how:

1 Pick the replacement shot. Mark an In point where you'd like the shot to begin.

2 Copy the shot by pressing Command + C.

3 Highlight the destination in your Timeline with the Select Tool.

4 Contextual-click, and choose Paste Attributes. Select Content for the Video (audio if wanted).

5 The new shot replaces the old. It's the same duration and has all of the same effects applied.

This is a huge timesaver when building bumpers, lower-thirds, promos, or any other type of edit where there's repetition.

Paste Attributes

Attributes from big ben:
☑ Scale Attribute Times

Video Attributes:
☑ Content
☐ Basic Motion
☐ Crop
☐ Distort
☐ Opacity
☐ Drop Shadow
☑ Motion Blur
☐ Filters
☐ Speed
☐ Clip Settings (capture)

Audio Attributes:
☐ Content
☐ Levels
☐ Pan
☐ Filters

Cancel   OK

"Tell Me What's On Your Mind"—Render Status Bar

Sure your Timeline had lots of red segments, but why? Have you been neglecting your machine? Did your tower get jealous when you took the laptop home with you? It's hard to really know why an effect needs to render and what is blocking real-time performance.

Or at least it used to be hard. Final Cut Pro 6 is a lot more willing to share. As long as you have Tooltips active (see your User Preferences) you can better tell what's going on. Just roll your cursor over a red segment and hover. Render status bars now provide detailed Tooltips as to why a segment with red render status bars can't play back in real-time.

Now, if we could just use the same trick to figure out why our kids and spouses get mad sometimes.

Get to the Point (the Edit Point that is!)

Editing is all about subtle manipulations of edit points and to help you do that faster it helps to have a quick way to navigate between them. Here are two easy ways to do that.

Use the V key. When you hit V on the keyboard, Final Cut Pro will navigate the playhead to the nearest edit point and select both sides of the edit point. From here, you're in a perfect place to do a roll edit, launch the Trim Edit window, etc.

Once an edit point is selected, use the up and down arrows on the keyboard to quickly navigate between edit points. Because the first point is already selected, using the up and down arrow keys will keep other edit points selected as well.

Choosing Your Part

Have you ever needed to select just a small portion of a clip to remove it from the Timeline? Maybe you have wanted to add an effect to just a small section of a clip without affecting the rest of the clip? Well, the Range Selection Tool is for you!

The Range Selection Tool is hidden under the Edit Selection and Group Selection Tools on the tool palette. You can also select it by using the keyboard shortcut GGG.

Once you have activated the tool, your cursor will become a crosshair. Simply click on your clip and drag left or right to select the portion of the clip you want. Notice a couple things:

- If you have linked audio, the audio will be selected as well.

- Your Canvas turns into a two-up display. If you dragged to the right with the tool, the two-up display will show you a static In point (left hand side) and as you drag to the right your Out point (right side) updates as you drag. If you dragged to the left you would see the opposite.

Once selected, you could do a lift edit (delete) or a ripple delete (shift + delete) to remove this section of clip. The cool thing is you can also apply an effect to just this portion of the clip! Either drag a filter from the Effects tab in the Viewer or choose Effects > Video Filters.

Now, when you load the clip into the Viewer and click on the filters tab you'll notice in the keyframe graph area your effect has only been applied to that portion of the clip—this is noted by the two thin black lines below the Timecode Ruler.

Save the Layout

All Timeline layouts can be saved so you can quickly call them up. Next to the Toggle Timeline Track Height bars is a submenu called the Timeline Layout popup. Simply arrange the Timeline how you want, and turn on the desired view options. Then save your work for later.

ON THE SPOT

CHAPTER 12

Multiple Camera Angles
Getting Results with Multiclips

When executed properly, a multicamera shoot can save enormous time in the post-production process. You can virtually eliminate synchronization issues, plus you've got additional angles to cut to. That is, if you do things right.

photo iStockphoto.com

Screw up the field side of it and you've just got more tapes with matched shots and bad timecode. Getting a multicamera edit to work is as much about pre-production and accuracy in the field as it is about what happens in post.

If you subscribe to the "fix it in post" mentality, then your multicamera edits can be downright painful. With these challenges in mind, let's explore ways to improve both the field and edit side of the production.

231

Plan for the Shoot

Just dropping a bunch of cameras at a location will not give you great coverage. Successful directors know they must plan out their shots to map out coverage. Here are a few important things to make sure of:

- **Map Out Coverage:** What sort of angles do you need? A two-person interview looks great with three cameras but a concert event might need eight cameras to capture the experience.

- **Use a Floor Plan:** You'll need to create a floor plan for your shoot that identifies talent and camera positions. Be sure to plan this out ahead of time and distribute to all of your crew.

- **Plan for Lighting:** Camera coverage will have a HUGE impact on your lighting strategies. Try to avoid lights getting too far behind cameras and operators; otherwise, you'll get unwanted shadows on the set.

- **Make Sure You Have Enough Power:** Eight cameras plus a three-ton grip truck's worth of lights can put a big drain on a circuit. Make sure you have identified where your power is coming from and that you have enough extension cords/stingers to get you the needed juice.

This is my Camera Darryl and my Other Camera Darryl

Want to use Multiclips in Final Cut Pro? Just grab any bunch of cameras, right? Unfortunately not. You need to match your cameras up fairly well.

- **Aesthetics:** Be sure to match settings across cameras. You'll want your color settings as well as options for shutter speed to match. Ideally, all cameras will be identical or closely related so they appear the same. This may mean a little extra planning (and even rentals) on your part.

- **Technical:** You'll need to identify Shooting Format, Codecs, Frame Size, etc. While Final Cut Studio is more efficient at mixing frame rates, the multicamera technology is not. Your clips need to match on all fronts, acquisition format, codec used, frame size and frame rate. If in doubt, test it out (well before the shoot).

What About Timecode?

If you want to synchronize your cameras to one another, then timecode is essential. Accurate timecode makes creating multiclips easy. But what happens if you can't afford the hardware needed to pull it off? From easiest to hardest, here's how to judge the need for timecode.

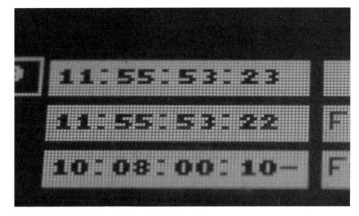

photo iStockphoto.com

- **Studio Cameras with House Sync:** If you are shooting in a studio, you're probably recording a switched feed already. Go ahead and record isolation feeds for the essential angles. Be sure to specify to the studio manager or engineer that you'd like all the timecodes to match.

- **Time of Day Timecode:** While this timecode can be harder to digitize (due to potential breaks) it also works well for creating a multiclip.

- **Slave Cameras Together:** A DP can often "jam" two cameras together. By taking the timecode out of one camera and feeding it into the other, sync is possible. Even some of Panasonic's FireWire-based cameras have this option.

- **Use a Clapboard:** You may think it's silly, but a film-style clapboard is an easy way to synchronize your cameras. You get both a visual and audio marker, plus every shot is already labeled for logging purposes.

- **Audio Sync Point:** Expand your waveforms and look for identical information. It might be a cough or the start of applause. Just find something in common on all tracks.

- **Visual Sync Point:** Look for common action in all shots. It might be the opening of a door or the clasp of a handshake. While not terribly accurate, this is your last stand at synchronicity.

A Digital Countdown

Looking for a way to sync things up when you're in the field? One way is to put a digital counter on set and point all your cameras at it. This can be a stopwatch or a laptop with a counter running, for example. Another useful thing is to create a countdown movie to put on your iPod or iPhone.

1 Create a New Sequence.

2 Edit Slug into the sequence with a one-minute duration.

3 Select the Slug and add the Timecode Generator effect (Effects > Video Filters > Video > Timecode Generator).

4 Double-click the slug to load it into the Viewer for modification.

5 Adjust the filter so the text is larger and fills most of the screen.

6 Choose File > Export > Using QuickTime Conversion...

7 Choose iPod or iPhone from the format menu.

8 Add the movie to your iTunes library and sync.

9 When on set, just start the movie and point the cameras at the screen. You'll have an easy visual indicator to sync with.

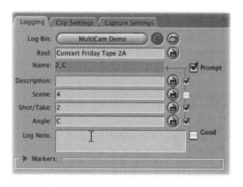

Log and Digitize

Once your footage is shot, it's time to load it into Final Cut Pro.

- Capture each tape into individual clips. You should make a new clip for each time the cameras were 'cut.'

- Be sure to assign an angle number for each clip that you capture. It is a good idea to use angle numbers that match your camera diagram. The Angle property determines how a clip is sorted within the multiclip.

- Be sure to log carefully around timecode breaks.

Note: While tapeless formats don't need to be digitized, you'll still want to organize your media with angle numbers and descriptive metadata.

Good Color in the Field

One way to address color calibration between your angles is to use a calibration card when shooting. This is relatively easy if you just remember to put a fresh color balance card on your clapboard for each shoot.

One of our favorites is the QP Card, an affordable reference card (http://www.qpcard.se). Priced at less than $5 per card, this is a great investment in accurate color.

- They are small and lightweight, easily fitting in your gear bag.

- Relatively inexpensive and disposable, so you can use a fresh card periodically. Old cards tend to fade in the light.

- It's adhesive on the back so you can easily attach it to your clapboard.

- With a white, black, and neutral grey surface, color correcting with Final Cut Pro's three-way color corrector is a snap.

- $5 spent per shoot is well worth hours saved on color correction. In most circumstances, just three clicks per angle will calibrate across each camera.

Just What Are Angles?

The multiclip requires angle numbers for each clip or name. If you forget to add the information while logging, Final Cut will try to deduct the angle number from the clip name or other information.

- **Angle Property of the Clip:** This is usually entered when logging and can be a number or a letter. Final Cut Pro interprets letters (such as A–F) as angle numbers 1–6, respectively.

- **Clip Name Using Cinema Tools Clip-naming Conventions:** If you plan on working with film material, then use the Cinema Tools standards; for example, F-4-B1 where F is the scene, 4 is the take and B1 is the camera.

- **Reel Name:** It is common practice to use the reel name to indicate the camera used to acquire the footage.

- **Media Filename:** If no other information is present, then Final Cut Pro examines the names of the files when it tries to sort angles.

Aud Rate	48.0 KHz
Aud Format	16-bit Integer
Angle	C

I Forgot—Assigning Angle Numbers After Capture

We admit it. Sometimes we forget to assign angle numbers while logging. That's okay; Final Cut Pro didn't get to where it is by being inflexible.

❶ Select a clip in the Browser that you need to modify.

❷ Right-click on the clip and choose Item Properties > Item Properties.

❸ Scroll down until you see the Angle field.

❹ Enter a number or letter in the Angle field.

❺ Click OK.

Synchronize with Timecode

If your clips have matching timecodes, then multiclip creation is extremely easy.

❶ Select the angles you'd like to use in the Browser.

❷ Choose Modify > Make Multiclip.

❸ The Make Multiclip dialog opens and shows the angle order and a graphic representation of the media.

❹ Choose Synchronize using Timecode.

❺ If you decide not to include a clip, deselect its checkbox.

❻ When ready, click OK.

❼ A new multiclip is created.

Synchronize with Clip Details

If you lack syncing timecode or any easy visible cue like a clapboard, then you'll need to attempt to align your clips up in the Timeline.

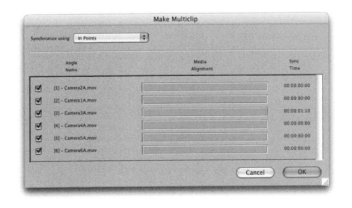

1. Edit all of the angles into your Timeline.

2. Expand the audio track height and make sure that Show Audio Waveforms option is enabled.

3. Nudge the tracks left or right until they sync up. Look for spikes in the waveforms such as the clapboard to ease synchronization. You can also listen to two tracks at a time and nudge the tracks until you minimize any echo.

4. Once the clips are aligned, you'll need to perform some match framing to identify In points.

5. Select the first clip and press F to match frame back to the source clip.

6. In the Viewer, press I to mark an In point.

7. Without moving the playhead, select the next clip in the Timeline. Press F to match frame again to load the clip into the Viewer. Press I to mark an In point.

8. Repeat for all of the remaining clips in the synced Timeline.

9. Select all of the angles you'd like to use in the Browser.

10. Choose Modify > Make Multiclip. The Make Multiclip dialog opens and shows the angle order and a graphic representation of the media.

11. Choose Synchronize using In point.

12. When ready, click OK.

13. A new multiclip is created.

Are Your Drives Fast Enough?

Do you plan on editing multiclips? Then you're going to need some fast hard drives. If your multiclip has five angles, then your drive must be able to play back five streams of video in real-time. This is perhaps the greatest challenge when it comes to multiclip editing. Here are a few approaches to maximizing your system's performance.

- Use the fastest scratch disk available on your system.

- Never use the system boot drive.

- If you own a Mac Pro, consider putting two serial ATA drives in and using Disk Utility to stripe them together for performance.

- You can reduce real-time playback quality in the Canvas. In the Timeline you can lower the Playback Video Quality and Playback Frame Rate.

- Be sure to use RT Extreme and change the sequence to Unlimited RT.

Offline RT Returns

If your system just can't keep up (it's okay, it happens to all of us) you can still get by. Experienced users may remember using the Offline RT format to conserve disk space. While space may no longer be a concern, smaller file size means better performance.

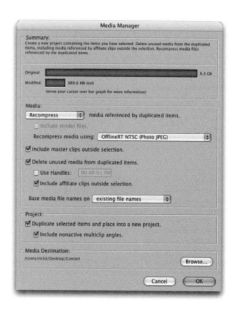

❶ Create the multiclip and sequence as you normally would.

❷ Select the multiclip and sequence in the Browser, then right-click and choose Media Manager.

❸ In the Media area choose Recompress and specify one of the Offline RT codecs that most closely matches your footage. (Offline RT can reduce file size by 700%).

❹ Choose to duplicate items and place them into a new project. You'll also want to include nonactive multiclip angles.

❺ In the Media Destination area specify a location for the files.

❻ Click OK to transcode the media to a new destination.

Note: Depending on the number of angles and format of your video, this may be the only way to edit your multicamera material. Current drive technology, while fast, can't really keep up with 16 streams of HD video.

From Offline to Online

When you finish editing your Offline RT material, you can convert it back to online resolution.

❶ Click on the completed sequence in the Browser.

❷ Right-click and choose Media Manager.

❸ In the Media area choose Create offline and specify the codec you'd like to use for the final sequence.

❹ Click OK to create a new sequence. Specify a destination and name, and save the file.

❺ You can now reconnect or redigitize.

- If the media already exists on your hard drives at the high resolution, right-click and choose Reconnect Media.

- If the material needs to be captured, right-click and choose Batch Capture.

- Unless you need a lot more media, uncheck the box next to Include master clips outside selection and uncheck Include affiliate clips outside selection.

❻ Once the media is reattached at the final resolution, you can simplify your sequence for output.

❼ Duplicate the sequence and open it.

❽ Right-click on the multiclip in the Timeline and choose Collapse Multiclip(s).

❾ The modified sequence requires less overhead on the drives as it does not need to play all clips in real-time.

❿ Output your show as needed.

Creating a Multiclip Sequence

If your footage from the multicamera shoot contains synchronized timecode, you can use the Make Multiclip Sequence command. You can use the command to create a sequence from your clips. The Make Multiclip Sequence command can deal with gaps in clips (such as for tape changes) by using the timecode synchronization offset.

❶ Select multiple clips in the Browser, or select a bin of clips.

❷ Choose Modify > Make Multiclip Sequence. The Make Multiclip Sequence dialog appears.

❸ Final Cut Pro groups clips together with identical starting timecode numbers. Additional clips with unique starting timecode numbers are grouped into separate multiclips.

❹ Choose a method from the Timecode Synchronization popup menu:

- Use Starting Timecode.

- Use Overlapping Timecode.

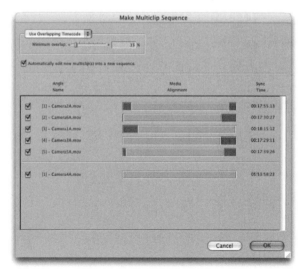

❺ Depending on which timecode method you choose, do one of the following:

- Enter a value in the Starting timecode delta field, and then click Update to resynchronize the multiclips.

- Adjust the percentage in the Minimum overlap field.

❻ The clips are arranged into new multiclip groupings. You can repeat the above steps until you are satisfied with the groupings.

❼ Choose the Automatically edit new multiclip(s) into a new sequence option, which will create a sequence that contains the new multiclips.

Customizing the Keyboard

Before you start to edit your multiclip sequence, consider rearranging a few things to make it easier.

1 Choose Tools > Keyboard Layout > Customize.

> Note: While a Multicamera keyboard layout exists, you will likely want to customize your default layout.

2 Click the Unlock button to modify the keyboard layout.

3 In the Search field, type Angle to narrow the buttons.

4 For the numeric keypad, remap Cut Video to Angle 1 to the 1 key.

5 Repeat for angles 2–9.

6 When done, close the keyboard layout menu to save the changes.

> Note: if you're using a laptop on the road, consider picking up a USB numeric keypad. You can find these at just about any office supply store or computer store for around $25. This will give you more keys for greater control.

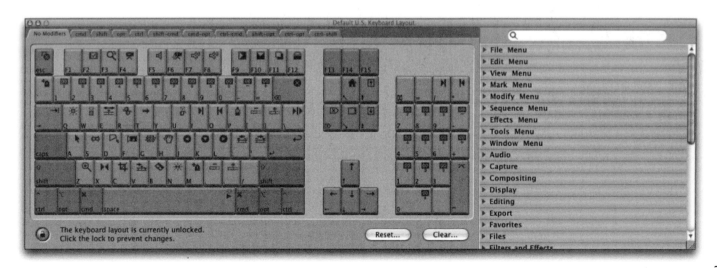

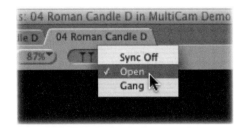

Set to Open

Once you've added a multiclip to your Timeline, be sure to make one small, but important, change. Click the Playhead Sync button in the Canvas and switch it to Open. This way the multiclip will load into the Viewer and stay synchronized with the playhead.

Using the Viewer

When editing a multiclip, you will spend much more time in the Viewer than the Timeline. You can use the Viewer to display, rearrange, resynchronize, and cut between all the angles in a multiclip.

www.brindleybrothers.com

- **Display:** The Viewer can show 1, 4, 9, or 16 angles at a time. One angle is pretty worthless and 16 angles can get quite small on most monitors. To change the number of angles displayed, click the View popup menu.

- **Identify Angles:** The Viewer uses colored outlines to identify active angles (blue for video, green for audio).

- **Rearrange Angles:** Command-click the angle you want to move. Drag it over another angle to reorder the Viewer window. Release the mouse button and the angles are rearranged.

- **Delete an Angle:** Command-click the angle you want to remove. Drag it outside the Viewer, release the mouse button and the angles are deleted.

- **Cutting:** You can cut angles while the sequence plays. Just click the angle in the viewer you'd like to use. Keep in mind that a customized keyboard is a more tactile way to "punch" a show and change angles dynamically.

When You Should Collapse

At the end of a hard edit day, sometimes you just want to melt into the couch and collapse. Final Cut Pro feels the same way after a multiclip edit. Playing back all those uncompressed streams of video is hard. Give your system a break before final output.

1 Duplicate the Multiclip sequence so you have a spare to reference.

2 Open the duplicate and select all of the media in the Timeline.

3 Right-click and choose Collapse Multiclip(s).

4 The sequence is simplified and the original source material is cut into the Timeline.

If you need to make changes, you can always trim the shots in the Timeline. If you need to make dramatic changes, return to the multiclip sequence.

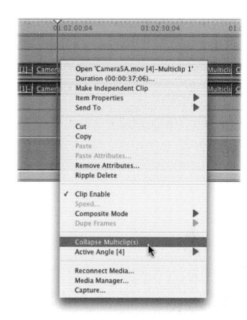

Change Angles After Switching

If you attempt to cut to an alternate angle on an existing switch point, Cut to Angle doesn't give the right result; use Switch Angle instead.

- If you have a multiclip edit in a sequence that has been switched on the fly, during playback, and the playhead is now parked on a frame between edits, using Cut to Video Angle 1 (or whatever angle) will switch the following clip, not the current clip under the playhead.

- Instead of using Cut to Video Angle 1 use Switch Angle 1 instead and you'll get the results you expect.

ON THE SPOT

Crisis Management
Troubleshooting and Recovery Techniques

It's always darkest just before it goes completely black. That's how it feels as your deadline approaches and your system starts to act up. Clients are waiting, the FedEx guy has his feet up on your desk drinking his second cup of coffee, and if you're really quiet you can actually hear the gremlins laughing.

Most of the time, it only takes a few tricks to crush the gremlins and get your project out the door. This chapter will help you troubleshoot what's going wrong and provide tips for fixing it. (The odds are that it's between 3 and 5 a.m. when you're reading this, and there's no one to call who won't hang up on you.)

Take a deep breath, and slowly read this chapter's tips. Sometimes the light at the end of the tunnel isn't another oncoming train; sometimes it's really your show getting put to tape.

When in Doubt, Shut Down and Restart

Things can and do go wrong. A simple reset to your system is often the best way to "cure" software problems. Don't just click Restart, however; let the system fully reset itself by shutting down. As a favorite engineer used to tell me, "Shut down, count to 20, restart—if there's still a problem, then call me."

Test It

If you think you have a problem, you need to isolate it and test it thoroughly. By taking the time to gather the right information, you'll make it easier for others to help you.

- What are the symptoms of the problem?
- When does the problem appear?
- Is the problem specific to one machine, or does it repeat on several machines?
- When did the problem start happening?
- Have you installed any software lately?
- Is it a video-only problem? Audio-only?
- Can you replicate the problem consistently?

Unexpected Quits

Okay, this may seem obvious to some of you. Make sure you have the latest "blessed" versions of Final Cut Pro, Apple QuickTime, the operating system, and any third-party drivers required for your system (AJA, Pinnacle, and so on). By "blessed" we mean the versions and combinations that Apple lists on its website. Go to www.finalcutpro.com, and click Support. We had a client complain about Final Cut Pro's stability on a beta of the operating system and of QuickTime. Yes, they were public betas, but that doesn't mean you have to install them.

True Uber-Geekdom: FSCK

If you're having system problems and want to clean the disk, check partitions, and so on, here's a way to fix problems without any third-party applications: Start up in single-user mode, and run FSCK. Uh, what was that?

FSCK stands for "file system check," and the –fy you'll type just says to go ahead and fix any problems it finds. Here's the drill:

① Restart your Mac.

② Immediately press and hold Command + Option + S. You'll see a bunch of text begin scrolling on your screen. (Cool, you're now a geek.) Soon you'll see the Unix command line prompt (#). Don't cry; it's still your Mac—you're just a true Unix god—well, demi-god.

③ Type **fsck -fy** (that's fsck + space + minus + f + y).

④ Press Return.

The FSCK utility will do its magic, running some text across your screen. If there's damage to your disk, you'll see a message that says: "FILE SYSTEM WAS MODIFIED."

If you see this message, it found some problems and fixed them—repeat steps 1 and 2 until that message no longer appears. It's normal to have to run FSCK more than once; the first run's repairs often uncover additional problems.

When FSCK finally reports that no problems were found and the # prompt reappears, type **reboot** to restart or type **exit** to start without rebooting. Then press Return.

Rebuilding Permissions

This sounds like something from etiquette class, but this little activity can save hours of headache throughout your system. In the Utilities folder in the Applications folder, there's an application called Disk Utility. Under the First Aid tab there's a button to repair permissions (Repair Disk Permissions). Select your drives and let it rip. You should run it a couple of times. It's amazing how so many of those little quirky problems will go away.

"I Can't Even Open My Project File" (Or Other Flaky Activities)

Corruption can happen a lot of places, even in Final Cut Pro:

❶ Look in the Autosave Vault. Before panicking, simply try going back a few versions. Do a search for Autosave in the Finder. Look in the folders for a backup of your project file. Work your way backward through the recently saved copies.

❷ Create a new user account. Create a new user account for testing purposes. This is a great way to see if the problem is a corrupt preferences file. Most Final Cut Pro preferences files are stored in the user's settings. Open the System Preferences panel under the blue Apple. Click Accounts. Click on New User. Create one call test, and give it admin privileges. You can assign it a password or not. Only use this account for troubleshooting (you may want to keep it for the future).

Now, log out, and log in as the new user. Try opening Final Cut Pro. It should open with no active project files. If it opens, you've narrowed the problem down to bad user preferences (see next tip) or a bad project file.

❸ Test the project file. Next, open the project file that was causing the problems. (If it was stored in the other user folder, you won't have access to it. Log in as the original user, make a copy of the file, and move it to a shared location such as the media folder or the top level of your hard drive—not the desktop—that's owned by the user.)

If it opens, you've confirmed it was the preferences. If it crashes, it could be bad media or renders, or something has become corrupt in the application or the OS.

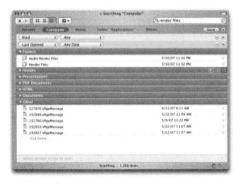

❹ Delete the render files. Delete all the render files. Don't worry—you can rerender a lot faster than you can rebuild the project. To find render files, look on your media drives for the Render Files and Audio Render Files folders. Terminate them with extreme prejudice. Yes, it's Apocalypse Now for your render files.

Try reopening the project. Success? If not, try hiding the media files from the project. Disconnect the media drive, or drop the media into another folder. If the project opens with the media offline, you've got a bad media file. (An alternative is to open the project file on another machine—same rules apply.)

⑤ Recapture the media. If you determine you have a bad file, you can either load/relink media back into the project in small groups or batch recapture the media from the original tapes. If you're still getting tanked, send the project to a friend to see if it'll open on their machine. This is the best way to determine if you're having a hardware, application, or operating system issue.

⑥ Still broken? At this point, you may need to call your reseller or a consultant.

Disable Extensions

In the "old days," you'd turn off your extensions when booting, but OS X doesn't have extensions, right? Well, actually it does, and you can boot into Safe Boot/Safe Mode to see if the problem is caused by a non-Apple extension:

① Shut down your Mac all the way. (Choose Shutdown from the Apple menu, not Restart.)

② Press the power button, and wait for the chime.

③ Immediately after the chime, press and hold the Shift key. When the gray apple and spinning gears show up, let go.

Zap the PRAM

PRAM is the Parameter RAM, which is an area of RAM that's used to store information about your computer. It stores things such as startup device, date, time, time zone, mouse speed, and the like.

If the information in the PRAM becomes corrupted, odd and spooky things can occur; you can clear the information and reset it to factory settings.

To reset PRAM, follow these steps:

① Restart your computer while pressing Command + Option + P + R.

② As the computer begins to restart, you'll hear the startup chime repeat. Continue pressing the keys until the chime has sounded three or more times.

③ Release the keys, and the startup should complete.

Get More Help

Yes, we know you can find it in the Help menu, but these are killer startup shortcuts for OS X that we never can remember—so here they are, straight from the Help menu.

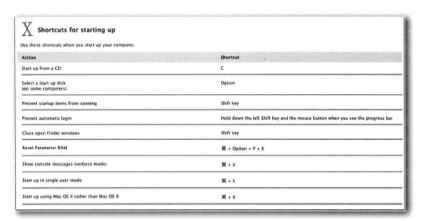

X Shortcuts for starting up

Use these shortcuts when you start up your computer.

Action	Shortcut
Start up from a CD	C
Select a start up disk (on some computers)	Option
Prevent startup items from opening	Shift key
Prevent automatic login	Hold down the left Shift key and the mouse button when you see the progress bar
Close open Finder windows	Shift key
Reset Parameter RAM	⌘ + Option + P + R
Show console messages (verbose mode)	⌘ + V
Start up in single user mode	⌘ + S
Start up using Mac OS X rather than Mac OS 9	⌘ + X

Start up from a CD: Hold down the C key on startup.

Eject CD on startup (which is great if you're stuck in an endless boot to the CD system folder: Hold down the mouse button on startup.

Select a startup disk (on some computers): Hold down the Option key. You'll see all disks that have bootable system drives. This includes Windows if you're using Boot Camp.

Prevent startup items from opening (great for troubleshooting): Press the Shift key.

Prevent automatic login (if you want to start up from a different user, even though you have auto login turned on): Hold down the left Shift key and the mouse button when you see the progress bar.

Close open Finder windows: Press the Shift key.

Reset Parameter RAM: Press Command + Option + P + R.

Show console messages (verbose mode): This makes you look really knowledgeable and freaks out other Mac users—press Command + V.

And, of course, if you have a frozen Mac (we're talking spinning beach ball of death, ice-age frozen): Hold down the power button for several seconds and several seconds more until it reboots.

Dashboard Killer

We'd be lying if we told you we didn't like the Dashboard and the multitude of widgets that it uses. The problem is if your Dashboard looks anything like ours (read way too many widgets to count) quite a bit of system memory is used to run those widgets.

Well, many people's first thought is to close the application to reclaim that memory. Guess what? You can't quit the Dashboard! Well, not in the conventional sense anyway. Here are two ways to kill the Dashboard application, one easy and one geeky.

- There are a couple applications on the market that let you kill the Dashboard application. A simple one is called Disable Dashboard Utility (do a search on versiontracker.com). It's really two small applications; one to deactivate and one to enable the Dashboard.

- If you're an uber Unix geek you can also kill the Dashboard by opening up the terminal and typing the following commands:

To turn Dashboard off type:

Defaults write com.apple.Dashboard mcx-disabled -boolean YES

To turn Dashboard back on type:

Defaults write com.apple.Dashboard mcx-disabled -boolean NO

- For either of these commands to take effect you have to restart the Dock by typing: killall Dock

Note: When using these methods it will still look like the application is active, but closer inspection in the activity monitor will show Dashboard and its widgets are not active.

Get Rid of Your Cache

No, not your money! Final Cut Pro saves waveforms and thumbnails it displays in the interface as small little files in what are called caches. Most of the time these files are benign and since they're really small they seldom need to be deleted. However, sometimes when things start to go wonky, like waveforms not displaying and clips displaying the wrong thumbnail, it's a good idea to delete these files.

1 Inside Final Cut Pro, open up System Settings (Shift + Q).

2 In the middle of the first tab, you will find your current waveform and thumbnail cache locations. (Notice you can locate these anywhere you'd like.)

3 Note the location, hide FCP (Command + H) and navigate to that location in the Finder and delete all the files in those folders. Make sure you empty your trash.

Waveform Cache: (Set...) 161.7 GB on Macintosh HD:Users:amigo:Documents:Final Cut Pro Documents

Thumbnail Cache: (Set...) 161.7 GB on Macintosh HD:Users:amigo:Documents:Final Cut Pro Documents

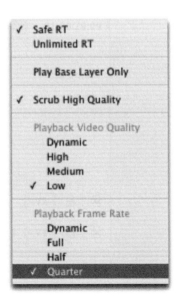

Ugly Playback

This is one of our favorite gotchas. Recently, a client called us and was extremely frustrated; he was rather worried that somehow his tricked out Final Cut Pro system was possessed and had ruined all of his media. After calming him down a bit, he described the symptoms as really staggered and jumpy playback and it looked like the footage was really low rez even though it was high def.

After a few more questions the fix was clear. In the RT pull-down on the Timeline, settings for Playback Video Quality and Playback Frame Rate were set to low and quarter respectively. No wonder he was getting ugly playback!

If you have similar symptoms, the RT menu is often one of the first places to check. While there are many combinations here, we find that setting both Playback Video Quality and Playback Frame Rate to Dynamic will offer the best balance of real-time playback and quality.

Lost Window, Part 1: No Canvas

As obvious as this one is, we get calls almost weekly from folks telling us that the application is broken because all they see are their Browser and their Viewer windows. The others are gone. This is a simple fix that we'll keep between us: You have no sequences open. Open any sequence from your Browser, and—Boom!—there are your Canvas and Timeline windows.

Lost Window, Part 2: Minimize

OS X has a great feature called Minimize. It hides any open window in the Dock. Unfortunately, a lot of folks hit this one by accident and "lose" one of their key editing windows. So look in your Dock, and see if any of those lost windows are just hanging out waiting to be found.

The hack WindowShade X lets you convert this button to allow you to roll up your window or minimize in place. Better yet, the haxie allows you to disable the Minimize feature entirely just within Final Cut Pro. This is a great solution until Apple restores this feature in a future OS.

Lost Window, Part 3: Hidden Windows

Being fans of keyboard shortcuts, we love to use Command + 1–6 to toggle which window is active. However, if a window is already active and you use its keyboard shortcut, it actually hides the window. (You can also create this problem by cycling and unchecking these windows in the Window pull-down.)

The solution again is easy: Either reuse the shortcut, revealing the window, or go to the Window menu pull-down, and check the appropriate "hidden" window.

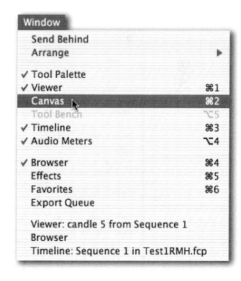

253

Contain Yourself

If you're having problems putting your project to tape because of dropped frames or crashes, try creating a self-contained movie file, drop it into a new sequence, and use sequences to print/edit to video. Yes, this will eat up a lot of disk space, but it may be the only way to get that opus out to your client.

Stuttering Video

If your video playback is jerky in your Canvas or Viewer, you may need to adjust your View settings. Click the Zoom popup menu and select Fit to Window, or press Shift + Z. You should set both the Viewer and Canvas to this setting, especially if you frequently change window layouts. This way the video size will scale to match the window and give you the smoothest playback.

My Render Files Are Gone

If they're really gone, don't worry—you can always rerender. However, usually lost render files are a case of, "I've targeted my render file location under System Settings > Scratch Disk tab to a drive that's no longer attached to my machine." If this is the case, plug it in and link the lost render files back to the project.

Another option is that the folder containing the reference files could have been moved. To find all the reference files on your hard drives, do a search in the Finder for the render files and folder...you'll be amazed at what you'll find.

By the way, this is a great way to clean house and get back some lost hard drive space.

What's That Exclamation Point?

A lot of new users call us up asking about that exclamation point or nice green check mark on their image. We tell them that Final Cut Pro has an Artificial Intelligence engine, and it's approving of the shot or edit. Or, if there is an exclamation point, then there's content that's inappropriate for people younger than 18. They thank us and hang up the phone.

After about five minutes, they call us back and ask if we were pulling their legs. Well, Final Cut Pro does have a secret AI engine. If we told you more, we'd be put on double-secret probation, but the exclamation point and checkbox actually mean something else.

They're used to determine if your video is broadcast safe/legal. An exclamation point means you're not broadcast safe, and a green checkbox or one with an up arrow means you're okay. Now how did this get turned on? Well, the keyboard shortcut for this is Control + Z, so people often accidentally hit it when trying to do an Undo (Command + Z) or a Fit to Window (Shift + Z).

Where's My Image?

This one happens all the time. "My video is gone, my video is gone!" There's a good chance you've slipped into one of the wireframe modes used for fast previews of motion graphics. Simply highlight the Viewer or Canvas that's affected, and press the W key until the picture returns.

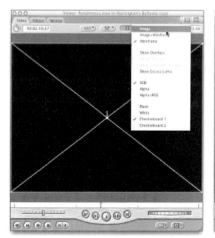

Photo Credit Blue Ridge Balloon Company

Can't Add a Dissolve

When creating a transition between clips, you're essentially overlapping the two clips. If you've set your In and Out points too close to the end of the clip, you won't have enough space for the transitions to occur. You can use the Slip tool to adjust the shot so there's more overlap. For future edits and logging, it's a good rule of thumb to allow at least one-second "handles" beyond your marks.

Number Lock

MacBook Pro and PowerBook users beware: This one gets even us some of the time. If you look on the right side of your keyboard, you'll notice that there are small numbers on some of the keys. This is essentially a numeric keypad. How do you access it? Simple—you just push the Num Lock key if you want a numeric keypad (just like the ones on a full-size keyboard). This sounds convenient until you accidentally push the Num Lock key, which is right next to your Volume Up key. Let's just say panic ensues when you can't log in to your trusty laptop and only a third of the keys seem to work. Be sure to check the Num Lock key, and see if it's lit up. Chances are you want this "feature" off.

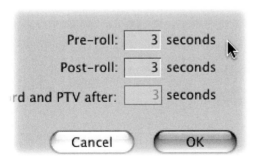

Win the Battle of the Pre-Roll

If you're trying to batch capture and your system keeps aborting because of "not enough pre-roll," you can go into the Audio/Video Preferences settings and go to the Device Control Presets to create a new preset and reduce the amount of pre-roll needed to capture. Remember, some decks have minimum pre-roll requirements. In this case, use the Capture Now setting, and you be the pre-roll button. If you're still hitting a "can't capture" wall, dub the tape onto another tape with existing control track at the head of the shot.

Where Has My Audio Gone?

See your picture, but can't hear it? You may need to check several things:

1 Is the computer volume turned up? (We had to ask.)

2 Are the speakers powered on and connected? (We had to ask that, too.)

3 Check View > External Video, and be sure it is set to off. By the way, you can create a button and a keyboard shortcut that will turn external video off.

4 Check your Audio/Video Settings, and set Audio Playback to the Built-in audio controller or the hardware card that you use for monitoring.

What's That Beeping Sound?

When you play your Timeline, do you hear a loud series of beeps? This is your clue that you have run out of RAM to preview your unrendered audio tracks (or your microwave dinner is ready).

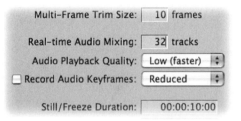

Remember, you may think you're only using six or eight audio tracks, but if you mix sample rates, add filters, or even have cross dissolves between tracks, Final Cut Pro may see those six to eight tracks as 20–24 tracks. The result is you're more likely to "break" real-time previews. Follow these steps:

1 You can increase the number of tracks set in your User Preferences. Simply put a higher number in the Real-time Audio Mixing box. Eight was the default for way back in Final Cut Pro 1.0 (which ran on a G3), so chances are you can up that to 16, 32, or even 64 (and that "new" G7 25GHz machine will surely play all 99 tracks).

2 Render the section. Audio renders are usually quick and free up memory for your cool eight-track quad-split with color-correction cross-wipe transitions.

Your System or Your SAN?

With SAN solutions like Apple's Xsan becoming more and more common in post-production environments, one of the hardest things about troubleshooting a problem is trying to figure out if the problem is local to your machine or if it's being caused by a problem on your media (fiber channel) or metadata (Ethernet) network. Here are a couple of easy methods to start narrowing in on the problem.

The problem may lie with your local system if:

- Project files open on other machines with the same OS, QuickTime and pro apps software.

- You have lots of unexpected quits or cannot open pro apps software.

- You have display issues like waveforms not redrawing and thumbnails displaying on the wrong clips.

- Your machine does other weird things like not mounting drives and peripherals, displays weird things on screen, etc. These things may point to a hardware failure.

The problem may lie with your SAN if:

- Media plays back fine on local systems, not just on the SAN.

- Consistent drop frames occur even though SAN throughput is sufficient.

- Media and project files do not open on multiple machines, indicating corruption.

- Users are not able to access files or otherwise don't have permission to open files.

90 Percent of Problems Are Cable Problems

Most people assume the worst when their edit system starts acting up. If you're getting a signal or device control problem, it might not be your machine (or even your software). A $10 cable can tear down an entire edit session. Follow these steps:

❶ Shut down the computer to avoid any improper dismounting of media drives.

❷ Isolate the suspected problem device.

❸ Be sure to reseat both ends of the cable.

❹ If that doesn't work, try swapping out the cable.

❺ Continue to add devices until the problem recurs. Then repeat this cycle. You might be surprised how many times this works.

Remember, there's more than just FireWire cables; there are USB cables, RS-422 cables, monitor cables and extensions, and fiber-optic cables. Even your audio and video cables (RCA, BNC, XLR) could be culprits. "What, no video? Oops, my RCA came unplugged."

Dropped FireWire Frames—Not Really

Say you're dropping frames right off the bat...every time you try to capture. This is not a problem. Depending on your FireWire drive, bridgeboard, and computer, you may always drop the first frame of video on every capture. Don't worry; everything catches up 1/30 of a second later. Just capture an extra one-second handle, and turn off the Abort on capture on dropped frames option in the User Preferences window. And go, go, go.

Just to make sure that the only place you're dropping frames is the first frame, highlight the captured clip(s) in your Browser, and select Tools > Long Frames > Mark. You should see a little yellow marker at the beginning of the shot—and only there.

If you have long frame markers in other places, see many of the tips in this chapter.

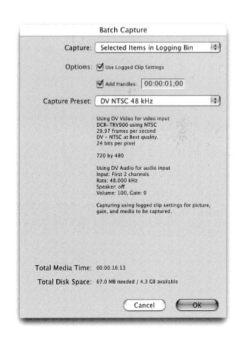

Back In Time—Converting to Older Versions

Officially there is no way to go back to earlier versions of Final Cut Pro from a later version. However, it is possible, within some limits, to go back to previous versions of Final Cut Pro (4.1 or later) using XML export and import. The common ground between Final Cut Pro 6, 5, HD and 4.1 is Final Cut Pro XML version 1. Final Cut Pro 6 also supports up to version 4 of XML export but that will not open in any earlier version of Final Cut Pro. Final Cut Pro XML will support effects and titles.

To export:

❶ Select what you want to take back to the earlier version—to send the whole Project back, make sure no bin, clip or sequence is selected.

❷ Choose File > Export > XML...

❸ In the Export XML dialog select Apple XML Interchange Format, version 1 from the Format popup menu:

- This selection is very important—version 2 XML will not open in any version of Final Cut Pro before version 5.

- If going from version 6 to 5 or 5.1, you can choose to use the more robust version 2 XML.

❹ Click OK to export.

❺ You will be asked for the name of the exported XML file. The default will be the Project name.

❻ The export time will depend on the size and complexity of the project.

To import:

❶ Set the sequence setting to match the project timebase.

❷ Choose File > Import > XML. Navigate to the XML file and select it.

❸ Choose the appropriate options from the Import dialog.

❹ Complete the import.

Note: This method will not work if there are certain version specific effects or options enabled. Those features, when imported into previous versions of Final Cut Pro, will be reported as noncritical errors (and subsequently ignored). In general, this technique works very well if you need to travel back in time or exchange files with older systems.

Phil Hodgetts – http://www.digitalproductionbuzz.com/BuZZdex/

Flaky Machine? Clean it Out!

If your machine just keeps acting up, consider running some repairs. From rotating logs to repairing permissions, Unix has got some definite needs for cleaning.

Here are two great applications for keeping your Mac happy:

- **MacJanitor**: All UNIX systems use a set of maintenance scripts that run every day, week, and month. If you leave your computer running 24/7/365 then these scripts will take care of things for you. You do leave your computer on all the time, right? Probably not. That's why MacJanitor is so useful. You can run the OS X scripts manually to make sure that maintenance tasks get done.

  http://personalpages.tds.net/~brian_hill/macjanitor.html

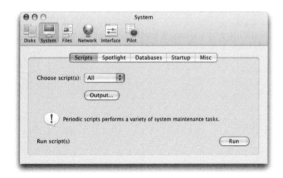

- **Cocktail:** A useful Swiss Army knife-style utility. This program tackles most general-purpose needs including maintenance tools and interface tweaks, all accessible via a "comprehensive graphical interface." Cocktail tackles disks, system, files, network, and other issues. Cocktail is one of the first places we turn to if our machines just aren't running right.

  http://www.maintain.se/cocktail

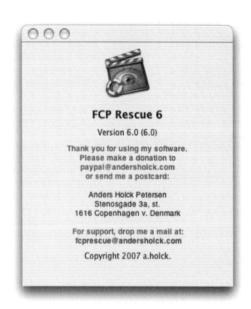

Final Cut Pro Preferences Are Essential

A lot of Final Cut Pro's behaviors are determined by your preference files. Once you get your system just right, you'll want to save your preferences. If your system is acting up, you might need to trash them. Fortunately two utilities exist to make this process easier:

- **FCP Rescue:** Fortunately FCP Rescue makes it easy to backup, trash, or restore preferences. The utility is a breeze to use and makes it simple to save, restore, or trash all of your settings. Best of all, it's totally free!

  http://fcprescue.andersholck.com/

- **FCP Attic:** FCP Attic also allows for the backup, restoration, or trashing of preferences. Unlike FCP Rescue, it allows you to specify a location for the backup. Plus, you can move preferences easily between multiple machines. This extra power comes at a slight cost, however, currently at $15.

  http://chesa.com/store/

Keep Your System Up to Date with Version Tracker Pro

While Software Update is a great way to keep your Apple software up to date, what about all the other programs on your hard drive? That's where Version Tracker Pro comes in. You can quickly scan your computer and check for updates for all installed software. This program saves a ton of time by automating the checking of multiple websites. We find it a great way to keep our machines happy. After all, staying current often means the difference between crashing and stability.

http://www.versiontrackerpro.com

Don't Cross the FireWire Streams

Do you have both FireWire hard drives and a FireWire Deck or IO device hooked up to your system? If so, don't plug them into the same bus or you're asking for trouble. You see, all the FireWire ports on your Mac are tied to the same card. And to be honest, it doesn't work very well to try to send video in opposite directions.

For best results, spend the money on a separate FireWire card. These are available for both towers and laptops for around $60 and is money well spent. We highly recommend hooking up your deck to the system port since it won't get unplugged often. Put your drives into the new card, so all the frequent plugging and unplugging will just wear out the $60 card and not the $3,000 computer.

Shared Project Files

Maybe you're lucky and you have a huge 42TB Xsan set up for central storage in your facility—besides being technically really cool, we're super jealous! Xsan and other Storage Area Networks (SANs) are a perfect way to share media files and project files.

One area that can quickly get people into trouble is opening a single project file at the same time on different machines. Perhaps no other Final Cut Pro-related Xsan issue causes more corruptions, headaches and lost work.

The fix is simple. DO NOT open the same project file on multiple machines at the same time. Of course there are times you will want to open the project file at the same time, so here are a couple of ways to get around the issue.

- Duplicate the project file and label it with a suffix like for _bob_72207 where Bob is the person getting the file and the numbers are the date.

- If you don't like duplicating project files (to prevent clutter) make sure that you ask others on the SAN before opening. An easy way to do this is by using iChat and enabling Bonjour messaging. That way everyone can talk without having to leave their edit suite/office and it doesn't require they have an AIM or .Mac account.

Shared Project.fcp

ON THE SPOT

CHAPTER 14

The Finish Line
Learning Advanced Finishing Techniques

Spit and polish! That's the difference between an average show and one that shines to your client. You've slaved over the creation of your opus and are ready to take it to the world. Often it's the last 5 percent of effort that elevates your show and your editing skills from the rest of the pack.

It's all in the details. Are your video levels legal, is your audio balanced, do your renders need rendering? We took you up to the finish line; in this chapter, we'll show you how to cross it with style.

In this race, it's best to take a break before your sprint into the home stretch. A rested editor with some time and distance will see mistakes that an exhausted editor will miss after the 22nd hour of editing. So take a time-out. Go get yet another cup of coffee, watch a cartoon, take five, listen to "Take Five" (every good editor should know classic jazz), and come back to your show with fresh eyes.

Photo Credit Time Image

In) ⟳ Mon 4:36 AM

Macintosh HD

balloonride

BallonRideMovie   balloon landin
BallonRideMovie   balloon landings
BallonRideMovie   balloon landings

Previewing Edit

Photo Credit Blue Ridge Balloon Company

Little Things

When finishing a show, it's the little things that make all the difference. The difference between good and great can be as small as 5 percent. If at all possible, never finish a show at the end of your Shift. After several weeks (or even months) of work put into the average project, it's worth tackling it fresh in the morning.

Check for Flash Frames

Before we print to tape, we step through our finished shows one edit at a time, just to make sure we don't have any black flash frames. Use the up and down arrow keys to take you from edit point to edit point. If your Canvas shows a black frame (or unintentional frame), you have a flash frame. Switch to trimming, and you can take the offending frames out.

Bad Dissolves

It's very easy to get flash frames in transitions. They can be caused by a shot change at the end of your clip. This happens a lot when editing together previously cut material. It's not your fault really; you can't always know that a transition will use parts of the clip you couldn't see when you started the edit.

❶ The easiest way to check is to enter Trim Edit mode. Double-click an edit to enter trim mode. You need to be right on the cut or just let your fingers do the work by pressing Option + 7.

❷ Press the space bar to review the edit. Watch it closely, looking for a scene change midtransition. Often a one- or two-frame roll edit will solve the problem and not change the feel of the show.

❸ Press the down arrow to move to the next edit or the up arrow to move to the previous edit.

Learn to Cut with L-Cuts

Experienced editors know that changing picture and sound at the same point (a straight cut) can be very disruptive. It's more noticeable when both elements change suddenly, which can be jarring to the Viewer. A much better method is to try and use an L-cut (so called because of its shape in the Timeline). In this case, the picture edit happens before or after the edit.

These are especially helpful when editing dialogue because they give the editor better control over pacing and reaction shots. You can also use an L-cut to hide a continuity error. Although the difference may sound small, you'll soon discover what an impact they have on a professional edit. Follow these steps:

Photo Credit Blue Ridge Balloon Company

① Move through your Timeline and select edit points with the Rolling Edit Tool.

② Double-click to enter Trim Edit mode.

Use the comma (,) and period (.) keys to make minor one-frame edits. Better yet, click the Dynamic trimming box, and you can use the J-K-L keys to quickly trim your show.

Don't Get Bored When Choosing Transitions

Don't let bad transitions happen to good sequences. We often see editors get "bored" by a show because they've spent too much time on it. They lose any sense of judgment and resort to using "one of everything" from the Transitions menu.

Constrain yourself when using wipes. A few wipes go a long way. Transitions should only be used when needed to show a change in space or time. It's also a good idea to follow a directional transition with an identical transition in the opposite direction. As a cinema classic once said, "Wax on, wax off."

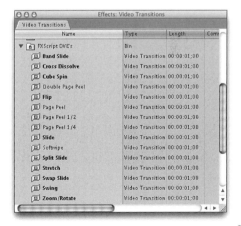

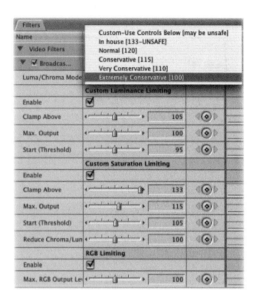

Broadcast Safe

Making your show broadcast safe is one of the paramount tasks in any finishing workflow and one way to help achieve broadcast safe is with the Broadcast Safe filter (Effects > Color Correction > Broadcast Safe). The thing is, most people apply the Broadcast Safe filter and assume that's all there is to it. In reality, simply applying the Broadcast Safe filter doesn't always achieve broadcast safe results, especially if the footage is really illegal to begin with.

- As a general rule of thumb, it's always a good idea to color correct your footage first and then use the Broadcast Safe filter as a safety net for those pixels that might be illegal.

- Using the Broadcast Safe filter, the easiest way to get better results is to change the Luma/Chroma Mode pull-down to Very or Extremely Conservative. The other options in the pulldown don't really succeed at making your show broadcast safe.

- It's also important to note that when you choose anything other than Custom from this pull-down the sliders and controls below do not have any effect on the result. They only work if you choose Custom.

- Speaking of Custom, using this mode is the best way to get great results. For a good explanation of all the controls check out the Final Cut Pro user manual, page III-526 or 1311.

Client Text.txt

Verify Lower-Thirds and Titles

To ensure against misspelled lower-thirds and titles, get a document directly from your client with all the correct spellings or names, ranks, and serial numbers—well, you know what we mean.

Or create one yourself, and have them review and sign off on it.

Now all you need to do is copy and paste the text back into Final Cut Pro, and you've ensured that you have the client's "approved" spellings of everything!

Veja Dupe

Ever get that feeling like you've seen a shot before? It's easy to lose track of every shot cut into your show. It's an unintentional gaffe to repeat a shot in a show unless it's for special storytelling purposes. But how can you find those sneaky dupes?

Don't worry; Final Cut Pro makes it easy:

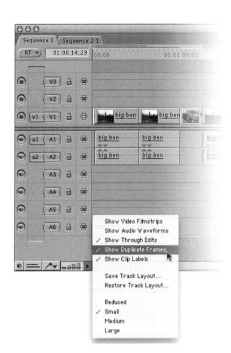

1. Check your Dupe Detection settings. Press Option + Q to call up your User Preferences panel. Unless you're working in film when you should use at least one frame of handle, you can set the threshold up to 15 frames.

2. Open Sequence > Sequence Settings (Command + 0), select the Timeline tab, and specify Show Duplicate Frames. You can also access this more quickly from the Track Layout menu at the bottom of the Timeline.

3. Six different colors are used to mark duplicated frames: red, green, blue, white, black, and purple. Final Cut Pro will mark the duplicate frames along the bottom edge of a clip in the Timeline. If you have more than six duplicated clips, the colors are reused. If a duplicate clip has a motion effect applied, duplicate frame indicators will not appear.

4. You can contextual-click a clip with duplicate frames to see a shortcut menu. One of the options is Duplicate Frames. It'll show you a list of all repeated clips and indicate how many frames were repeated.

5. You can choose an item from the list, and the playhead will jump to that point of your sequence. This way you can review each shot and decided if changes are needed.

Faster, Faster!

We didn't believe this at first either, but the G5 and MacPro internal hard drives are fast enough for uncompressed video—not your factory-installed hard drive, as the system folder and program files clog it down. The key is to buy a Serial ATA drive, often priced below $1 per gigabyte. Installation is a snap (see http://www.info.apple.com/usen/cip/pdf/ g5/073-0806.pdf for details) and it only takes a few minutes. In no time you can be using uncompressed graphics and video in your Timeline.

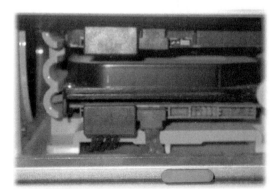

Cut for Broadcast? Then Cut to Clock!

Did you know that most hour-long shows on broadcast TV are actually less than 45 minutes and that most half hour shows are about 22 minutes? Wow, that's a lot of commercials!

One of the most important aspects of finishing a show is making sure that it is "cut to clock." Each segment in the show, breaks, as well as the entire show length, must adhere to certain lengths. Every network is different, but make sure you get a copy of the clock from your specific broadcaster and don't deviate from it.

Create a Checklist

Every show we work on goes exactly as planned and there is never a mad rush during finishing to get the show completed—yeah right! Let's face it—the finishing process is a busy time. And while you might think that you will remember everything there is to do to finish the show, chances are you will not. An easy way to help make sure you cover everything that needs to be done is to create a checklist.

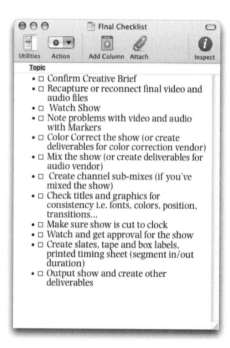

The checklist can, of course, be amended with project specific tasks, but here is a general list that you can adapt for your needs.

1 Recapture or reconnect final video and audio files.

2 Watch the show.

3 Note problems with video and audio with markers.

4 Color Correct the show (or create deliverables for color correction vendor).

5 Mix the show (or create deliverables for audio vendor).

6 Create channel submixes (if you've mixed the show).

7 Check graphics for consistency, i.e., fonts, colors, position, and transitions

8 Make sure show is cut to clock.

9 Watch and get approval for the show.

10 Create slates, tape and box labels, printed timing sheet (segment in/out duration).

11 Output show and create other deliverables.

Multiple Versions

So you've just completed your high definition masterpiece when you find out that you need to create a standard definition letterboxed version of the show. Thankfully, this is pretty easy inside Final Cut Pro.

❶ Create a new sequence and load a new sequence preset (for example, Apple Pro Res 422 NTSC).

❷ Take your high def sequence and nest it in the new one you just created.

❸ If you're asked if you want to conform this sequence to the new one, choose No.

❹ Voila! You now have a letterboxed version of the show because FCP maintains aspect ratio of the original sequence its scale was reduced to fit in the 4×3 frame.

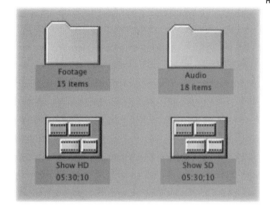

Additionally, after you nest the sequence you can open it in the Viewer and increase its scale to 70% (this will, of course, depend on your acquisition source—70% is derived from HDV footage). This will essentially edge crop the original HD sequence. Just be very careful—if the footage was not shot 4×3 safe you could be cutting off important action and/or framing.

Pan and Scan, My Man!

Ever wish you could easily reframe a shot that an absent-minded videographer or director forgot to frame correctly? Well, one very cool and easy way is to use a feature in Color called Pan and Scan.

❶ Send your sequence to Color (File > Send To > Color).

❷ Select your shot in the Color Timeline and select the Geometry Room (Command + 6).

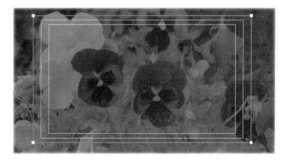

❸ Make sure the Pan and Scan tab is chosen in the bottom right-hand corner of the room. Using the Position, Scale and Rotation Tools, reframe your clip as you see fit. Be wary of the aspect ratio control because we want to keep the aspect the same and only reframe the shot.

❹ After you're done, be sure to render the clip(s) and choose File > Send To > Motion to reconnect the files back in Final Cut Pro.

Jamming Out in the Edit Suite

We've had online sessions where getting the audio mix finalized was virtually impossible—not because of the material but rather because the client and producer just kept talking about where to order lunch. As we turned the volume up to hear better, they just kept talking louder. Finally, they asked us to turn the speakers down, at which point we pointed out that we were happy to go take a break and return when we could finish our audio edit.

My more recent solution is to block the noise out. Although you might look funny to others in your office, a good pair of studio monitoring headphones goes a long way. Block out the environmental noise, and focus on your audio edit. Plus, you'll no longer have to worry about your client's habit of talking on their cell phone during the session.

We also like some of the new high-end noise-canceling headsets. They filter out all of the machine hum (computers, desk, air conditioner, and so on), and let you focus on the show's audio.

Why Is There That Shot at the End of My Tape with the Boom Mic in It?

If you've ever asked this question (and it's okay if you have), here's the answer: At the end of shooting at each location, a good audio engineer will record room tone or natural sound. This sound is meant to be used in your Timeline to fill in any gaps.

Why? Well, there's a big difference between computer silence (the absence of any audio in the Timeline) and "true" silence. All locations on this planet have some sort of noise, whether it's the whir of machinery, the pumping of ventilation, or the chirping of birds in the background. Use the room tone between sound bites. Better yet, lay a continuous bed of it below all of your bites from a particular location. This goes a long way to smooth out the rough spots.

Narrow Your Focus

Trying to "troubleshoot" your mix? Most editors will intently listen to their show, as if intensity alone could move the edit from a "fine" cut to a "final" cut. Intense focus is a good thing, but make things a little easier by narrowing your focus. Problems will stand out in your audio track when you listen to the elements separately.
Use these tips:

- Turn off your audio monitors to listen to tracks (or pairs) individually.

- If you've added audio edits to your music, do things transition smoothly, or are you trying to hide your music edits?

- Are there any loud breaths, gasps, or "guttural" sounds in your narration or sound bites? Throat clearings and coughs can be easily cleaned up.

Photo Credit Hemera Photo Objects

Little Upcuts

No matter how good of an audio editor you are, the more edits in your vocal tracks, the more likely you are to have small pops in your track. We usually add several four- or six-frame audio dissolves to all audio edits on a narration track. These short dissolves go a long way to smooth things out in your vocal track.

After adding the dissolves, be sure to listen to your mix. You want to make sure that when you add that dissolve you're not picking up extra audio clips (random words and double breaths) from the media in the clip's handles.

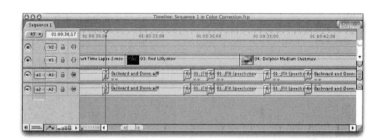

Delete Unused Tracks

Under the Sequence menu, there's an option to delete unused audio and video tracks—use it!

273

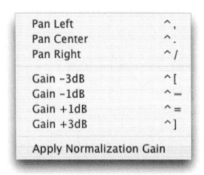

Pan Left	^ ,
Pan Center	^ .
Pan Right	^ /
Gain −3dB	^ [
Gain −1dB	^ −
Gain +1dB	^ =
Gain +3dB	^]
Apply Normalization Gain	

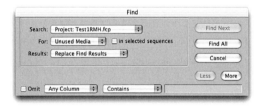

Sometimes a Zero Is Good

Depending on how you capture audio, this one may really cause you problems. Be VERY careful when mixing your show for final output. In the nonbroadcast world, you'll generally want to pan your narration tracks to center (or "zero them") so the voice comes out evenly from both speakers. This is true whether your audio is from a split track source (with camera and boom mic) or a single mono file imported from a CD. Follow these steps:

1 Use the Select Track Forward tool to highlight an entire track of studio.

2 Press Control + period (.) to pan the track to center.

Offline—Online?

There's nothing worse than getting a Media Offline screen in the middle your show. Want a quick way to check your sequence for offline media? No problem. Follow these steps:

1 Press Command + F to launch the Find dialog box.

2 Select the correct project, and choose Used Media. Specify that you want to Replace Find Results.

3 Click Find All.

4 Look in the Results box for any clips with a red line through them. You'll quickly discover any offline clips used by that sequence.

The Road Test

One of the final steps in mixing an audio CD is the road test. Audio engineers and producers will often burn a CD, pop it in a car, and drive around town. Why? Well, it's to see how the mix sounds in a "real-world" setting.

What does this mean for you? Well, you should really try out your mix in its intended viewing area. A video meant for playback in a sports stadium will have a different mix than one going to an in-store kiosk.

Photo Credit Hemera Photo Objects

An LCD TV

One of the final techniques used to check our videos is playback on an "LCD" TV. We don't mean a fancy flat-screen set. Rather, we mean the "Least Common Denominator" television set. We keep a $150 TV/VCR combo unit around just for these purposes. It's a good idea to watch your show like the rest of the world. Joe and Jane Public don't have high-resolution monitors with a Blue-Gun for professional calibration. See things through your customer's eyes every once in a while.

This low-tech approach shouldn't replace a broadcast monitor but rather complement it. We keep both a calibrated high-end broadcast monitor and a cheap TV set in our edit suites. That way we can see both the highest and most likely denominators while we're editing our shows.

Using Both Mics

Oftentimes a tape will have sound on both channels. However, it's likely that two different microphones recorded the sound. Using a camera mic and combining it with a lavaliere or boom mic often accomplishes this.

You'll want to control which mic is used. Sometimes it'll be both, sometimes only one. Be sure to adjust the levels of the two mics until things sound right. Most importantly, pan both of these mics to the center so your speakers reproduce the sound evenly.

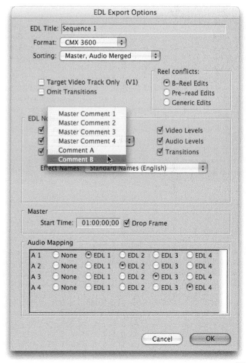

If You Need an EDL

Good news for those of you who need to use EDLs to move your sequences to an online or linear system. You can choose to include Master Comment Information. Simply choose to export Comments 1–4 or Comment A–B in the EDL Export dialog. You can now get additional notes to the online editor so they have a better idea on how to handle complex tapes or shots.

Grading Made to Order

So you're excited about learning Color, Apple's new color correction and grading program, but you just haven't quite gotten around to really learning the application? No worries; you can still get some very good results by using Color's pre-built color effects. Here's how:

❶ Select your sequence you wish to grade and choose the File > Send To > Color. Name the Color Project (it defaults to the name of the sequence) and click OK.

❷ Color will launch. Select a shot in the Timeline you wish to grade. Go to the Color Fx room (4th tab from the left at the top of the interface or Command + 4).

❸ From here you can choose individual parameters to grade your clip on the left-hand side of the room or on bottom right-hand side of the room there is a tab called Color Fx Bin. Choose this.

❹ Here you'll find pre-built "looks." Simply drag one of the looks out into the center of the room to apply it.

❺ Many times this is all you will need to do, but if you want to tweak the look, click on the Parameters tab (next to the Color Fx Bin tab you just clicked). Now, select one of the parameter tiles in the center part of the room and change whatever parameters you want.

❻ When you're done you need to render the clip(s). To do this choose Render Queue > Add Selected (Shift + Command + A) to render selected clips or Add All (Option + Shift + Command + A) to render all the clips you graded. Next, click on the Render Queue Room (Command + 8) and choose Start Render (Command + P).

❼ Lastly, choose File Menu > Send To > Final Cut Pro.

Back in Final Cut Pro, a new Timeline is created named the same as your original but with (from Color) added to the end. Your graded clips have automatically connected themselves to the new renders from Color.

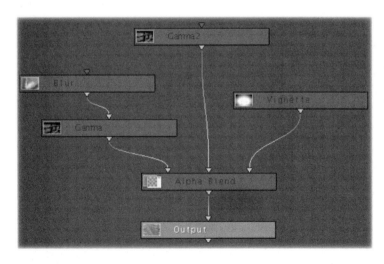

Blur for Legal Sake

One thing we find ourselves doing all the time is having to blur logos and other objectionable content for broadcast. This is mainly done, of course, so a network doesn't get sued! Although this process is sometimes time consuming, it's a necessary evil.

1 Find the shot that needs to be blurred and duplicate it by holding Shift + Option and dragging the clip onto the track above its current location.

2 Load the top clip into the Viewer and apply a Gaussian Blur filter to the clip. Don't worry, the whole clip will go blurry. This is normal!

3 Next, apply the Mask Shape filter. Choose the shape that matches best and adjust the horizontal and vertical scale controls to suit the item that needs to be blurred.

4 Position the center point of the item to be blurred.

5 The trick now is that you need to keyframe the center point (and sometimes the scale controls) to match the movement of the object. Depending on the amount of movement, you may have to keyframe quite a bit.

6 Next, add a Mask Feather filter and adjust to taste. This will aid in taking care of the hard edges of the blur.

For complex objects that need to be blurred you could also use the 4-point and 8-point garbage mattes. The only difference with the technique described above is that you would keyframe point positions. Also, there is no need to add the Mask Feather filter as the Garbage Mattes have feather built in.

For those of you who abhor keyframes and seek more automation in your life, this same task can also be accomplished in Motion with masks and the Match Move behavior.

Don't Stop

Oftentimes you'll want to play a sequence through to get the producer's or client's feedback. This is a great way to get important comments to improve the show. However, they'll probably want you to stop on each "error." This is bad for several reasons. You'll lose any sense of timing or rhythm to the edit. Additionally, it's common to stop for a change, only to discover that the "missing" shot in question happens 10 seconds later.

Instead of stopping, encourage your suite mates to watch the show all the way through. Tell them you'll mark all the "problem areas."

❶ Agree on a word such as 'mark' to signal that a shot should be flagged for review.

❷ Position the playhead at the start of the video track, and press Play.

❸ Tap the M or ' key to add a marker on the fly.

❹ Afterward, you can move between markers rapidly. Press Shift + the up or down arrows to jump between markers.

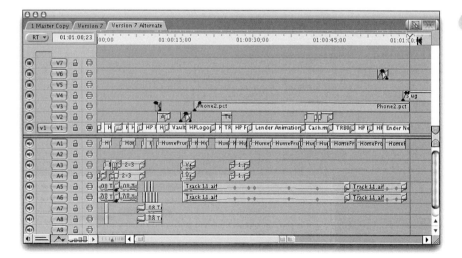

Go Low (In Your Timeline)

Before you finish your show, try to clean the Timeline up. Get your show back down to as few tracks as possible. Editors have a tendency to build their shows upward. Unfortunately, a "tall" show is often harder to move though because of all the scrolling. This compounds itself, making it more difficult for future revisions. If you want to drag a track straight down, simply hold down the Command key when dragging.

Window Burns

You've sent your client a dub and are waiting for feedback. Eventually you get a call that goes something like this:

Client: Just got that dub and it's great. I've just got a couple of changes.

Editor: Okay, no problem.

Client: That one shot with the guy in the blue shirt, it needs to come out.

Editor: You mean just after Jane's sound bite?

Client: No, it's after the shot with the kids in it.

Repeat the previous conversation until both sides think significantly less of the other.

Want an easier way to get client feedback on a show? Make a window burn. Put the timecode across the bottom of the screen so you and your client can look at the actual timecode and reference something far more accurate than a VHS counter.

To set a sequence timecode, follow these steps:

❶ Create a new sequence with the same settings as the sequence you want to output. This will be your output sequence.

❷ Drop your edited sequence into the output sequence.

❸ Apply the Timecode Reader filter to your media clip (Video Filters > Video > Timecode Reader).

❹ Control + click your video track, and choose Open in Viewer.

❺ Adjust size and position so it's easier for your client to view (be sure to keep safe title area in mind).

Bonus: If you're using Compressor 3, be sure to check out the built-in Timecode filter. This is a great option for going to the web or DVD.

Poor Man's Uprez

Sometimes you don't have the time to do an online session and ingest your clips as uncompressed, or maybe you just don't have the equipment to support the process. Either way, here is a quick way to achieve uncompressed space via software. Just be aware that this method won't make your video look better, but what it will do is give you great bandwidth for color correction (versus DV or HDV, for example), and make your text and graphics look as good as possible.

① Start by creating a new sequence and load the uncompressed 10-Bit preset.

② If you're working in HD simply change your frame size and pixel aspect ratio to the flavor of your choice. Click OK to save the changes to your new sequence.

③ Find your original sequence in your Browser and drag it to the Canvas. Make sure you're holding down the Command key as you don't want to nest this sequence (Command will make all the clips come in as individual clips, not as a nest) and choose Overwrite. Also make sure you have the same number of video and audio tracks as your original to ensure clips don't get lost.

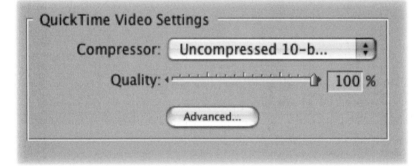

④ All of your clips will be placed in the Timeline and simply choose to render the sequence.

If you're going back to tape make sure your hard drives are fast enough to support uncompressed playback (might be a big issue if you're attempting to do this with HD).

If your final output is DVD or the web, don't worry about not being able to play it back, as you'll simply output the file through Compressor and don't need real-time playback.

Change Your Viewpoint

If you're watching your videos in the same edit suite every day, you'll eventually develop "blind spots." Try moving things around a bit. Lay off a VHS, and take it to the conference room (or even home with you). Put a copy on your laptop, and watch it there. The key is to test it in different environments.

Careful on Recapture

While it's a common workflow these days to capture at full resolution and never look back, many people still use offline–online workflows for working on big projects. When it comes time to go to the online stage, one thing that seems to frustrate a lot of people is that Final Cut Pro requests something like four hours of media to be ingested when the show is only half an hour!

What's the deal? It is quite simple, really, and has to do with a few settings in the media manager.

❶ Select the sequence you want to online and choose File > Media Manager.

❷ In the Media section choose Create Offline from the pull-down and set your sequences to the codec you'll be using for your online session.

❸ Make sure Include master clips outside selection is UNCHECKED. If this is checked you could be bringing along a ton more media than is needed from marked master clips.

❹ Choose to delete unused media and add handles (usually 1-2 seconds is sufficient).

❺ Make sure Include affiliate clips outside of selection is UNCHECKED. If this is checked you could be bringing along affiliate clips media located in other sequences.

❻ UNCHECK Include nonactive multiclip angles. It's always a good idea to flatten multiclips before media managing, but if you didn't flatten your multiclips, unchecking this makes sure that nonactive angles are not included.

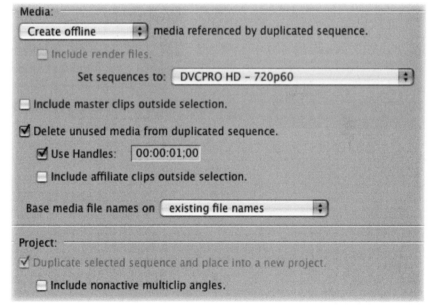

281

ON THE SPOT

CHAPTER 15

A Place for Everything
Media Management and Backup

One of the biggest calls for help we hear is from editors who have "misplaced" their media, render files, or entire projects. This chapter helps you plan ahead so that doesn't happen—and, if it does, you'll know where to look for them.

It's also inevitable that your client will call to make changes to last year's project, just as you empty your trash, deleting his files from your hard drive. Well, if you follow some of our backup strategies and tips, you'll have the project back online in no time (of course, billing out big bucks for those changes). All it takes is a bit of advanced planning, a CD or DVD burner, and a few good tips.

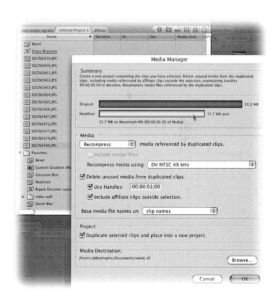

A Simple Beginning (Working in Low-Res)

No matter what format you shoot on or capture from, you can digitize to a lower resolution. If you have gobs of footage or want more real-time layers, consider capturing to an OfflineRT format from the beginning. Several third-party cards have their own offline formats. These low-resolution formats are a tremendous space saver. When you're done, see the tip "Back from the Trip." Remember, DV is low resolution for HD and SD.

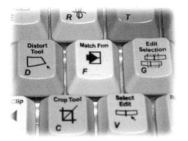

Where Did I Come From?—Part 1

You may want to quickly find a clip that's been edited into your Timeline. Simply park over a clip, and make sure its track is selected. Press F to match frame to the source clip. The original source should load into the Viewer with In and Out marks preserved.

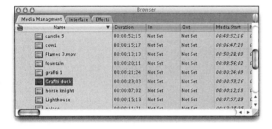

Where Did I Come From?—Part 2

Have a clip in your Timeline but want to find the original clip? This sounds easy—just search your Browser. But what if you have several hundred clips organized into multiple bins? Don't worry—put the computer to work. Press Shift + F to locate the clip in the Browser.

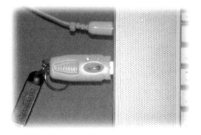

Safety Is In Your Hands (Using Portable Drives)

A project file is a very valuable thing. Consider investing in a USB thumb drive. Virtually all work under OS X and provide an excellent way to back up project files and graphics during an edit session.

"Golden Parachute" (How to Make a Perfect Backup)

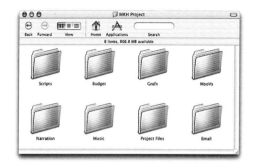

We're often asked about our backup strategies. What do we save, what do we toss, where do we store things on our drives? Here's one methodology that works for us: We create two folders for each project: a "clips folder" on one of our media drives and a "golden parachute folder" on our apps drive. In the clips folder we include all captured media that we have access to that comes from the original videotape (with timecode), all render files, and our Autosave Vault.

The golden folder contains everything else: our project files, graphics, still photos, music, narration, PSDs, script, budget, correspondence, and any QuickTime files that were created in other applications. We back this folder up every time we work on this project. It has all of the elements we'd need to re-create the show minus the footage we can recapture. (Usually this all fits on a single CD-R disc, but occasionally, if we have a lot of animations, we use a DVD-R.)

When the project is done, we save the archive (this folder) with the source tapes. In a year, if our client comes back to make a change, we now have everything at our fingertips, including the script and budget. (How may times have you asked your graphic artist for a file six months later only to hear, "Uh ... it's somewhere ... maybe on the backup server"? You'll never see that file again!) This works great.

Now when it's time to clean house, you can simply throw away your project media folder. We tend to keep golden folders on our drive as long as possible.

A Safer (Autosave) Vault

Your Autosave Vault backs up files to your main drive by default. In our experience, the main drive is more likely to experience corruption or damage because of heavy use, viruses, and so on. A better idea is to set the Autosave Vault to archive to a different drive. This way you have extra protection if a drive or machine goes down. (A good rule of thumb is never save your project and your Autosave Vault to the same drive.)

A More Useful Subclip

When you create a subclip, it can't access the original media. This may cause problems if you need to trim or add a transition. It's a good idea to remove subclip limits. This command can be done to a group of subclips.

❶ Select the subclip(s) in your Browser window.

❷ Choose Modify > Remove Subclip Limits.

24p Remove Advanced Pulldown

Most 24p cameras have two modes: 24p Standard and 24p Advanced. Why, you ask? Well, it depends on your intended output.

Shoot 24p Advanced:

- If you intend to do an actual film out or integrate the material with actual film.

- You intend to use Final Cut Pro's Advanced (2:3:3:2) Pulldown Removal.

Shoot 24p Standard:

- You're going for a "film look" but intend to stay on video.

- You plan to intercut with film that has been transferred using 3:2 pulldown and will stay on video as your final deliverable.

  For a lot more on 24p, be sure to check out http://www.adamwilt.com/24p/

Stock Project

Working on an episodic television or a quarterly corporate magazine? Create a standard starting point. A master project allows you to use a template that contains all your transitions, graphics, music, lower-thirds, and so on. Follow these steps:

❶ Take a successfully completed project, and save a copy using Save As.

❷ Organize your bins for graphics, sound effects, titles, music, and so on.

❸ Create subsequences for the opening, bumpers, and closing segments.

❹ Close and save the project file.

❺ At the Finder level, locate the project file. Highlight the project file, and press Command + I to call up the file's information. Lock the project file.

❻ In the future, just launch the project. You'll have to do a Save As to save the project.

This is a great way to "fast-start" a project. All of the stock elements you need are quickly at hand. You'll save valuable time because you won't need to search and import your common files. (By the way, this tip works for daily, weekly, monthly, quarterly, and annual shows. But if you only cut once a decade, you shouldn't hold your breath.)

Video Max Show
Starter

In-Progress Archives

What many folks don't realize is that the SuperDrives can write to an RW disc. The write speed is generally half of what it is for regular R discs, but what do you care if you're burning overnight? It's a good idea to create a project archive that contains all of your non-timecode files. You can burn to CD-RW to back up smaller projects or to DVD-RW to back up larger projects. If you find yourself archiving to disc often, be sure to check out Roxio's Toast for its streamlined approach to disc burning.

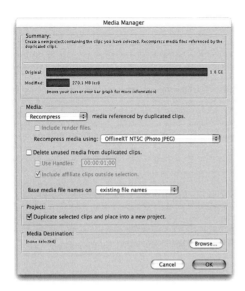

On the Road Again

Once upon a time, we dreamed of a day when we could actually get sunshine in our edit suites. Thoughts of a window and some fresh air seemed nice, but so far away. These days, we routinely get out of a dark edit suite and see the light of day (at such luxurious locations as Starbucks or Caribou Coffee).

How, you ask? OfflineRT. Many people write this technology off as not important. "Why work at two different resolutions? It just means more work." But this isn't the case. OfflineRT is 1/8th the size of DV-25 and less than 1/40th the size of SD. On an 80 GB laptop you can easily get more than 40 hours of media and still have room for most of your applications.

❶ Capture at your preferred high-quality format (DV-25, DVCPro 50, 8 bit, 10 bit, HD, and so on).

❷ With your laptop powered down, plug in a FireWire cable between your laptop and desktop.

❸ Power up the laptop while holding down the T key. This will place the laptop in Target Disk mode. You'll see a huge FireWire icon as your desktop. Meanwhile, the laptop will appear as an icon on the primary machine's desktop. Your laptop now acts like an external hard drive that you can read and write to. (It's a really good idea to have your laptop plugged into an electrical outlet; go ahead, do it now—we'll wait.)

❹ Select all the shots and sequences in the Browser you want to move to your target disk.

❺ Contextual-click, and choose Media Manager. A dialog box will appear giving you several options. There are several choices to make, but they're simple decisions.

❻ From the Media area, choose to Recompress media referenced by duplicated clips. Choose OfflineRT NTSC or OfflineRT PAL depending upon your footage format.

❼ Because you intend to reference the high-resolution footage, don't delete any unused media.

8 Likewise, you should base media file names on existing file names.

9 Under the Project area, check the box to Duplicate the selected clips and place into a new project.

10 If you're working with multiclips (and want to still edit), then be sure to check Include nonactive multiclip angles.

11 Under the Media Destination area, specify a volume for the media to trans-code to.

12 Click OK.

The speed of this process is based upon the processing speed of your computer. On a slower machine it can be timely, but the results are worth it. You'll get more layers of RT effects and zippier response from your machine. Edit away, see the world, drink lots of espresso ... when you get back, it's a simple process to reconnect to the high-resolution footage.

Effective (Project) Communication

At the end of the day, probably the most important part of editing and post-production is communication. This communication can be internal with other people on your team, with vendors or probably most frequently with your clients.

Besides backing up media and project files, another important thing to back up is communications documents. Most likely these are emails, but may also include instant messages, change orders, and workflow documents. Having an archive of this communication is a good way to protect yourself (or your company) if issues with the project should come up at a later date.

However you choose to back up these items, it's important that you back them up to a safe place, and no, your computer is not a safe place! If your machine were to fail, you'd have some problems. We prefer to create a hard folder for each project, and at the end of the project, populate it with paper communications as well as CDs of email and instant message archives.

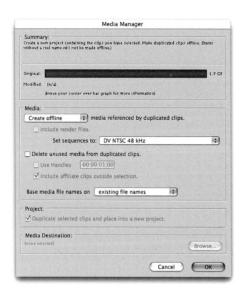

Back from the Trip: The Beginning

You've completed your project in OfflineRT and are ready to go "high-res." It's a good idea to clean up your project and minimize how much footage you need at a high resolution. The process is the same if you need to redigitize or relink to high-resolution media:

❶ Duplicate your project file. Select all the sequences and any additional clips in the Browser you want to move to your high-resolution project.

❷ Contextual-click, and choose Media Manager. A dialog box will appear giving you several options.

❸ From the Media area, choose to Create offline media referenced by duplicated clips. Set the sequence settings to match the resolution of the original media or the resolution you intend to finish in.

❹ Previous versions would frequently get confused if you deleted media from duplicated clips. However, if the media has been previously captured, you should leave this box unchecked.

❺ Check the Include master clips outside selection option to impact how much media is retained in the master clips of the new project. This option will include both the part of clips used in selected sequence as well as media between In and Out points in the clip.

❻ Uncheck the Include Affiliate Clips Outside Selection option. Otherwise you'll have too much media to load.

❼ Save the file to a new destination.

❽ Close the current project and the newly created project. All of the clips will come up as offline (signified by a red line slashed through the clip in the bin).

Back from the Trip: Reconnecting Existing Footage

To reconnect existing footage, follow these steps:

❶ Highlight your sequence file, and contextual-click. Choose Reconnect Media, and specify to connect Offline Media.

❷ Final Cut Pro will attempt to relink the media files for you. Be careful, however, because it may default to your low-resolution footage first. Scroll left in Column view, and check which folder you're in. You may need to manually locate the high-resolution bin.

❸ Highlight the clip, and be sure that the Reconnect all files in relative path box is checked.

❹ Continue reconnecting until the project is online. You'll need to rerender all effects.

Back from the Trip: Capturing at a Higher Resolution

To capture at a higher resolution, follow these steps:

❶ Highlight your sequence file, and contextual-click. Choose Batch Capture.

❷ Capture your media using standard workflow.

❸ Highlight any graphic and sound files, and choose to reconnect media.

❹ You'll need to rerender all effects.

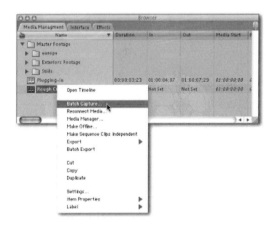

Disk Images for Tapeless Media

Are you riding the wave of tapeless acquisition and post-production? Formats like Panasonic's P2 and Sony's XDAM are very cool. The main benefit of these formats is speed of ingest, although there are others like increased metadata support.

One overlooked area is proper backup of these tapeless formats. After you transfer the footage, chances are you'll want to use the P2 card or XDCAM disc again. But if something happens to your media and you've already erased the card/disc, there really is nothing you can do. Now that's scary!

An easy way to back up this media is, after you mount the card/disc and transfer the media, you can then create a disk image. Before we do this, just be aware that you will need lots of extra hard drive space because not only does the media take up room on your drives, you also have the disk image. It's probably a good idea to invest in a large FireWire drive that does nothing else but store the disk images.

❶   Launch the disk utility (Applications > Utilities > Disk Utility).

❷   Select the card/disc in the source list on the left-hand side of the window and then click the New Image button on the tool bar.

❸   In the dialog that pops up give a name for the image (name this the same way you'd name a tape) and choose a location.

❹   It can take some time to create an image of the card/disc; factor that into your workflow.

If you are a P2 user, you can also create a disk image directly from the Log and Transfer window in Final Cut Pro. To do this, simply select the P2 volume in the Browse area of the Log and Transfer window and from the action menu choose Archive to Disk Image.

We are sometimes asked why not just back up the folders manually from a card/disc instead of creating a disk image. Well, the answer is simple. A disk image is a self-contained file and, as such, you're not going to be able to delete files and folders by accident like you might be able to if you just archive the folders. This is especially important because both P2 and XDCAM require a strict file structure.

Dates for Sequence Backup

If you have ever taken over editing on a project for someone else, you probably know how frustrating it can be to try to locate the correct sequence you're supposed to be working on if the previous editor didn't have good media management skills. Likewise, even if you were the only editor on a show, have you ever had the problem of locating the correct version of the show among countless versions and sequences? Well, here is a simple fix.

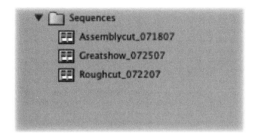

Make sure you put the date onto the end of the sequence. Name it something like Greatshow_072507. If you are doing a lot of changes to a sequence and want to be extra safe, you could break it down even further by putting the time of day on the end, for example, Greatshow_072507_Morning.

Get into the habit of naming and backing up your sequences with the date. Trust us, this easy system has avoided headaches countless times.

The Drive Archive

Over the years, we have been fortunate enough to work with the same clients over and over again. Typically, these return clients will want to use pieces from older projects in their new projects and in some cases, quite of bit of older material.

In the past, archiving projects to disk simply to have that drive sit on a shelf wasn't really an option, mainly because of cost, but now with hard drives being so cheap, we regularly factor in the cost of a 500GB–1TB drive into project costs. That way we can archive whole projects (most of the time media-managed by FCP) to the drive.

Some clients balk at the initial upfront cost of the drive, but when we explain that next year, when they come back to work on their annual video, we won't have to re-ingest footage from tape or go searching for graphics. They quickly understand the value of these "live" archives.

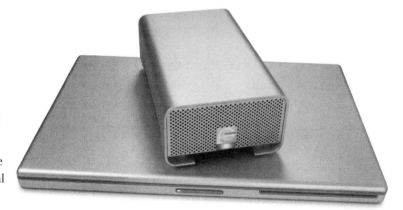

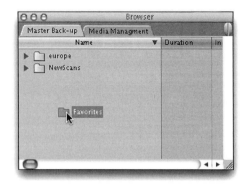

"Master Backup Project"

This tip is useful if you're upgrading, moving from system to system, or deleting your Final Cut Pro User Preferences. A lot of folks don't realize you can drag a favorite/ custom filter, motion, or transition directly into your Browser. Create a project and label it as **Master Backup**. Now drag your Favorites folder out from your Effects tab, and drop it into your Project tab of your Browser. Also, if you've created any titles or lower-thirds that you want to save for future use, open their projects and drag them across into your Master Backup project. Save this project. You now have a backup of all your favorites to restore on your machine, to another user account, or to transfer to another edit system.

.mac Has Got Your Back

Apple offers an excellent service for online storage, tools, and utilities. One of those utilities is Backup, which is designed to synchronize some of your key system settings. Any file can be added to Backup and be told to archive to your iDisk (the Internet storage that comes with a .mac account). Be sure to add your active project file to the backup list and tell it to archive every night. This is an excellent way to preserve a clean copy of the project file.

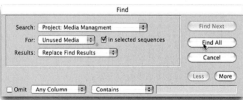

What's Left?

Need to determine what footage hasn't been used? Highlight one or more sequences, and press Command + F. Ask Final Cut Pro to show you unused media. All of the clips will be shown in the project, which can be useful when hunting for B-Roll. This way you can find shots that haven't yet been cut into your show.

Out of Space?

Running out of disk space fast? Well, you can delete media without throwing away logging information. Remember, with all of the clip information, you can always recapture material that has timecode.

❶ Press Command + F to launch the Find dialog box.

❷ Select Unused media from the dialog box, and click Find All.

❸ In the Results window, select all the clips.

❹ Contextual-click, and select Make Offline.

❺ Choose Delete Them from the Disk option if you're confident.

Alternatively, you can choose Move Them to the Trash if you want a "trial" delete. Check your sequence to make sure no media went offline unintentionally. The easiest way to do this is to contextual-click the sequence icon, and select Relink Media. If the Offline box is grayed out, there are no clips offline. Erase whenever you want.

The key advantage of this method is that you're not throwing away logging information. If you discover you need a clip in the future, you can easily recapture the clip.

We Do It Every Night

It's ESSENTIAL to make a backup copy of your project at the end of an edit session. Creating a thumb drive, burning a removable disc, even emailing yourself the zipped project file is a great way to make a copy of your work. When you least expect it, things will go wrong. As long as you have a copy of the project file and your source tapes (with timecode), restoring a project is a fast process. BACKUP NOW … or regret it later.

If you have a .mac account, set it up to automatically back up your active project's folder.

Color Code Your Project

Taking the date method one step further, another easy way to manage sequences is by color coding them. Using this method, all rough cut sequences might be red, fine cut sequences blue and final sequences green.

To color code your sequences, simply right-click on them in the Browser then choose Label > Color of your choice. Notice how the colors are named by default? Well, that's because color coding can also be used to color code your clips. We want to have the labels make sense for sequences, so let's change these default names.

❶ Open up User Preferences (Option + Q).

❷ Click on the third tab over called Labels.

❸ Name the colors as you see fit. We find using stages in the editing process, like rough cut, fine cut and final cut work well.

❹ Click OK to save your changes.

Just in case you were wondering, you can't change the actual colors—maybe in the next version!

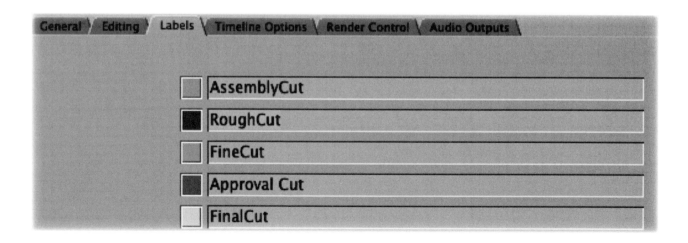

Why You Need Batch Capture

Have you ever needed to go on a road trip across state lines or to a location out of town? Some people forget the first rule of video (plan!), and just jump in the car and try to go instantly. This option is prone to many issues (and usually leads to arguments).

Several editors we meet don't harness the power of the Batch Capture feature. They rely on the inefficient Capture Clip or, worse, the potentially dangerous Capture Now. So what's the big deal? The video goes into the computer, right?

Getting into Capture mode takes time. You'll see increased stability and efficiency if you do all of your capturing at once. Plus, performing a Batch Capture lets you put the computer to work while you change gears. Let the computer spend 30 minutes capturing on its own, and you can work on picking music, switch to a second machine and work on graphics in LiveType or Photoshop, or even just return voice and email.

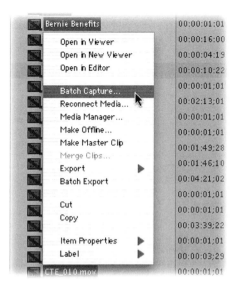

Follow these steps:

❶ Define which bin is your logging bin. This is where clips will be stored. It's a good idea to have a separate bin per source tape. This makes it easier to Batch Capture and archive.

❷ Review and log your footage. Mark In and Out points like always. When a clip is defined, click the Log Clip button or press F2.

❸ Before a Batch Capture, save your project. Bringing video in is one of the most demanding tasks on the application. You're most likely to crash during capture.

❹ When ready, click Batch Capture or press Control + C. You can only Batch Capture if your camera or deck supports device control. Most FireWire devices and professional video decks are supported. You may need to get a special deck control cable and USB-to-serial adapter to use older professional decks.

❺ The best part of the Batch Capture feature is that it's an automated process. You can leave your system unattended while it captures the logged clips. So your system will not hiccup, you'll need to change a few preferences. Under the General Settings tab, be sure to uncheck the Abort capture on dropped frames and Abort capture on timecode break boxes.

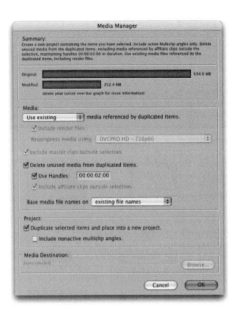

Trim the Fat

Perhaps you were a little bit less than careful when ingesting your footage and now you have 10 hours of footage for a 10 minute show! Don't worry, we can help you trim the fat. One thing before we begin, though. THIS IS DESTRUCTIVE! Please make sure you have a backup of your media (tapes or archives of tapeless formats). Also, it's a good idea to only do this if you're sure there won't be major changes to the show.

❶ Select the sequence you wish to trim in the Browser.

❷ Choose File > Media Manager.

❸ From the Media pull-down, choose Use existing.

❹ Check the Delete unused media from duplicated items box.

❺ Check Use handles and add a couple seconds of handles.

❻ Uncheck Duplicate selected items and place into a new project if you'd like to stay in this project, or check it to create a new project. The new project will contain only the sequence you have selected and master clips folder with the trimmed media.

❼ If you have the duplicate selected items and place in new project box checked, you also have the option to Include nonactive multiclip angles. Check this if you aren't sure if you will be switching back to other angles or uncheck it if you're satisfied with the current selection of angles in a multiclip.

❽ Click OK to start processing the media. If you chose to create a new project, you'll be prompted to name and save the project.

Depending on how your project is set up, you may also see a dialog labeled Additional Items Found. This is Final Cut Pro's way of double-checking other open projects that reference the media you're about to process.

- Clicking Add will bring along that additional media in other projects;

- Continue will not bring along that media, but may make the clips offline in the other projects;

- Abort cancels the operation.

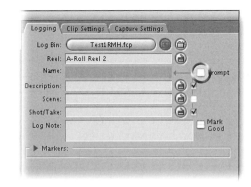

Power Log

Did you realize you can log faster than real-time? Try these three tips to get your footage in fast:

- Simply tap the L button multiple times to play the tape faster. With practice you can ramp your playback speed up and still understand the dialogue. All of your logging controls still work.

- Better yet, log while viewing. Tap I to mark an In point, and then press F2 to simultaneously add the Out point and log the clip.

- Uncheck the Prompt box in the logging window. After you name the first clip, all subsequent clips will be progressively numbered or lettered.

Look Before you Dig: Capture Settings ...

Surprise, you have a choice to make when digitizing (Okay, you have LOTS of choices to make when digitizing). But here's one more that's important. When batch capturing, you need to specify if you want to Use Logged Clip Settings or not. This is an important decision. You are telling Final Cut Pro to capture with the settings the computer had while logging, or to override and use the current capture settings.

- Use Logged Settings if you are sure the clips were logged properly.

- Uncheck this box if you'd like to capture at an alternate resolution like OfflineRT.

- You should uncheck this box if you captured your clips as video only and need to capture audio as well

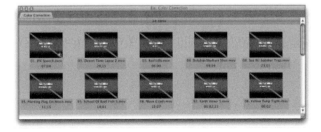

ON THE SPOT

CHAPTER 16

Out of the Box
Exporting and Publishing Your Program

Good editors think outside the box, and great editors don't even know there's a box. (The best editors are kept in a box and are only let out to edit!) We hope this book has already allowed you to exceed the limitations of your box. With that said, this chapter focuses on mastering and delivering your magnum opus.

The days of delivering just a video master are long gone. Clients now expect you to multipurpose their shows. In addition to a tape version, you're often asked for a DVD master, a CD master, multiple Web versions, a streaming audio file, and even frame grabs.

This means you must once again wear many hats beyond just being an editor. That's okay, because this chapter will make a hat rack out of you.

Reference Movies

Need to save some space? Reference movies allow you to work with your video clips or sequence files in other applications. Think of a reference movie as a pointer back to the original media, a lot like a link on a web page. Follow these steps:

1 Choose File > Export QuickTime Movie.

2 Name the file, and choose to not make the movie self-contained. This will save you disk space by referencing back to the media on your local drives. That being said, the media can't be deleted, moved, or on a different machine that's unreachable via a network.

3 Import the file into your other video application, and start working.

Reference movies are useful when working in After Effects, Cleaner, iDVD, or other applications where you want to work with a large video file. This is a useful way to export a sequence or longer segment of clips as one file. If you want to permanently save the video clip, be sure to check the Self-Contained box. Just remember that an hour-long show at DV-quality will need more than 12 GB of space!

A Cheaper DVD—Part 1

Need to test your DVD for computer playback? You want to see how the whole thing plays back from the optical drive (any skipping or crashes)? Tired of wasting discs? It's possible to burn your DVD content to a CD for playback on a computer. If the computer has a drive that can read both CDs and DVDs, then this trick works fine:

1 Simply author your disc, and save the VIDEO_TS and AUDIO_TS folders.

2 Burn these folders to a data disc using Toast or other third-party disc-burning application.

3 In Apple's DVD Player application, choose File > Open DVD Media.... Navigate to the TS folder on the CD, and open the file.

> Note: If you're not concerned about performance on optical media, then just use the same method to open the folder that contains the build files for your DVD and test.

A Cheaper DVD—Part 2

If you're using Toast or other DVD-burning software to burn your DVDs, you can harness the power of a DVD-RW. Not all players will recognize a rewriteable disc, but if yours does, a DVD-RW is a great way to save money during the testing stage.

Slates: What Needs to Be There?

Slates are useful for a lot of things. The following are what we put on ours (and why). These aren't the only things you might try, but it's a good place to start:

- **Title of show:** That way the duplicator or broadcaster knows the right tape is in the machine without having to fast-forward into your show.

- **Run time:** Duplicators are really happy when they put the right length tape in their recorders, and broadcasters like to know if that spot is 30 seconds or a minute.

- **Audio mix:** Mixed, discrete tracks, stereo, mono, and multiple languages are lots of options. And don't forget to tell them what levels your tone is set to: −12 db, −18 db, −20 db, or even 0 db if you're going analog.

- **Date and version:** If you do lots of versions of a show or a weekly show, adding the date helps stop confusion.

- **Production company:** They lost the box, and now they know who the production company is—oh yeah, when the network loves the show, they know who to hire!

- **Phone number:** Now they know how to get ahold of you to praise your work—or curse you if your levels are all messed up.

- **Audio:** If you're combining a slate with your countdown, you may want to add audio. Use short beeps that match the tone under your bars. There should be no audio or picture after the 2-pop on your tape.

Stomp It

Need to make clips smaller? Final Cut Pro has an excellent compression utility built in. If you intend to output to MPEG-2 or MPEG-4, Compressor is your application of choice:

1 Mark an In and Out point on your Timeline to define the range.

2 Choose File > Export > Using Compressor.

3 Specify one or more settings from the preset list. Submit the job, and let it run.

4 If you're in a hurry, close your other open applications and let the compression tie up all your system resources.

You can also create additional presets for QuickTime encoding. All codecs (including third-party ones) that are properly installed will be available.

> Note: If you need to know more on compression, check out *Compression for Great Digital Video* by Ben Waggonner.

A Better Stomp for MPEG-4

If the presets in Compressor don't quite fit your need, tweak them! By clicking the Presets icon, you can call up lists of all the presets that Compressor uses. All you need to do is modify an existing preset, or make your own from scratch.

The following are some options to try:

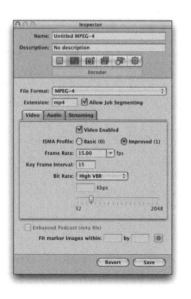

- For bit rate, the VBR options (which stands for variable bit rate) produce smaller file sizes and better quality. They take longer, however, because the processing time increases.

- Cutting the frame rate in half is a great way to save space. Something that originated in NTSC looks great at 15 frames per second for playback on a computer.

- Adjust the Audio Bit Rate setting. If you have the bandwidth (and the audio is important), increase it. A talking head, on the other hand, can be more compressed before you'll notice a big difference in quality.

Tips on Compression

The art of compressing files for the web or disc is a technology art form that stumps many people. With hundreds of options, settings, and sliders, it's no wonder. To demystify things a bit, here's a crash course on getting your file size down.

To start, have a five-minute QuickTime movie with DV NTSC compression at full size that's approximately 1 GB. Then follow these steps:

❶ Reduce the frame rate to 15 frames per second (512 MB).

❷ Reduce to Half Screen 320×240. This cuts both the height and width in half, as well as compensates for nonsquare pixels. If your compression application supports cropping, be sure to crop 10 percent of all sides to compensate for the space outside of Action Safe. (You're now at 128 MB.)

❸ If you have the option, be sure to deinterlace the video track. Interlaced video is for playback on a television, not a computer.

❹ You may also consider reducing the sample rate and size. The same math benefits apply. Reducing an audio track from 48 kHz to 22 kHz saves more than 2 times the space on the audio side. You're also likely to be able to go to an 8-bit mono file if it's for playback on a typical PC. Those two options combined will shave 75 percent off the audio file size.

❺ Add audio compression to taste; IMA 4:1, QDesign, and MP3 work well, depending on your codec.

❻ Save the Output settings as a preset or write them down. This way you can troubleshoot client changes or just replicate the settings on the next job because the client liked the results so well.

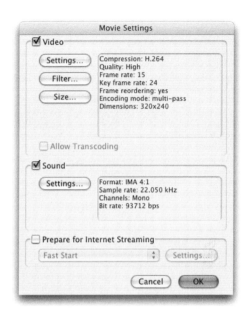

The Whole Enchilada (Entire Media)

Getting ready to Print to Video or Edit to Tape? Be sure to specify that you want to print the Entire Media; otherwise you'll only output between your In and Out points (useful if you mean to, but a pain if you didn't). In and Out marks will often affect exporting as well, so be sure to mark the area you want or clear the In and Out marks.

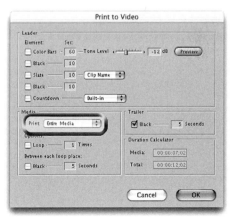

Being Discrete

So you've worked hard getting a perfect mix and have created submixes, outputted your show and are ready to archive your show as a self-contained QuickTime. In the past, if you were to do this, your audio would be mixed down to stereo or as grouped channels (i.e., stereo and dual mono).

Now, in Final Cut Pro 6 you can export individual discrete channels very easily.

❶ Open up the Sequence Settings (Command + 0) window for your sequence.

❷ In the General tab in the bottom right-hand corner there is an area labeled Audio Settings.

❸ Change the Config pull-down option to Discrete and click OK to save the change.

❹ Choose the File menu > Export > QuickTime Movie.

❺ Save the file as you normally would. Discrete channels will be saved in the export.

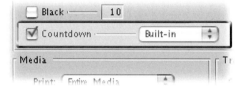

Count Down: "In 3 ... 2 ... 1"

Countdowns are often not needed on your master tape. People seem enamored by countdowns, though (maybe it's the fault of Wayne's World). You generally need a countdown in the following situations; otherwise, leave it off:

- If the piece is going on air, put a countdown on it. This includes news packages, programming, commercials, and video news releases.

- If the piece is for playback at a live event, put a countdown on it for cueing purposes. Make it a subdued countdown (such as small, dark gray numbers over black), and keep it silent.

- If the client specifically asks you for one.

Convert Between QuickTime and Avid

Have a bunch of animation files that were made for an Avid editing project? You may have some show graphics around that were compressed with Avid codecs. As long as you have the Avid codec installed on your system (it's free from the support page at Avid's site—www.avid.com/onlineSupport/browseCodec.asp), you can convert.

Follow these steps:

1 Follow the steps described in the "Use Converter" tip.

2 Add the files to Compressor's window by drag and drop. The QuickTime codec will properly decode the files.

3 Batch process to the format you need.

This conversion can happen in the Timeline as well, but batching the files proves faster from a workflow point of view.

> Note: If you need to do a lot of conversion, be sure to check out Automatic Duck's utilities for importing and exporting between Final Cut Pro, Avid products, After Effects, and Boris RED 3GL. They're truly a timesaver if you do a lot of work between programs.

PTV (What's That?)

Want to go straight to tape when you choose Print to Video without having to press Record on your deck and click OK? You need to turn on Auto Record and PTV after three seconds. To access this advanced control, you need to call up your Audio/Video Settings folder:

1 Choose Final Cut Pro > Audio/Video Settings.

2 Go to the Device Control Presets tab, and modify your current Device Control preset that has worked for you.

3 Check the Auto Record and PTV after: X seconds box, and specify a time to wait. Three seconds is usually enough.

> Note: The PTV setting is a function of your camera and deck and may not be supported by all devices. This is a hardware option, not a software setting.

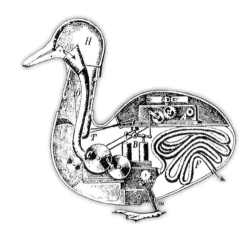

Pre-roll:	3	seconds
Post-roll:	3	seconds
☑ Auto Record and PTV after:	3	seconds

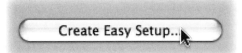

Making Presets

Hardware settings can be tricky. We can't tell you how to configure every third-party device you may want to add to your system, such as a DV converter, but we can suggest a few things to make life easier:

- RTFM: Be sure to check with the manufacturer on how to configure your audio/video settings. Many devices have very specific options to get their decks or converter boxes working "seamlessly."

- When it works, save it. Be sure all Device Control presets and A/V devices are named and saved.

- With the correct settings active, create an Easy Setup. An Easy Setup will store Sequence, Capture and Device settings. This will allow you to change settings from one menu. It isn't uncommon to have several configurations for capture and output depending on the hardware devices you have hooked to your system. These are stored inside your Custom Settings folder ([System Drive] > Library > Application Support > Final Cut Pro System Support > Custom Settings). You should back this folder up anytime you add easy setups.

Audio Mixdown ... Where Are You?

When outputting material to tape, an Audio Mixdown feature was a recommended precaution to ensure you didn't drop frames. In Final Cut Pro 4 or newer, however, the option has moved from its familiar place. Choose Sequence > Render Only > Mixdown (or press Command + Option + R). You can also map this as a button, and place it into the Timeline button bar.

Send Your Client an MP3

Have a client with low-bandwidth? Consider sending them an MP3 of your program. We'll often do this when we want to lock in an audio mix for a piece that's music-dependent or after the rough cut is complete on a documentary-style piece. Follow these steps:

❶ Choose File Export to AIFF(s).

❷ Export at a sample rate of 48 kHz, a sample size of 16 bit, and the files at the Stereo Mix setting. Starting with a high-quality source file will result in better compression.

❸ Import the resulting file into iTunes. You can drag it into the library, or choose File > Import.

❹ In iTunes, you need to set your MP3 settings. Go to iTunes > Preferences, and then click the Advanced button in the Toolbar and click the Importing tab. The MP3 Encoder and Good Quality settings work well.

❺ Highlight the track you want to convert.

❻ Choose Advanced > Convert Selection to MP3. iTunes will convert your AIFF into an MP3 file quickly.

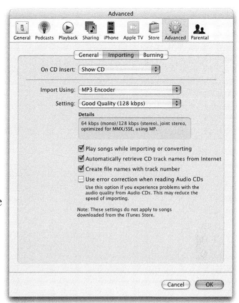

By default, the file will be added to your library. Simply select the MP3 file in your iTunes window, and press Command + R to reveal the file. Email it to your client, and wait for feedback. Both Windows and Mac machines have the ability to play back MP3 files included with any modern operating system.

A Loop is a Loop is a Loop

Need to make a show loop for a client's tradeshow booth or front entry? Final Cut Pro makes it easy for you to make money. In the Print to Video or Edit to Tape dialog boxes, you can specify how many times a show should loop. You can also add black in between each segment. Feel free to use the Bars and Tone options because they'll only be added to the first pass; all of the loops will contain just the program content.

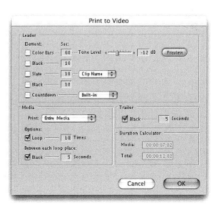

Built for Speed

So you've just won the lottery and have decided to spend all of the money ... on new Macs! Cool Beans, you're a geek (just like us!) Okay, back to reality for a second. If you have multiple Macs in your shop, you can use them for faster rendering in Compressor by creating a render cluster. Here is how it works.

❶ Make sure all of your machines are on the same network (high-speed Ethernet connections are a must).

❷ One machine must act as a traffic cop for the network, so choose that machine and then open up System Preferences on that machine and choose the Qmaster preference pane.

❸ Under Share This Computer as: choose QuickCluster with services.

❹ Name the Cluster with a simple name.

❺ Click Start Sharing.

❻ On all the other machines on your network, open up the Qmaster preferences and Under Share This Computer As: choose services only and click Start Sharing.

❼ In Compressor create a batch with settings and destination of your choice.

❽ When ready, save the batch, then submit the job.

❾ In the dialog box that pops up, change the Cluster pull-down to the cluster you previously named.

❿ Submit the batch. Your batch will now be processed by all of the machines you've set up on the network.

There are other ways to set this up that give you even greater control.

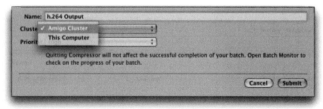

- Check out the Compressor manual for more help with those setups.

- For this process to work as it should, all machines should have the same versions of software installed.

- Be sure the same versions of custom presets are loaded on all machines.

Final Cut Pro Movie ... What's My Name Again?

The Export menu keeps evolving. Be sure you understand the two most important options in this menu:

- **QuickTime Movie:** This is the same as a Final Cut Pro movie. The file is exported using the sequence settings for size, frame rate, compression, and so on.

- **Using QuickTime Conversion:** This opens all of the formats supported by QuickTime. By checking different boxes and pull-down menus, you can access several different formats including AVI, DV Stream, and Image Sequence. This is the method for getting a file out, so it can be used in other applications or platforms that don't recognize or have the capacity to play back your video file with the Source Compression setting applied.

Levels and Pan in OMFs

Maybe you're the type of editor who really likes to get a basic mix of your show working real well, but ultimately you won't be mixing the audio. That task will be done by a dedicated audio person. One way this is done is with OMF files.

In the past when Final Cut Pro exported an OMF file, all level and pan information that you set up were lost. This meant that the audio editor had to start from scratch mixing the show.

Now in Final Cut Pro 6, level and pan information can stay with the clip if you choose. This is a great way to give the audio editor a good idea of what you were looking for in the mix and then they can use their skills to take the mix to the next level.

❶ To export an OMF with level and pan information intact, choose File > Export > Audio to OMF.

❷ In the dialog box that pops up, choose your sample rate and bit depth, amount of handles, and if you want to choose crossfade transitions.

❸ Then choose to include levels and/or pan information.

> Note: It's always a good idea to ask your audio editor if they want this information included in the OMF.

311

When You Need Something Else

Compressor and the export options in Final Cut Pro are excellent; however, they aren't Windows-centric. Although the MPEG and QuickTime options play perfectly fine on PCs, you'll run into client bias for other formats. Consider the following programs for additional output needs:

- Sorenson Squeeze (http://www.sorensonmedia.com)

- Episode and Episode Pro (http://www.telestream.net)

- Flip4Mac (http://www.flip4mac.com)

- Autodesk Cleaner and Cleaner XL (http://www.autodesk.com)

Export Video in a Flash

Doing a lot of video work for the web? Need to export as Flash Video files? Would you like to do it directly from Final Cut Pro?

If you have Flash CS 3, this dream can be a reality. When you install Flash, a QuickTime export plugin is installed on your system.

❶ In Final Cut Pro, choose File > Export > Using QuickTime Conversion.

❷ In the format pull-down you have an option for FLV (flash video).

❸ Click Options and you can fine tune the settings for the export.

Edit to Tape (Tape is Not Dead)

The Edit to Tape function is a great mystery to some. "Why would I use it and how?" Edit to Tape allows you to perform timecode-accurate assemble and insert edits onto a linear tape. Remember, what type of edit you can perform is a function of your video deck, not of Final Cut Pro. Assemble edits let you start recording at a specific spot in your show, but you need to record all the way to the end of the program. Insert edits allow you to replace just one shot or group of shots, without having to re-record the end of the show. And frame-accurate timecode insertion is a function of the deck, too. If you're in the market for a new deck, be sure to ask if these features are supported.

How (and Why) to Start at 1:00:00:00

If your show is going to hit air or even make that picky duplicator happy, your program should start exactly at the one-hour mark. This means you need to start your bars and tone at 58:30:00, giving you enough time for slate and countdown. (By the way, countdowns are only needed for programs going to air; they just annoy duplicators.)

Most DVCam and Mini DV machines don't allow you to stripe timecode with a preset number. To complicate things, Final Cut Pro doesn't allow you to stripe timecode onto your tape as you record your show (again, this is usually a function of the deck; they need a timecode-in capability).

Here's a trick we've used: The solution is to go "out of house" and have a friend with a deck that can generate timecode (or even a duplicator) create a couple of DV tapes with timecode that starts at 58:00:00. Now you can simply clone the timecode from your DV camera to your DV deck. Make sure you're connected FireWire-to-FireWire, and start the playback on the striped tape before you hit the Record button on the record deck. What you should get is a perfect clone of the timecode on the new tape.

You don't need to record the whole tape. Just take it to a few minutes past the one-hour mark. Using the Edit to Tape command, you can target your In point at 58:30:00, perform an assemble edit, and you're golden.

> Note: Be sure to give the Edit to Tape window a try and see if you can get the desired results.

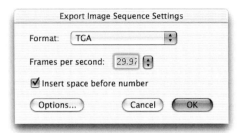

When All Else Fails

There's a sure-fire way to get your video out of Final Cut Pro and into another editing system: an image sequence. Essentially you output a still for every frame of video. You can then import these stills into another video application and work with them. This is one method that's sure to work, but it's a little cumbersome. Follow these steps:

1. Mark a range in your clip or sequence by setting an In and an Out point.

2. Choose File > Export > Using QuickTime Conversion.

3. From the Format drop-down menu, select Image Sequence.

4. Click the Options button, and select a format and the appropriate frame rate. Targa is very popular with PC-based animators; PCT is more popular with Mac-based artists.

5. Create a new folder, and specify the destination.

6. Click OK.

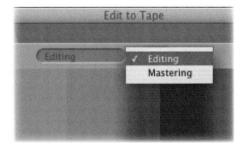

Mastering versus Editing Modes

Another area of the Edit to Tape window that confuses people, especially when they're a little foggy on the ideas of assemble and insert editing, is the difference between Mastering and Editing modes.

Mastering mode is the default mode of the Edit to Tape window. When you're in this mode you can select the Mastering Settings tab and choose to add leader and trailer information when you export. Also, in the mastering mode you can only set an In point on the tape because the output is defined by the length of your selection (sequence, clip, etc. and yes, Ins/Outs are respected, if marked).

Using the Editing mode, you cannot choose to add leader and trailer information, but you can choose both an In and an Out point on tape. Because of this you can essentially perform 3-point edits back to tape frame accurately (yep, just like you would in the linear editing). Using the Editing mode, if you noticed a mistake on tape, for example, you could simply re-edit the shot back on to the tape and not affect the rest of the program.

Idiot-Proof DVDs

Here's a DVD Studio Pro tip for you (okay, we're a little off-topic, but we haven't gotten around to that book yet). Have you ever had to talk a client through how to start a DVD (sounds dumb, but hey, many clients are technologically illiterate)? You can create DVDs that just start automatically when inserted.

❶ Import your MPEG-2 and Audio file (AIFF or AC3) into DVD Studio Pro. If you are being lazy (lazier?) you can just import a self-contained QuickTime movie.

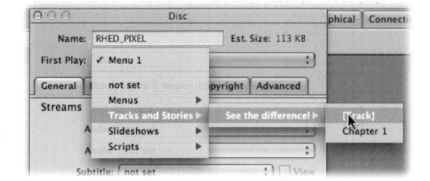

❷ Add your files to your video track and name it.

❸ In your Outline tab, click on your disc and name it.

❹ Leave the disc icon selected, and then switch to the Inspector.

❺ Set the First Play action to be the video track. Be sure to navigate First Play > Tracks & Stories > < *Track Name* > > [Track].

❻ If you'd like the disc to loop, keep reading, otherwise, skip ahead. Select your track in the Outline view. Then in the Inspector, set the End Jump so the track jumps back into itself (yes, it's like a black hole). This is great to make DVDs for kiosks or entryways.

❼ You can now click the Burn button (we sometimes call it the Homer button).

❽ Give the DVD to your client and rest assured; if their DVD player can play DVD-Rs, they will see your video.

Deliver on Disc—Test on Disc

If you intend to deliver a file on CD or DVD, you need to burn the file to disc and then play it back. Why? Well, the file may be too large and exceed the data rate of your playback device. Don't assume that your client has a high-speed drive. Burn to CD, and test it on a machine that's similar to your client's. Once you have a working setting that your client is happy with, be sure to save it and use it in the future.

DVD ROM

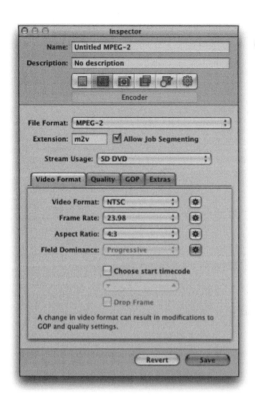

Compressor Confusion: Is 24p for Me?

Think it would be really cool to convert your 29.97 interlaced video into P progressive? Think again. Only material with a native frame rate of 24p, such as film, some HD, or Varicam, should be compressed using the 24p settings. With standard video there is no 3:2 pulldown to reverse Telecine.

Now what if your source material is 24p? Don't convert it to 29.97 prior to transcoding. Going directly into Compressor at 24p will result in higher quality image at a lower compressed bit rate. The secret is that the Compressor MPEG-2 encoder sets internal MPEG-2 frame flags, so DVD players will apply the *3:2 pulldown* process for display on 29.97 fps interlaced NTSC TV sets.

Is your head spinning? Here's the proper workflow using Apple's end-to-end 24p editing and delivery solution (Cinema Tools with Final Cut Pro). The workflow typically goes like this:

- **Film:** Shoot film > Telecine > 30 fps video > capture into Final Cut Pro > remove pulldown with Cinema Tools > edit 24p video > Export with Compressor > create masterpiece in DVD Studio Pro.

- **Video:** Shoot 24p Video > capture natively into 24p Final Cut Pro > edit 24p video > Export with Compressor > create masterpiece in DVD Studio Pro.

Video Pop-Up Maker

1. Enter your info

Video URL http://photoshopforvideo.
Video Title Fading Filters
Image URL http://www.photoshopfor

(Start Over)

Preview

click here to download

Embedding Video in a Web Page Without Coding

If you don't have an HTML authoring tool and don't know the code for embedding QuickTime in a web page, just do it online and have the code for a popup videoplayer generated for you. To generate the embed code for a video that's online, say if you want to embed it in your portfolio site, just jump on over to http://embedthevideo.com.

> Note: DO NOT enter the www in front of the address ... it breaks the page. Need more than QuickTime support? Try the site http://freevideocoding.com/.

Phil Hodgetts – http://www.digitalproductionbuzz.com/BuZZdex/

Timecode Burn-in and Encode in One Step

Timecode burn-in is used to assist in referencing back to parts of show. Typically this has been used on VHS tapes for producers so they can comment on shows, etc.

These days it's more common to use QuickTime files and DVDs for this type of work. Since you're going to have to encode the video anyway (most likely using Compressor), why not add timecode burn-in at the same time?

Fortunately, a great new feature in Compressor 3 allows you to do this.

❶ Inside Final Cut Pro select the sequence you want to export.

❷ Choose File > Export > Using Compressor.

❸ Inside Compressor select the setting you'd like to apply to the file. With the setting active, select the Inspector window and click the Filters tab.

❹ Choose Timecode Generator.

❺ Change the settings for the Timecode Generator as you see fit.

❻ Apply the setting to the clip in the Batch window.

❼ Submit the job.

> Note: If you're trying to choose the Timecode Generator for an Apple preset you'll notice there are no filters in the Filters tab of the Inspector. To be able to add the Timecode Generator to one of the Apple presets, you'll have to duplicate it first (then it becomes a custom preset).

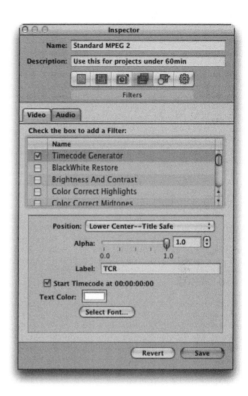

Client Screening—.mp4 Screeners

Need to get your work out there? Be sure to check into using MPEG-4. You'll need to get your client to upgrade to QuickTime 6 or 7 (it's free). The file sizes are significantly smaller, they encode blazingly fast in Compressor, and the quality is outstanding. We still like Sorenson movies, but .mp4s have quickly become our first choice.

It Rocks.mp4

Go to YouTube

What people tend to forget is that you are sending YouTube a master for them to compress; therefore, send the highest quality you can, that fits within their limitations. YouTube.com is well know for being the busiest video-sharing site, but unfortunately, YouTube uses the much older Sorenson Spark codec for their video encoding. This was the "improved" video format for Flash 7 but is based on the very old H.263 video conferencing codec. Even when new, this was an old, inefficient codec.

Many people send YouTube an already compressed video, and are disappointed when they see the quality that results on YouTube. That's because most of the information was first thrown away by the encode before upload, so there was little quality left to be encoded to Flash 7.

The goal is to give YouTube a master that they can use for encoding:

- YouTube has two limitations: no more than 10 minutes per video and no larger than 100 MB per video.

- YouTube converts everything that is uploaded to Flash 7 video at 320×240.

- Remember the good old days of VHS distribution? You wouldn't give the duplicator a VHS copy of the show to duplicate. No, you'd give them the highest quality master you could. Therefore, to get the best quality from YouTube, give them a high quality "master" that is close to 99 MB.

Here's how to pull this off:

❶ Use QuickTime Pro or Final Cut Pro to export to .mp4 with H.264 video.

❷ Export as MPEG-4 with H.264 and set the size to 320×240. There is no point providing more resolution than YouTube's finished size. By going direct to that size means that you can devote bandwidth to making that master look great, instead of sending excess size that will be scaled down. The bonus is that you get to control de-interlacing and scaling.

❸ From here on there are two choices: calculate the maximum data rate that will keep the file under 99 MB, or use some general purpose settings.

Phil Hodgetts – http://www.digitalproductionbuzz.com/BuZZdex/

Info, Info, Info!

We've mentioned this a few times in various tips, but it is worth repeating. Proper documentation of tapes, memory cards, optical media, and drives is essential! This is particularly important when you're doing a handoff to a vendor.

Here are some thoughts about documenting items in your project:

- Label both the tape and box for tapes and make sure they match! It doesn't do you any good if the box says one thing and the tape says another.

- Make sure memory cards (Flash and P2) and optical media (CDs, DVDs, XDCAM) are labeled. Typically, these types of media have places to label them. Avoid stickers or other labeling methods, as these might get in the way of the physical mechanisms in readers/players.

- Make sure external drives are named in the Finder and label the drive. Make sure the labels match.

- Make sure your various pieces of media are accompanied with paper documentation of their contents. For example, a log sheet of a show master might include segment ins/outs, durations, as well as audio assignments. A DVD might include a screen shot printout of the contents of the disc.

Widescreen to VHS

This tip should have been in the first edition (thanks to Rick Finley for pointing it out to us). What happens if you have a widescreen video that you need to give to your client on VHS? Sure, DVD players have a widescreen option, but VCRs don't.

❶ Create a new standard aspect ratio sequence.

❷ Drag your widescreen sequence into a 4:3 Timeline as if it were a clip.

❸ Select the edited clip (which is really a sequence) and press Return or Enter to load it into the Viewer.

❹ In the Motion tab, choose the Distort area and set the aspect ratio to −33 to compensate for the widescreen shape.

❺ Render and then output.

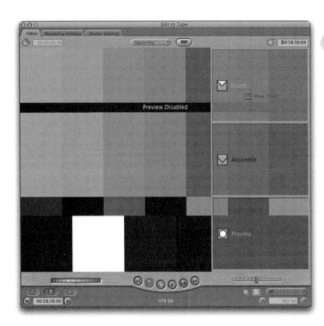

Insert or Assemble?

Instead of the Print to Video command or the dreaded crash record, you prefer to use the Edit to Tape functionality in Final Cut Pro. Congrats! Edit to Tape gives you lots more flexibility in getting back to tape.

One area that confuses people (even those who have been using Edit to Tape for a long time) is the difference between doing an assemble edit and insert edit in the Edit to Tape window. Here is the difference:

- **Assemble:** An assemble edit records video, audio, timecode and control tracks onto a tape all at once, replacing whatever was previously on the tape. An assemble edit will also not create a smooth Out point when the program is done recording, meaning that the control track will be broken.

- **Insert:** An insert edit lets you choose what will be replaced on the tape. You can select to insert audio, video, timecode, etc. Because an insert edit never breaks the control track on a tape, both the In and Out points are smooth.

So which one is better? Wherever possible, use an insert edit. Insert editing works best by blacking (striping) a tape with timecode and then inserting your show onto the tape at the timecode you choose.

Browsing the Finder—Adobe Bridge

Need to sort through a lot of files at the Finder level? Then consider the robust Adobe Bridge, which is part of the Adobe Creative Suite bundles. The latest version of Bridge lets you view nearly every graphics type plus view video clips and even flip through scripts saved as PDF files. With large previews and customizable layouts, this is a great way to media-manage your files in a hands-on way.

Crash Record

Come on! The FedEx guy will be here in half an hour!

Ever heard that before? Sometimes when you need to get things out fast, the only option is a crash record.

❶ To perform a crash record, simply back up your playhead in your sequence to the start.

❷ Make sure Final Cut Pro is setup to output to your device by checking View > Video Playback and View > Audio Playback and View > External Video > All Frames.

❸ Put a tape in your deck and put the deck into record.

❹ Wait a few seconds and then press play for your sequence.

Doing a crash record is not ideal. Using Print to Video or Edit to Tape are better options because of the following:

- Timecode will start at 0, unlike an Edit to Tape option where you would stripe the tape with timecode of your choosing first.

- You have no ability to put leader information on tape, like bars and tone or slates, unless they were already in your sequence.

- A slight nudge of the keyboard or mouse could stop playback.

Browsing the Finder—OS 10.5

One of the most useful features of OS 10.5 is Quick Look. You can now view the contents of files without even opening it. You can browse a folder and flip through documents and watch full-screen video. This is a great way to organize graphics and stock footage when you first add them to your project folder.

ON THE SPOT

CHAPTER

17

Cinema Tools

Compressor

DVD Studio Pro

Final Cut Pro

LiveType

Color

Motion

Soundtrack Pro

Mixing It Up
No App is an Island!

With the release of Apple's Final Cut Studio, it is pretty likely that you are using more than just Final Cut to create your masterpiece. As a matter of fact, most of Apple's Pro Video Apps, Audio Apps, iApps, and even the OS all work together to make your life easier and your shows look better. That's the beauty of using Apple ... because when the hardware, OS, and applications all come from the same people ... everything works, and it works well.

The following tips cover just some of the ways you can leverage the Apple Pro video workflow. So now you can really impress your clients; make even more money; buy faster, more tricked out Macintoshes; edit more shows; make more money; hire younger, more caffeinated editors; make even more money ... and oh yes ... laugh all the way to the bank. (Just because you read this chapter.)

iDVD

GarageBand

iTunes

iPhoto

iMovie

iWeb

Why iLife?

The simple answer—because it's cool. We love the pro apps, but Apple's consumer apps have PLENTY of professional power if you approach them right. They come free with any new computer and cost only $79 if purchased separately. That's less than $15 bucks an application—we pay more for shareware.

iMovie: Need to do a quick string out of clips? Or need to capture some footage so you can do web compression? No need to tie up Final Cut Pro. You can run iMovie on an older Mac and capture DV only. Use this machine for quick web compression or simple demo reels.

Final Cut Express can now open an iMovie project. Be aware, though, that the media does not have timecode. Also, sound effects, audio levels, and transitions are not imported. We'd stay away from this feature.

iDVD: We know so many pros who are embarrassed that they use iDVD. Don't get us wrong; we use DVD Studio Pro all the time. But sometimes you just need a quickie disc that has a basic menu and a couple of clips.

iPhoto: Need to manage your still photos? Yup ... and iPhoto does a great job. Plus it still plays well with Photoshop, as you can set it as an external editor (iPhoto > Preferences > Edit photo: In application... click the Select Application button and choose Photoshop).

Probably the cheapest photo doctor ever. iPhoto is great for cropping your pictures to a perfect 4×3 aspect ratio, quickly removing red eye, and "healing" those ugly pimples on Aunt Edna's nose!

iTunes: This great application can be used to manage your stock music collection as well as to convert CDs to 48 kHz AIFF files.

GarageBand: Wow! What a cool app. Pick yourself up a $99 USB audio keyboard and you can whip up your own stings for animated logos and temp tracks. If you have any musical talent, you can even make full blown music for your videos and DVDs.

iWeb: Need to create web pages in a jiffy? iWeb is an easy-to-use tool for basic web page authoring. It's an easy way to make a client review site to keep all parties on track.

Having a Good Time, Faster!

Ever find rendering in LiveType to be a drag? We sure do. It's annoying to be able to only render one item at a time, plus then you will most likely have to render again when you key the text into your Final Cut Pro Timeline. Fortunately, this is as much a thing of the past as parachute pants.

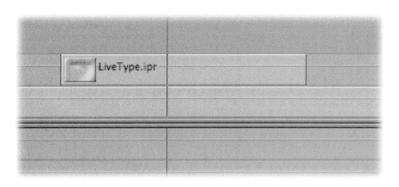

❶ Import the LiveType project files into a bin by choosing File > Import or by dragging them in.

❷ Load the project file as a clip and edit into your show.

❸ If needed, you can contextual-click and choose Open in Editor. LiveType will be launched and you can make your changes.

❹ Close and save the LiveType project and it will update automatically in the Final Cut Pro Timeline.

Oh, if that wasn't cool enough, the same thing applies to Motion projects as well!

GarageBand Jam Packs—What a Bargain!

Want to add onto GarageBand? Then be sure to check out the different Jam Packs— each adds more Software Instruments (again, that USB keyboard is a must). Plus you get a bunch more Apple Loops, which you can use in Soundtrack Pro as well. All you need to do is Index your system drive where GarageBand stores its loops.

When an MP3 is the Only Way

Sometimes the only audio you have is an MP3 or an unprotected AAC file (tracks bought from the iTunes music store can't and shouldn't be used in your show). If you don't have access to the original files, you should convert the compressed files to an AIFF file for use in Final Cut Pro.

❶ Drag the file into iTunes.

❷ Choose iTunes > Preferences, then click on the Advanced button and click the Importing tab.

❸ Choose AIFF and set the sample size to 16 bit and the sample rate to 48 kHz. Specify if the file is stereo or mono.

❹ Click OK.

❺ Load the compressed file into iTunes by drag and drop or choosing File > Open.

❻ Highlight the files you want to convert and choose Advanced > Convert Selection to AIFF.

❼ To reveal the converted file, highlight it and press Command + R to reveal it at the Finder level.

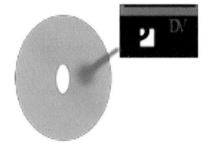

Rip from a DVD-R

While at the Los Angeles Final Cut Pro Users Group, we saw a useful demo for a wonderful product called DVDXDV. It allowed you to extract movie files from DVD-Rs that were created on a DVD-R or DVD+R burner. It extracted the tracks into self-contained QuickTime movies for editing in Final Cut Pro. It was simple to use and produced clean results. Note it's for pulling movies from DVD-R discs that are not copyright protected (such as source footage from a client). Everyone was impressed, especially when they found out it only costs $25 (an extended version sells for $80). Check it out at www.dvdxdv.com.

Send to Motion

One of the best things about the Final Cut Pro/Motion combination is the excellent integration between the two products. Apple bills this as the "round trip" ability and it is very fluid.

❶ Choose the items you want to export to Motion. You can either select sequence in the Browser or select items in an active Timeline.

❷ Choose File > Send To > Motion Project and choose a destination.

❸ You should also consider the following options:

- **Launch Motion:** Open the selected items and project inside Motion.

- **Embed Motion Content:** This option places the Motion project as a clip in Final Cut Pro HD. As you make changes in Motion, it will update inside of Final Cut.

❹ Click Save.

If you have any problems with an exported clip, you can try re-exporting it from the Final Cut Pro Timeline. You can also adjust the pixel aspect ratio settings in Motion's Media tab of the Inspector.

Zipped Emails

If you need to send a project file over a network or through email, it's a VERY good idea to create an archive first. Most servers can't recognize the .fcp file type extension. While OS 10.3 and newer comes with the ability to archive built-in, we sometimes find that it creates less-than-compatible archives. A better idea is to take advantage of Stuffit, which gives you much greater control over archives.

A Round Trip with Color

Like many of the other applications within Final Cut Pro Studio, round tripping is possible with Color.

➊ Select your sequence (you can only send sequences to Color) and choose File > Send To > Color.

➋ A dialog box will open describing your selection, as well as letting you name the Color project. The name defaults to the name of the selected sequence.

➌ After correcting and grading your footage you will need to render the clips in Color by choosing Render Queue > Add All and then choose Render Queue > Start Render.

➍ Then from inside Color go to the File Menu > Send To > Final Cut Pro. This will generate an XML file that FInal Cut Pro will use to reconnect to the rendered clips from Color.

> Note: You don't have to worry about keeping track of the XML file as it's passed seamlessly between Color and Final Cut Pro.

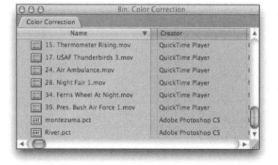

Go Cut Creator, Go!

Ever wanted to know where a clip came from? Well, now you can (which is a good idea if you need to make edits using Edit Original). Just make sure to activate the Creator column in your bin. If you don't see it, contextual-click on the headings area in your bin and choose it from the popup list.

Open Up and Theme and Modify

Did you know that you could modify the prebuilt templates in iDVD?

1. Control-click on the iDVD icon and choose Show Package Contents.

2. Navigate the following path: Contents > Resources.

3. Duplicate the theme you want to modify and rename it.

4. Control-click on a theme and choose Show Package Contents.

5. Navigate the following path: Contents > Resources.

6. You can now modify the graphics in Photoshop.

7. You can also open the movies in QuickTime Pro and apply color-changing filters. Move on to After Effects or Final Cut Pro for advanced options.

While you're there, you can throw away the PAL movies if you don't need them. You can also trash any templates you don't use to gain back hard drive space.

Score to Picture

Do you know that you can bring a QuickTime movie into Soundtrack Pro? All you need to do is drag a self-contained movie into the Video Well in the main window. This is a great way to score music, as Soundtrack Pro automatically syncs the video clip to your Soundtrack Pro Timeline. It's important to note that large movies can cause a performance hit. You can drag in a half-screen movie or even an MPEG-4 to cut down on RAM usage.

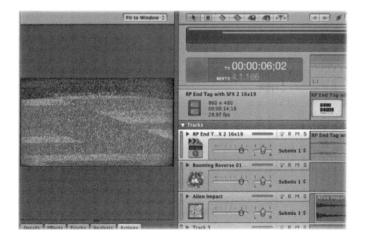

Motion Templates in Final Cut Pro

For the past few years Apple has been pushing Motion as a tool that should be in every editor's toolbox. The problem has been, not every editor has had the time or patience to learn Motion. In Final Cut Pro 6, Apple recognized this and has integrated Motion templates directly inside of FCP.

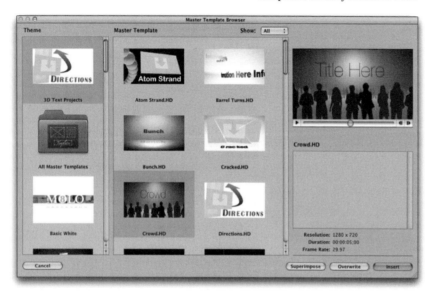

To launch a Motion template in Final Cut Pro you have three options:

❶ Choose the Effects tab in the Browser > Master Templates.

❷ Choose the Generators pull-down in the Viewer > Master Templates.

❸ Choose the Sequence menu > Add Master Template.

Choose the template that you want and load it into the Viewer. Once the template has been loaded in the Viewer, clicking on the controls tab will let you change various parameters of the template. There is only one catch:

Not every parameter of a template is editable in Final Cut Pro. Text entry, size, tracking and populating drop zones with footage are the only parameters you can adjust inside Final Cut Pro.

If you need to edit a template to, for example, change the text color, or swap out a background, you need to edit the template in Motion. Here's how.

❶ Edit the template from the Viewer into your sequence.

❷ Right-click on the template and notice at the top of the contextual menu you have two options: Open in Editor and Open Copy in Editor. Since the template is a prebuilt one from Apple, you can't save over it (it's locked) so you need to choose Open Copy in Editor.

❸ Make your changes in Motion and save the file. Your changes will update in FCP.

Note: You can make your own templates within Motion for use in Final Cut Pro. Doing this the Open in Editor behavior described previously would edit that template and then, back in Final Cut Pro all instances of that template would be changed. If you chose Open Copy in Editor and make changes, only that one instance will be affected. In the previous example, you could choose to open an Apple prebuilt template in the editor (not as a copy), but you would have to do a Save As from Motion, and then in Final Cut Pro do a manual reconnect to the file you just made.

An Unnecessary Drop in (Motion) Quality

So now that you're all about using Motion Templates directly in Final Cut Pro, there is one thing you should be aware of—Motion Template quality.

1 Launch your Sequence settings (Command + 0).

2 Choose the Render Control tab.

3 At the bottom of the window in the Master Templates and Motion Projects section, choose from between Draft, Normal, or Best.

4 You can also choose to render at Best Quality when outputting a file.

Just keep in mind, like many other settings, changing things here will only affect the current sequence. If you want to make these changes the default for other sequences, you need to make the change in User Preferences (Option + Q) and choose the Render Control tab.

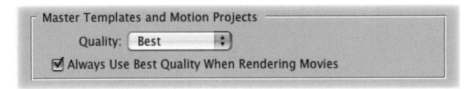

Shake It Up

Perhaps you've seen that small independent film *Lord of the Rings*? All kidding aside, one thing that many effects-driven blockbusters have in common is Shake. Shake is Apple's industrial-strength compositing application and at $499 it's accessible to almost everyone who wants to make their next blockbuster!

Shake and Final Cut Pro integrate nicely and here's how:

❶ You can export clips or whole sequences to Shake. To do so, select your clips or sequence and go to File > Send To > Shake.

❷ This will bring up a dialog box where you can choose the name of the resulting new sequence in Final Cut Pro, the name of the Shake Script (a shake script is synonymous to project file), as well as the name of the File Out Node in Shake. Finally, you can also choose to automatically launch Shake if you have it installed.

❸ This process does a few things. It creates a new Shake Script, a placeholder QuickTime file is created on disk and in your Final Cut Pro project which ultimately will be populated by the render from Shake (the File Out Node).

We Get Around

Tired of constantly going to the Dock to switch applications? By pressing Command + Tab you can cycle between all open apps. What's nice is that you can clearly see which application you are switching to.

While you're switching, you can free up memory too! Just mouse over or continue to tab until you have an unneeded application highlighted. You can now press Command + Q to quit the application.

Anamorphic Fix

Sometimes you load a tape and forget to check the anamorphic box. It's okay, you can fix this oversight. It just involves a little "checking."

❶ Scroll to the right in your bin until you see the Anamorphic column. If it's not there, contextual-click on the column headers and select it.

❷ Check the Anamorphic column for all needed clips.

If you need to fix a sequence, the fix is pretty simple as well.

❶ Highlight the sequence you want to fix.

❷ Press Command + 0 to access the sequence settings.

❸ Check the Anamorphic 16:9 checkbox, then click OK.

Round Trip Scopes

Both LiveType and Motion lack scopes—fortunately Final Cut Pro has them. Remember, you can import a Motion or LiveType project into Final Cut Pro and it keeps a live link.

❶ Load a project file into a bin.

❷ Double-click to load the project into a Viewer.

❸ Choose Tools > Video Scopes or press Option + 9.

❹ Set the Video Scopes to monitor the Viewer.

❺ Switch back to Motion or LiveType and work. When you want to check your scopes, just save the project, then return to Final Cut Pro.

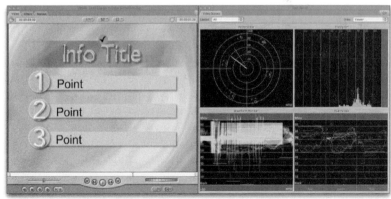

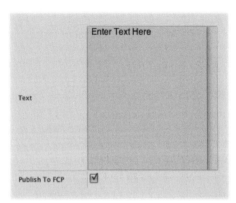

Publish Motion To Final Cut Pro

So, you've decided to take the jump and start learning Motion. One thing that you may be doing is creating Motion Templates. Did you know that you could save those templates for use in FCP just like the prebuilt ones from Apple? No? Here's how:

① Create your Motion project like you normally would, but because you're creating a template, make sure you leave things, like text, generic, like "Enter Text Here." Add particle generators, drop zones, replicators, and more to complete the look.

② Select your text, then click the Inspector tab in the Utility Pane (Command + 3).

③ In the Text tab at the very bottom there is a checkbox for "Publish to Final Cut Pro." With this checked the text will be editable inside of Final Cut Pro.

④ Choose the File Menu > Save As Template.

⑤ Name the template as you see fit. In the Theme pull-down notice that all of them are locked (unless you've previously created a theme). This is because all of the prebuilt templates and themes from Apple are locked.

⑥ Click on the New Theme button in the lower right-hand corner and name your theme category. Then make sure in the Theme pull-down your new theme category is selected.

⑦ Choose the appropriate format using the Format pull-down.

⑧ Using the Collect Media pull-down choose if Motion will "collect" all of the media used for this template or not. (Generally this is a good idea, because you don't have to worry about where the media that was used is located; Motion consolidates it.)

⑨ Have Motion create a QuickTime Preview of the template. Trust us, this helps!

⑩ Click Save.

Now, back in Final Cut Pro, add a Master template like you normally would. Notice, the template you just created is now available! Load the template into the Viewer and click the Controls tab. Any text you published to Final Cut Pro and Drop Zones you created (which come over automatically) are editable in here.

Note: If you need to move these templates from machine to machine, they are located in User > Library > Application Support > Final Cut Studio > Motion > Templates > Name of your Template.

Aperture to Final Cut Pro

Apple's Aperture is a fabulous professional-grade photo management and editing application. We use Aperture for all of our photo organization, and often find ourselves needing to get photos from Aperture to Final Cut Pro for use in a project.

Until recently, we were exporting the photos from Aperture to disk, and then importing them back into Final Cut Pro. That is until we discovered the free Aperture To Final Cut Pro plug-in by Connected Flow. There are several great features of this plug-in:

- Using the plug-in, you can choose the duration of the photos, transitions, and their duration.

- The plug-in will also create a new FCP project for you (and you can choose the sequence preset).

- You can assign an audio track and have the slides fit to the duration of the track.

- You can choose the file type (JPEG, TIFF, etc.) and custom names for the exported files.

Once you click the Export button, your photos will be processed and Final Cut Pro will launch the project you created with your photos already on the Timeline with transitions and durations matching what you chose. Now that is integration!

For more on this and other Aperture plugins, check out
http://www.aperturepluggedin.com/plugins/

Charts and Graphs with Keynote

We absolutely adore Apple's Keynote software. Besides importing PowerPoint files and creating beautifully animated 3D charts, it likes to share. In fact, it can create any QuickTime format. Just set up your document for a video size and export a QuickTime movie with the Export command.

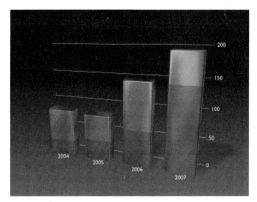

The authors would like to thank the following for making this book possible:

Gary Adcock

Steve Bayes

Joel Bell

Dorothy Cox

DV Magazine

Final Cut Pro User Groups

Mannie Frances

Jeff Greenberg

Rod Harlan

Phil Hodgetts

Scott Kelby

Ben Kozuch

Luke Lindhjem

Chris Main

Steve Martin

Brian Meaney

Dominic Milano

Patty Montesion

Jason Osder

Chris Phrommayon

Iva Radivojevic

Anne Renehan

Paul Saccone

Yan Shvalb

Mark Spencer

Douglas Spotted Eagle

Jessica Steigerwald

Paul Temme

Mark Weiser

Tom Wolsky